IBM WebSphere eXtreme Scale 6

Build scalable, high-performance software with IBM's data grid

Anthony Chaves

[PACKT] PUBLISHING

BIRMINGHAM - MUMBAI

IBM WebSphere eXtreme Scale 6

First published: November 2009

Production Reference: 1271009

Published by Packt Publishing Ltd.
32 Lincoln Road
Olton
Birmingham, B27 6PA, UK.

ISBN 978-1-847197-44-3

www.packtpub.com

Cover Image by Paul Bodea (paul@atelier26.ro)

Credits

Author
Anthony Chaves

Reviewers
Billy Newport
Jeremiah Small

Acquisition Editor
James Lumsden

Development Editor
Dhiraj Chandiramani

Technical Editors
Bhupali Khule
Pallavi Kachare

Copy Editor
Leonard D'Silva

Indexer
Monica Ajmera
Hemangini Bari
Rekha Nair

Editorial Team Leader
Akshara Aware

Project Team Leader
Lata Basantani

Project Coordinator
Joel Goveya

Proofreader
Joel T. Johnson

Graphics
Nilesh Mohite

Production Coordinator
Shantanu Zagade

Cover Work
Shantanu Zagade

About the Author

Anthony Chaves is a software developer interested in application scalability. He started the Boston Scalability User Group (BostonSUG) in 2007. BostonSUG features monthly guests who give talks about their work on building more highly scalable software.

After graduating from college, Anthony went to work for a large phone company in the Enterprise Services division. He developed software on Z/OS and Linux, bridging the gap between legacy applications written in COBOL and new projects using J2EE.

Anthony currently runs a software consulting company based in north-east Massachusetts. In the past, he has worked with large financial companies, data security companies, and early-stage start-ups.

Anthony's favorite development interests include many different methods of webapp user authentication and mobile sensor networks created with cell phones.

Anthony writes about software at `http://blog.anthonychaves.net`.

I would like to thank my beautiful wife Christina and daughter Olivia for encouraging me to face the challenge of writing this book. Thank you for putting up with me when working all night and well into the morning, and my grumpiness during the day.

I also have to thank Billy Newport for fielding my phone calls and emails filled with questions. He pointed me in new directions and helped me find what would be most useful to developers learning about WebSphere eXtreme Scale.

I would like to thank Packt Publishing for asking me to write this book and trying as best they could to keep me on any schedule.

About the Reviewers

Billy Newport is a Distinguished Engineer working on WebSphere eXtreme Scale and on WebSphere high availability. He's worked at IBM since September 2001. Besides his current activities, he helped add advanced APIs like the WorkManager APIs (JSR 236/237). Prior to IBM, he worked as an independent consultant at a variety of companies in investment banking, telcos, publishing, and yellow pages over the previous 13 years in over 10 countries. He graduated from the Waterford Institute of Technology in Ireland with a Bachelors in Applied Computing in 1989.

When not working at IBM, he's busy racing cars and running his drivers' education portal (http://www.trackpedia.com).

Jeremiah Small holds a BS degree in Computer Science from the University of Massachusetts at Amherst, and a Masters Certificate in Information Security from Boston University. He has over 13 years of experience as a software engineer and has designed and built highly-scalable, distributed systems in the education, security, and telecommunications industries. He is currently working for RSA, the Security Division of EMC.

Table of Contents

Preface

This is a book about in-memory data grids, particularly IBM WebSphere eXtreme Scale. An in-memory data grid (IMDG) lets us build more scalable data stores by partitioning data across many different servers. By "scaling out" across many servers instead of "scaling up" by using more powerful servers we can support more clients and data while keeping hardware costs low. One of the nicest things about working with eXtreme Scale is that it's easy to use. We don't need any special hardware or complicated software configuration wizards. It's as easy as downloading the light weight eXtreme Scale JAR file. The eXtreme Scale APIs are well defined and give us a lot of functionality.

This book explores many features of using an in-memory data grid starting from the object cache and going through using the compute grid functionality that lets us use the computing resources of the grid for business logic. We also explore how we can structure our data in a way that lets us take advantage of partitioned data stores.

What this book covers

Chapter 1: What is a Data Grid gets us up and running with IBM WebSphere eXtreme Scale. We download eXtreme Scale, add it to the build path, and get a small sample program running. We also explore some general in-memory data grid concepts.

Chapter 2: The ObjectMap API focuses on using eXtreme Scale as a key/value object cache. ObjectMap gives us a way to interact with the cache using familiar concepts associated with map-like data structures. We also look at working with distributed maps.

Chapter 3: Entities and Queries goes beyond a basic key/value object store. The Entity API lets us work with our objects using relationships between them. The Query API lets us use a SQL-like syntax to work with certain Entity objects in the cache.

Chapter 4: Database Integration explores areas where using a data grid makes sense and some areas where it may not make sense. Many applications already use a database and we can do some integration with eXtreme Scale to make cached objects persistent in the database.

Chapter 5: Handling Increased Load starts to look at some of the eXtreme Scale features that let us scale out across many servers. We cover configuration and dynamic deployments as well as the eXtreme Scale building blocks.

Chapter 6: Keeping Data Available covers more of the eXtreme Scale features that let us survive server or even data center failure. We also explore what happens when we add resources to or remove resources from a deployment.

Chapter 7: The DataGrid API goes beyond an object cache; a data grid provides compute grid functionality. By co-locating code with our data we're able to improve application performance and responsiveness.

Chapter 8: Data Grid Patterns looks at some problems that data grids can help us solve. We also show how we can structure our data to take the best advantage of a partitioned data store.

Chapter 9: Spring Integration deals with the popular Spring framework, which is used in many applications. Using eXtreme Scale with Spring is easy, and there are a few integration points that we cover. We can configure eXtreme Scale with Spring-managed beans. We can also instantiate eXtreme Scale objects using Spring.

Chapter 10: Putting It All Together provides an example of using eXtreme Scale with an existing project. Where do we start? What should we be aware of when migrating to a data grid? We also take a last look at what we can cache and where it is most helpful.

What you need for this book

You need a Java SDK to work with IBM WebSphere eXtreme Scale. Detailed instructions are provided in Chapter 1. Familiarity with a Java build environment is recommended. In this book, we occasionally mention the Eclipse IDE, though Eclipse is not required. The IBM JDK will require the least amount of effort to use these examples. Again, detailed instructions are provided in Chapter 1.

Who this book is for

This book is aimed at intermediate-level JavaEE Developers who want to build applications that handle larger data sets with massive scalability requirements. No previous experience of WebSphere eXtreme Scale is required.

Conventions

In this book, you will find a number of styles of text that distinguish between different kinds of information. Here are some examples of these styles, and an explanation of their meaning.

Code words in text are shown as follows: "This method takes an instance of a `java.util.Map` and adds all of its key/value pairs to the ObjectMap."

A block of code is set as follows:

```
BackingMap bm = grid.defineMap("payments");
bm.setNullValuesSupported(true);
bm.setTimeToLive(60 * 60 * 24);
bm.setTtlEvictorType(TTLType.CREATION_TIME);
bm.setLockStrategy(LockStrategy.PESSIMISTIC);
bm.setLockTimeout(20)
```

When we wish to draw your attention to a particular part of a code block, the relevant lines or items are set in bold:

```
try {
            pl.initialize();
            pl.loadPayments(args[0]);
    } catch (ObjectGridException e) {
            e.printStackTrace();
    } catch (IOException e) {
            e.printStackTrace();
    }
```

Any command-line input or output is written as follows:

```
startOgServer catalog0 -catalogServiceEndPoints catalog0:
galvatron:6601:6602
```

New terms and **important words** are shown in bold. Words that you see on the screen, in menus or dialog boxes for example, appear in the text like this: "A partition is made of even smaller pieces called **shards**".

Warnings or important notes appear in a box like this.

Tips and tricks appear like this.

Reader feedback

Feedback from our readers is always welcome. Let us know what you think about this book—what you liked or may have disliked. Reader feedback is important for us to develop titles that you really get the most out of.

To send us general feedback, simply send an email to feedback@packtpub.com, and mention the book title via the subject of your message.

If there is a book that you need and would like to see us publish, please send us a note in the **SUGGEST A TITLE** form on www.packtpub.com or email suggest@packtpub.com.

If there is a topic that you have expertise in and you are interested in either writing or contributing to a book on, see our author guide on www.packtpub.com/authors.

Customer support

Now that you are the proud owner of a Packt book, we have a number of things to help you to get the most from your purchase.

Errata

Although we have taken every care to ensure the accuracy of our content, mistakes do happen. If you find a mistake in one of our books—maybe a mistake in the text or the code—we would be grateful if you would report this to us. By doing so, you can save other readers from frustration, and help us to improve subsequent versions of this book. If you find any errata, please report them by visiting http://www.packtpub.com/support, selecting your book, clicking on the **let us know** link, and entering the details of your errata. Once your errata are verified, your submission will be accepted and the errata added to any list of existing errata. Any existing errata can be viewed by selecting your title from http://www.packtpub.com/support.

Piracy

Piracy of copyright material on the Internet is an ongoing problem across all media. At Packt, we take the protection of our copyright and licenses very seriously. If you come across any illegal copies of our works, in any form, on the Internet, please provide us with the location address or web site name immediately so that we can pursue a remedy.

Please contact us at copyright@packtpub.com with a link to the suspected pirated material.

We appreciate your help in protecting our authors, and our ability to bring you valuable content.

Questions

You can contact us at questions@packtpub.com if you are having a problem with any aspect of the book, and we will do our best to address it.

1
What is a Data Grid

We have many software packages which make up the so-called "middleware" layer. Application servers, message brokers, enterprise service buses, and caching packages are examples of this middleware layer that powers an application. The last few years have seen the introduction of more powerful caching solutions that can also execute code on objects stored in the cache. The combination of a shared cache and executable code spread over many processes is a data grid.

Caching data is an important factor in making an application feel more responsive, or finish a request more quickly. As we favor horizontal scale-out more, we have many different processes sharing the same source data. In order to increase processing speed, we cache data in each process. This leads to data duplication. Sharing a cache between processes lets us cache a larger data set versus duplicating cached data in each process. A common example of a shared cache program is the popular Memcached. A shared cache moves the cache out of the main application process and into a dedicated process for caching. However, we trade speed of access for caching a larger data set, this trade is acceptable when using larger data sets.

Typically, our applications pull data from a data source such as a relational database and perform some operations on it. When we're done, we write the changes back to the data source. The cost of moving data between the data source and the point where we execute code is costly, especially when operating on a large data set. Typically, our complied source code is much smaller than the size of data we move. Rather than pulling data to our code, a data grid lets us push our code to the data. Co-locating our code and data by moving code to data is another important feature of a data grid.

Because of their distributed nature, data grids allow near-linear horizontal scalability. Adding more hardware to a data grid lets it service more clients without diminishing returns. Additional hardware also lets us have redundancy for our cached data. Ease of scalability and data availability are two major benefits of using data grids.

A shared cache and a container to execute application code are just two factors which make up a data grid. We'll cover those features most extensively in this book. There are several different data grid platforms available from major vendors. IBM is one of those vendors, and we'll use IBM WebSphere eXtreme Scale in this book. We will cover the major features of eXtreme Scale, including the APIs used to interact with the object cache, running code in the grid, and design patterns that help us get the most out of a data grid.

This chapter offers a tutorial on how to get IBM WebSphere eXtreme Scale, configure our development environment to use it, and write a "Hello, world!" type application. After reading this chapter, you will:

- Understand the uses for a shared cache
- Set up a development environment with **WebSphere eXtreme Scale (WXS)**
- Write and understand a sample WXS application that uses the ObjectMap API

Data grid basics

One part of a data grid is the object cache. An object cache stores the serialized form of Java objects in memory. This approach is an alternative to the most common form of using a relational database for storage. A relational database stores data in column form, and needs object-relational mapping to turn objects into tuples and back again. An object cache only deals with Java objects and requires no mapping to use. A class must be serializeable though.

Caching objects is done using key/value tables that look like a hash table data structure. In eXtreme Scale terminology, this hash table data structure is a class that implements the `com.ibm.websphere.objectgrid.BackingMap` interface. A BackingMap can work like a simple `java.util.Map`, used within one application process. It can also be partitioned across many dedicated eXtreme Scale processes. The APIs for working with an unpartitioned BackingMap and a partitioned BackingMap are the same, which makes learning how to use eXtreme Scale easy. The programming interface is the same whether our application is made up of one process or many.

Using a data grid in our software requires some trade-offs. With the great performance of caching objects in memory, we still need to be aware of the consequences of our decisions. In some cases, we trade faster performance for predictable scalability. One of the most important factors driving data grid adoption is predictable scalability in working with growing data sets and more simultaneous client applications.

An important feature of data grids that separates them from simple caches is database integration. Even though the object cache part of a data grid can be used as primary storage, it's often useful to integrate with a relational database. One reason we want to do this is that reporting tools based on RDBMS's are far more capable than reporting tools for data grids today. This may change in the coming years, but right now, we use reporting tools tied in to a database.

WXS uses Loaders to integrate with databases. Though not limited to databases, Loaders are most commonly used to integrate with a database. A Loader can take an object in the object cache and call an existing ORM framework that transforms an object and saves it to a database. Using a Loader makes saving an object to a database transparent to the data grid client. When the client puts the object into the object cache, the Loader pushes the object through the ORM framework behind the scenes. If you are writing to the cache, then the database is a thing of the past.

Using a Loader can make the object cache the primary point of object read/write operations in an application. This greatly reduces the load on a database server by making the cache act as a shock absorber. Finding an object is as simple as looking it up in the cache. If it's not there, then the Loader looks for it in the database. Writing objects to the cache may not touch the database in the course of the transaction. Instead, a Loader can store updated objects and then batch update the database after a certain period of time or after certain number of objects are written to the cache. Adding a data grid between an application and database can help the database serve more clients when those clients are eXtreme Scale clients since the load is not directly on the database server:

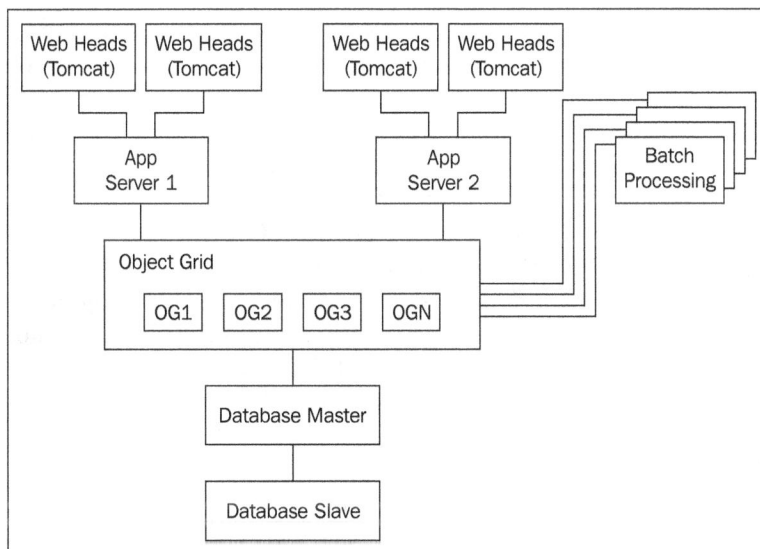

This topology is in contrast to one where the database is used directly by client applications. In the following topology the limiting factor in the number of simultaneous clients is the database.

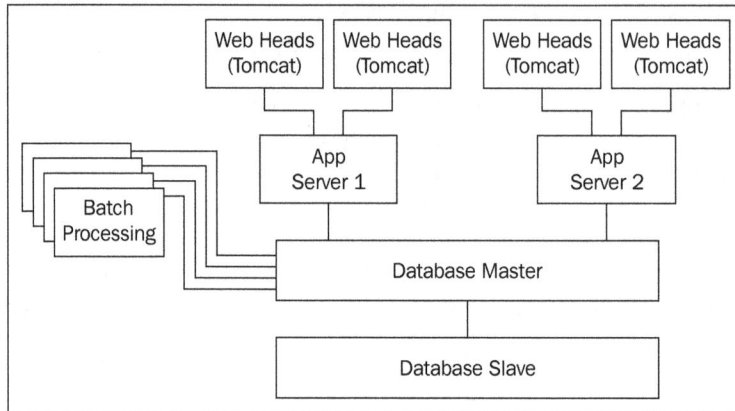

Applications can start up, load a grid full of data, and then shut down while the data in the grid remains there for use by another application. Applications can put objects in the grid for caching purposes and remove them upon application completion. Or, the application can leave them and those objects will far outlive the process that placed them in the grid.

Notice how we are dealing with Java objects. Our cache is a key/value store where keys and values are POJOs. In contrast, a simple cache may limit keys and values to strings. An object in a data grid cache is the serialized form of our Java object. Putting an object from our application into the cache only requires serialization. Mapping to a data grid specific type is not required, nor does the object require a transform layer. Getting an object out of the cache is just as easy. An object need only be deserialized once in the client application process. It is ready for use upon deserialization and does not require any transformation or mapping before use. This is in contrast to persisting an object by using an ORM framework where the framework generates a series of SQL queries in order to save or load the object state. By storing our objects in the grid, we also free ourselves from calling our ORM to save the objects to the database if we choose. We can use the data grid cache as our primary data store or we can take advantage of the database integration features of eXtreme Scale and have the grid write our objects to the database for us.

Data grids typically don't use hard disks or tapes for storing objects. Instead, they store objects in the memory, which may seem obvious based on the name **in-memory data grid**. Storing objects in the memory has the advantage of keeping objects in a location with much lower access time compared to physical storage. A network hop to connect to a database is going to take the same amount of time as a network hop to a data grid instance. The remote server storing or retrieving of the data from the grid is much faster than the equivalent operation on a database due to the nature of the storage medium. A network hop is required in a distributed deployment. This means that an object isn't initially available in the same address space where it will be used. This is one of those trade-offs mentioned earlier. We trade initial locality of reference for predictable performance over a large data set. What works for caching small data sets may not be a good idea when caching large data sets.

Though the access time of storing objects in memory is an advantage over a database hit, it's hardly a new concept. Developers have been creating in-memory caches for a long time. Looking at a single-threaded application, we may have the cache implemented as a simple hash-map (see below). Examples of things we might cache are objects that result from CPU-intensive calculations. By caching the result, we save ourselves the trouble of recalculating it again the next time it is needed. Another good candidate for caching is storing large amounts of read-only data.

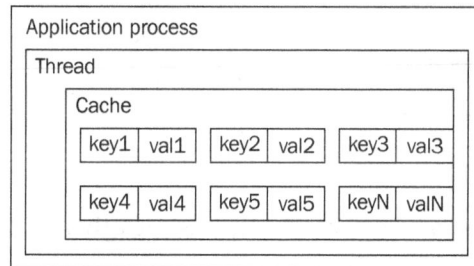

In a single-threaded application, we have one cache available to put data. The amount of data that fits in our cache is limited by the amount of JVM heap size available to it. Depending on the JVM settings, garbage collection may become an issue if large numbers of objects are frequently removed from the cache and go out of the application scope. However, this typically isn't an issue.

This cache is located in the same address space and thread as the code that operates on objects in the cache. Cached objects are local to the application, and accessing them is about as fast as we can get. This works great for data sets that fit in the available heap space, and when no other processes need to access these cached objects.

Building multi-threaded applications changed the scope of the cache a little bit. In a single-threaded application, we have one cache per thread. As we introduce more threads, this method will not continue to work for long:

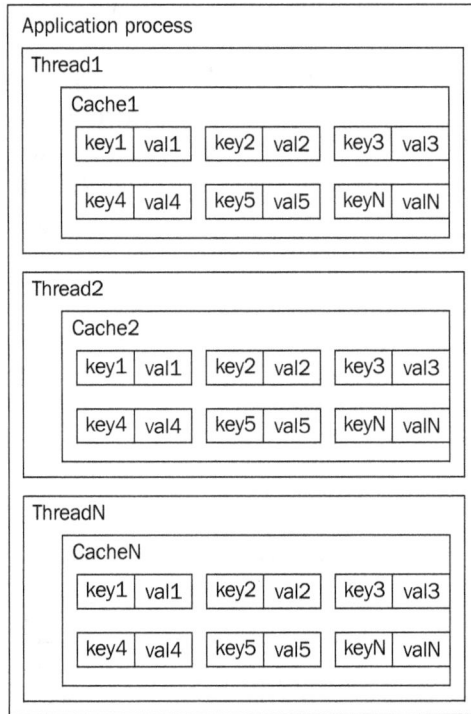

```
Application process
 ┌─────────────────────────────────────────────┐
 │ Thread1                                      │
 │  ┌─────────────────────────────────────────┐│
 │  │ Cache1                                   ││
 │  │  ┌──────────┐ ┌──────────┐ ┌──────────┐ ││
 │  │  │ key1│val1│ │ key2│val2│ │ key3│val3│ ││
 │  │  └──────────┘ └──────────┘ └──────────┘ ││
 │  │  ┌──────────┐ ┌──────────┐ ┌──────────┐ ││
 │  │  │ key4│val4│ │ key5│val5│ │ keyN│valN│ ││
 │  │  └──────────┘ └──────────┘ └──────────┘ ││
 │  └─────────────────────────────────────────┘│
 └─────────────────────────────────────────────┘
```

Each cache contains the same key/value pairs as the other caches.

As each of our N threads has its own cache, the JVM heap size must now be shared among N caches. The most prominent problem with this method of caching is that data will be duplicated in multiple caches. Loading data into one cache will not load it into the others. Depending on the eviction policy, we could end up with a cache hit rate that is close to 0 percent over time. Rather than maintaining a cache per thread, developers started to use a singleton cache:

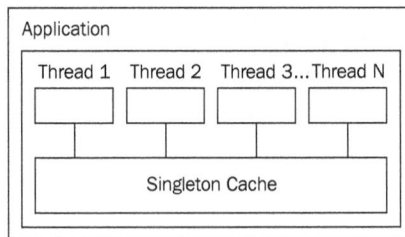

```
Application
 ┌───────────────────────────────────────────┐
 │  Thread 1   Thread 2   Thread 3...Thread N │
 │  ┌──────┐  ┌──────┐  ┌──────┐  ┌──────┐    │
 │  │      │  │      │  │      │  │      │    │
 │  └──────┘  └──────┘  └──────┘  └──────┘    │
 │  ┌───────────────────────────────────────┐│
 │  │          Singleton Cache              ││
 │  └───────────────────────────────────────┘│
 └───────────────────────────────────────────┘
```

The singleton cache is protected by the Singleton design pattern in Java. The Singleton design pattern (almost) assures us that only one instance of a particular object exists in the JVM, and it also provides us with a canonical reference to that object. In this way, we can create a hash-map to act as our cache if one doesn't already exist, and then get that same instance every time we look for it. With one cache, we won't duplicate data in multiple caches and each thread has access to all of the data in the cache.

With the introduction of the `java.util.concurrent` package, developers have safer options available for caching objects between multiple threads. Again, these strategies work best for data sets that fit comfortably in one heap. Running multiple processes of the same application will cache the same data in each process:

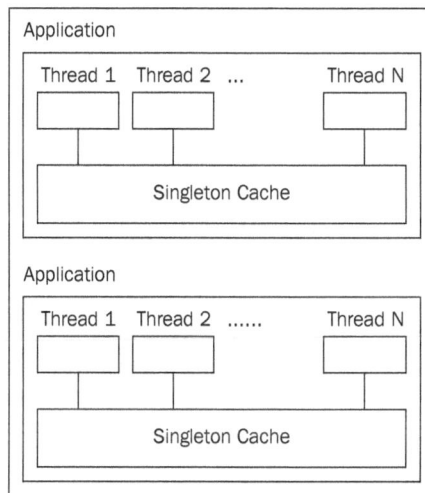

What if our application continues to scale out to 20 running instances to do the processing for us? We're once again in the position of maintaining multiple caches that contain the same data set (or subset of the same data set). When we have a large data set that does not fit in one heap, our cache hit rate may approach 0 percent over time. Each application instance cache can be thought of as a very small window into the entire data set. As each instance sees only a small portion of the data set, our cache hit rate per instance is lower than an application with a larger window into the data set. Locality of reference for an object most likely requires a database hit to get the object and then cache it. As our locality of reference is already poor, we may want to insert a shared cache to provide a larger window into the data set. Getting an object from an object cache is faster than retrieving the object from a database, provided that object is already cached.

What we really want is an object cache where any thread in any application process can access the data. We need something that looks like this:

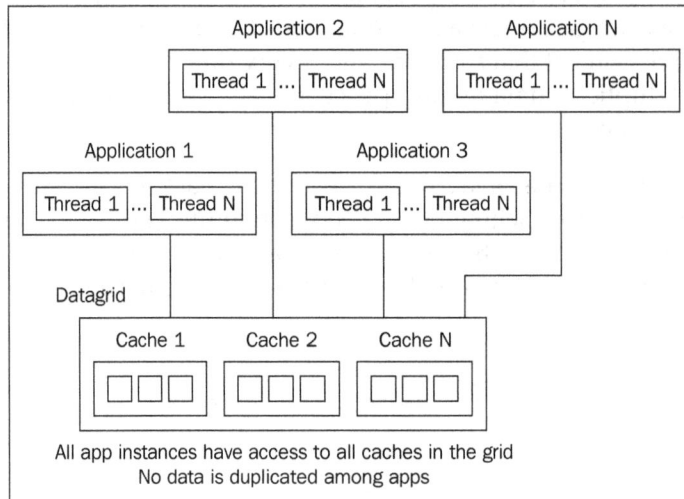

A data grid is made up of many different processes running on different servers. These processes are data grid, or eXtreme Scale processes, not our application processes. For each eXtreme Scale process, we have one more JVM heap available to an object cache. eXtreme Scale handles the hard work of distributing objects across the different data grid processes, making our cache look like one large logical cache, instead of many small caches. This provides the largest window possible into our large data set. Caching more objects is as simple as starting more eXtreme Scale processes on additional servers.

We still have the same number of application instances, but now the cache is not stored inside the application process. It's no longer a hash-map living inside the same JVM alongside the business logic, nor is it stored in an RDBMS. Instead, we have conscripted several computers to donate their memory. This lets us create a distributed cache reachable by any of our application instances. Though the cache is distributed across several computers, there is no data duplication. The data is still stored as a map where the keys are stored across different partitions, such that the data is distributed as evenly as possible.

When using an object cache, the goal is to provide a window as large as possible into a large data set. We want to cache as much data as we can in memory so that any application can access it. We accept that this is slower than caching locally because using a small cache does not produce acceptable cache hit rates. A network hop is a hop, whether it is to connect to a database or data grid. A distributed object cache needs to be faster than a database for read and write operations, only after paying the overhead of making a network connection.

Each partition in a distributed object cache holds a subset of the keys that our applications use for objects. No cache partition stores all of the keys. Instead, eXtreme Scale determines which partition to store an object in, based on it's key. Again, the hard work is handled by eXtreme Scale. We don't need to have knowledge of which partition an object is stored in, or how to connect to that partition. We interact with the object cache as if it were a `java.util.Map` and eXtreme Scale handles the rest:

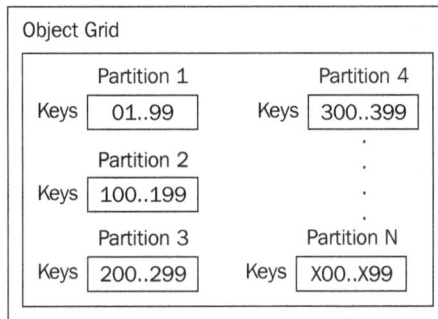

In-memory data grids can do a lot more than object caching, though that's the use we will explore first. Throughout this book, we will explore additional features that make up a data grid and put them to use in several sample applications.

Getting IBM WebSphere eXtreme Scale

IBM WebSphere eXtreme Scale is an in-memory data grid formerly known by the brand name Object Grid. There are two ways to get eXtreme Scale. First, eXtreme Scale is integrated with certain versions of IBM WebSphere Application Server. If you have a WebSphere Application Server 6.1 (or higher) deployment capable of integrating with WebSphere eXtreme Scale, then you should follow the instructions provided with your WebSphere software. WebSphere Application Server 6.1 contains additional features that are enabled only when WebSphere eXtreme Scale is present.

If you do not have an installation of WebSphere eXtreme Scale by using your WebSphere Application Server 6.1 license, then you can use the standalone edition. The standalone WebSphere eXtreme Scale trial edition is functionally equivalent to the full licensed version. Everything that can be done with the licensed edition can be done with the trial edition. The programming and configuration interfaces are identical. If you develop an application using the trial edition, it can be deployed to the full edition. All of the examples in this book have been tested with the WebSphere eXtreme Scale 6.1.0.4 FIX2 trial edition available as a multi-platform download. You can download the trial edition from IBM Developer Works at `http://www.ibm.com/developerworks/downloads/ws/wsdg/`. The file you're looking for is named `objectgridtrial610.zip`.

IBM strongly recommends that you use an IBM JVM for developing and running your WebSphere eXtreme Scale application. In the event that you use a non-IBM JVM, you should manually integrate the IBM **Object Request Broker (ORB)** with your JVM. Other ORBs might work, but they are not tested by IBM. The Sun JVM ORB does not work as of this writing. Please see `http://www.ibm.com/developerworks/wikis/x/niQ` for more information. You can download IBM Java developer kits from `http://www.ibm.com/developerworks/java/jdk/`. I created the examples with the IBM Development Package for Eclipse, though these examples will work with any of the JVMs listed there.

Setting up your environment

Unzip the `objectgridtrial610.zip` into an empty directory. Unzipping the file produces a directory named ObjectGrid. This directory contains everything you need to run local and distributed WebSphere eXtreme Scale instances.

In order to use the Object Grid classes in our first example, we need to add a few JAR files to our Java classpath. If you're using the command line tools, then add the following classpath option to your `javac` and `java` commands, while replacing the paths here with the appropriate paths for your environment and operating system:

```
-cp .;c:\wxs\ObjectGrid\lib\cjlib.jar; \
c:\wxs\ObjectGrid\lib\ogclient.jar
```

That's all the setup you need for the command line tools at this time. If you're using the Eclipse environment, then we need to add these JAR files to the project build path:

1. Create a new Java project in Eclipse.
2. Right-click on the project folder in the package explorer and select **Build Path | Configure Build Path.**
3. Open the **Libraries** tab and click **Add External Jars.**
4. Navigate to the `ObjectGrid/lib` directory and highlight the `cglib.jar` and `ogclient.jar` files. Click **Open**.
5. Click **OK** on the Build Path dialog.

We're now ready to work with a short sample to get our feet wet in the WebSphere eXtreme Scale world.

Hello, world!

An object cache stores objects as key/value pairs. The first thing we should do is define a class that we want to store in the cache. Let's store credit card payments for now:

```
public class Payment implements Serializable {
    private int id;
    private String cardNumber;
    private BigDecimal amount;
    private long version = 0L;
    // getters and setters omitted for brevity...
}
```

The Payment class is a simple POJO with getters and setters. As it may be used in a distributed eXtreme Scale deployment, it implements Serializable. That's it! All we need to use a class with eXtreme Scale's object cache is for it to implement Serializable.

Objects of type Payment will be the value part of the key/value pair when we store them in the BackingMap. The key should also implement Serializable if it is a class. The key, if it is not a primitive type, should also implement reasonable equals(Object obj) and hashCode() methods.

Now that we know what we will store in the cache, let's see what it takes to actually store it. In order to put objects in a BackingMap, we need the instance of com.ibm.websphere.objectgrid.ObjectMap. We don't interact directly with objects in a BackingMap. Instead, we do it by using a proxy ObjectMap.

We obtain a reference to an ObjectMap from the com.ibm.websphere.objectgrid. Session#getMap(String mapName) method. A Session lets us perform operations, like GET and PUT operations, in the context of a transaction.

A Session object is returned from the com.ibm.websphere.objectgrid. ObjectGrid#getSession() method. We get an instance of ObjectGrid from the ObjectGridManager#createObjectGrid() method.

```
public class PaymentLoader {

    ObjectGrid grid;

    private void initialize() throws ObjectGridException {
        ObjectGridManager ogm =
                ObjectGridManagerFactory.getObjectGridManager();
        grid = ogm.createObjectGrid();
        BackingMap bm = grid.defineMap("Payment");
    }
    // other methods omitted for now...
}
```

The PaymentLoader class has an instance variable grid which holds a reference to our ObjectGrid instance (seen above). The initialize() method sets up the ObjectGrid instance and defines one BackingMap used within the grid.

Let's take it one step at a time and walk through what we did. We want to interact with an **ObjectGrid** instance. The ObjectGrid interface is the gateway to interacting with WebSphere eXtreme Scale. It allows us to define **BackingMaps** and create **Sessions**. ObjectGrid instances are created with the **ObjectGridManager** interface. We get an ObjectGridManager reference by calling the helper class ObjectGridManagerFactory.getObjectGridManager(). ObjectGridManager is a singleton which provides access to methods which create local ObjectGrid instances, or connect to remote ObjectGrid instances. For now, we call the createObjectGrid() method on the ObjectGridManager. It returns an ObjectGrid instance which is exactly what we were looking for. There are several createObjectGrid methods on the ObjectGridManager that take varying arguments for naming grids and configure them through XML files. Right now this is unnecessary, though we will eventually need to use them. For now, createObjectGrid() meets our needs.

The ObjectGrid.createObjectGrid() method creates a local instance of an ObjectGrid. This means the grid lives inside the application process along with our business logic. At this point, the grid is API equivalent to any WebSphere eXtreme Scale topology we create. No matter how interesting our deployment becomes with partitions, shards, and catalog servers, we always use the same APIs to interact with it.

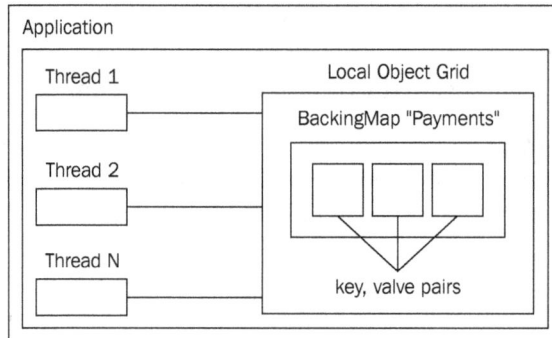

After creating the grid, we must define maps within it (as seen above). We store our application data inside the maps defined in the grid. Creating a map to store `Payment` objects is done by calling `grid.defineMap("Payment")`. This method creates and returns a BackingMap which lives in the grid and holds our `Payments`. If we were to store different classes in the grid, then we would call the `grid.defineMap(String mapName)` method for each one. We aren't limited to one BackingMap per class though. If we were to split up our `Payment` by card type, then our maps would be defined by:

```
BackingMap bmapVisa = grid.defineMap("VisaPayments");
BackingMap bmapMC = grid.defineMap("MasterCardPayments");
BackingMap bmapAmEx = grid.defineMap("AmExPayments");
```

Defining a BackingMap gives it a place to live inside the ObjectGrid instance. ObjectGrid instances manage more than one BackingMap. Creating the previous BackingMaps would give us a runtime grid that looked like this:

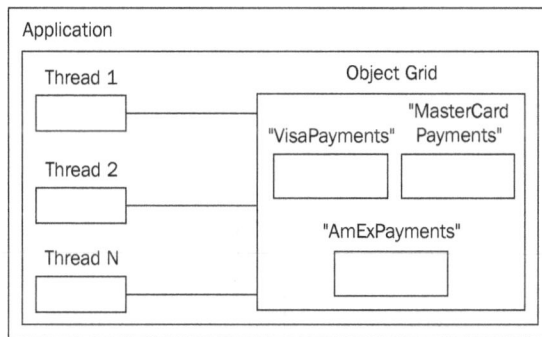

All BackingMaps must be defined before the call to `grid.initialize()`. An explicit call to `initialize()` is optional since the `grid.getSession()` method calls it if it has not been called by our application. A call to `grid.defineMap(String mapName)` will throw an `IllegalStateException` if the `initialize()` method has already been called. In the sample code, we rely on the implicit call to `grid.initialize()`, rather than explicitly calling it. This approach is acceptable as long as all BackingMaps are defined before the first call to `grid.getSession()`.

The most important thing to remember about BackingMaps is that they contain objects which live inside the ObjectGrid instance. Once an object is outside of the grid instance, we are no longer dealing with the BackingMap. We never directly interact with an object while it is inside a BackingMap. So how do we interact with objects in the grid?

Any interaction with objects in the gird must be done through an instance of ObjectMap. An ObjectMap is the application-side representation of the objects in a particular BackingMap. ObjectMap instances are obtained through the getMap(String mapName) method in the Session interface:

```
Session session = grid.getSession();
ObjectMap paymentsMap = session.getMap("Payments");
```

Sessions are used to gain access to ObjectMaps backed by BackingMaps that live inside an ObjectGrid instance. The ObjectMap instance can be thought of as a "near cache". Objects copied from remote ObjectGrid instances live inside the near cache when a "get" operation is performed. Objects in the near cache are synchronized to main ObjectGrid cache when a transaction commits. The following diagram should make the relationship clearer:

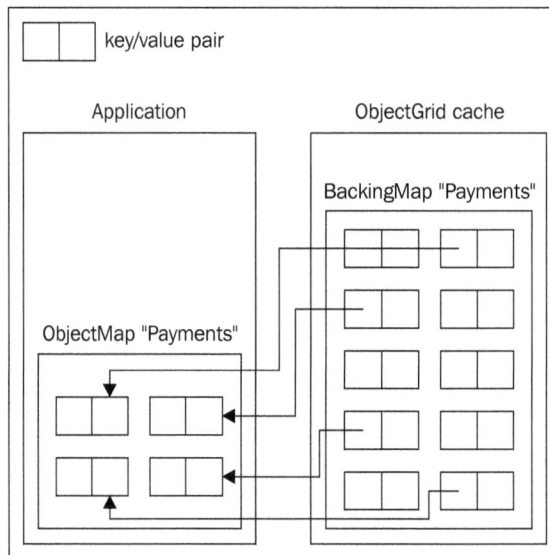

The previous diagram shows the BackingMap named Payment defined in our application. This BackingMap exists inside the ObjectGrid instance, and we cannot directly add, remove, or modify the objects inside it. Our sample code calls the grid.getSession() method (which actually creates the Payment BackingMap with an implicit call to grid.initialize()). The Session interface is used to create the ObjectMap object that lets us interact with the objects in the BackingMap named Payment with the call to session.getMap("Payment"). session. getMap("Payment") throws UndefinedMapException if it is passed the name of a BackingMap that does not exist.

Now that we have an ObjectMap, we can start adding objects to the cache. Interacting with an instance of ObjectMap is similar to interacting with `java.util.Maps`. ObjectMap contains methods to put objects in, and get objects out. The two simplest methods to use in this interface are `put(Object key, Object value)` and `get(Object key)`. While ObjectMap contains other methods to put and get objects in bulk, we'll use these two methods in our example:

```
private void persistPayment(Payment payment)
  throws ObjectGridException {
    Session session = grid.getSession();
    ObjectMap paymentMap = session.getMap("Payment");

    session.begin();
    paymentMap.put(payment.getId(), payment);
    session.commit();
}
```

The `persistPayment(Payment payment)` method uses the instance variable grid to get a Session. The `Session` instance can get a reference to the ObjectMap used to interact with the Payment BackingMap. We call the `Session#getMap(String mapName)` to get a reference to an ObjectMap. Once we have an ObjectMap, we can interact with it using GET and PUT methods.

When we want to put or get objects from an ObjectMap, we must do so under the context of a transaction. A transaction in WebSphere eXtreme Scale is similar in concept to a database transaction. The Session interface is responsible for transaction management, with explicit calls `session.begin()` and `session.commit()` or `session.rollback()` to start and end transactions. If a put or get on an ObjectGrid does not take place under an explicitly created transaction, then a transaction will begin and commit implicitly. Though implicit transactions may be usable for occasional one-off reads or writes, it is considered poor form to use them, and you are encouraged to call `session.begin()` and `session.commit()` in order to utilize transactions better and improve access to your BackingMaps:

```
session.begin();
paymentMap.put(payment.getId(), payment);
session.commit();
```

Starting a transaction alerts the grid that we are about to read from, or write to an ObjectMap. In this case, we are simply putting a Payment into the ObjectMap named Payment. Right now, that object only exists in our application context. The ObjectGrid instance does not know about it yet. The call to session.commit() signals that we are finished with our actions, and any changes made to any ObjectMap inside the transaction may be safely written out to their BackingMap inside the grid:

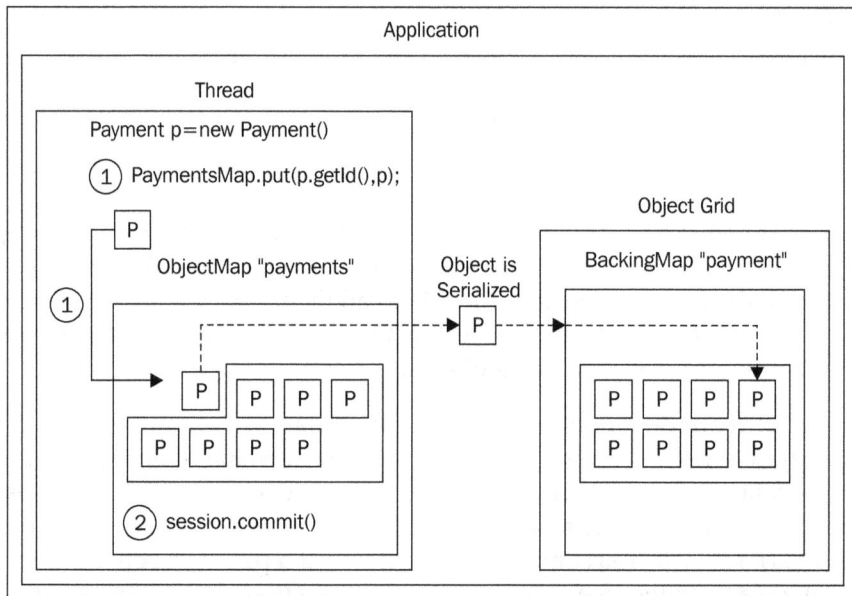

Eventually, we're going to get data out of the grid. In the event that we already have a reference to an ObjectMap, we can begin a new transaction in the Session and read from the ObjectMap using the get(Object) method. Our example shows what we need to do in the event we do not have a reference to an ObjectGrid on hand:

```
private Payment findPayment(int id)
  throws ObjectGridException {
    Session session = grid.getSession();
    ObjectMap paymentMap = session.getMap("Payment");
    session.begin();
    Payment payment = (Payment)paymentMap.get(id);
    session.rollback();
    return payment;
}
```

The `findPayment(int id)` method shows how to get a Payment out of the Payment BackingMap. Just like the `persistPayment(Payment payment)` method, `findPayment(int id)` obtains a reference to a Session and an ObjectMap for Payments. The `ObjectMap#get(Object key)` method returns an Object with the key ID. If that key does not exist in the map, then the get method returns null. We cast the Object returned from the get method into a Payment and return it after rolling back the transaction. We roll back because we did not change the payment object at all, and we only read from the map.

When we're done using the grid, we should make sure we don't leave the grid open to accidental operations. We call the `tearDown()` method to make sure our reference to ObjectGrid doesn't work anymore:

```
private void tearDown() {
    grid.destroy();
}
```

Finally, `grid.destroy()` frees any resources used by the grid. Any attempt to get a `Session`, or begin a transaction after calling `grid.destroy()`, results in a thrown `IllegalStateException`.

For completeness, here is the entire PaymentLoader class.package wxs.sample:

```
import java.io.BufferedReader;
import java.io.FileReader;
import java.io.IOException;
import java.math.BigDecimal;

import com.ibm.websphere.objectgrid.BackingMap;
import com.ibm.websphere.objectgrid.ObjectGrid;
import com.ibm.websphere.objectgrid.ObjectGridException;
import com.ibm.websphere.objectgrid.ObjectGridManager;
import com.ibm.websphere.objectgrid.ObjectGridManagerFactory;
import com.ibm.websphere.objectgrid.ObjectMap;
import com.ibm.websphere.objectgrid.Session;

public class PaymentLoader {

    ObjectGrid grid;
    static int pId = 0;

    private void initialize() throws ObjectGridException {
        ObjectGridManager ogm =
                ObjectGridManagerFactory.getObjectGridManager();
        grid = ogm.createObjectGrid();
        BackingMap bm = grid.defineMap("Payment");
    }
```

```
public static void main(String[] args) {
    PaymentLoader pl = new PaymentLoader();

    try {
        pl.initialize();
        pl.loadPayments(args[0]);
        pl.tearDown();
    } catch (ObjectGridException e) {
        e.printStackTrace();
    } catch (IOException e) {
        e.printStackTrace();
    }

    System.out.println("All done!");
}

private void loadPayments(String filename)
  throws IOException, ObjectGridException {
    BufferedReader br = null;
    try {
        br = new BufferedReader(new FileReader(filename));
        String line;
        while ((line = br.readLine()) != null) {
            Payment payment = createPayment(line);
            persistPayment(payment);
            findPayment(payment.getId());
        }
    } finally {
        if (br != null) {
            br.close();
        }
    }
}

private Payment findPayment(int id)
  throws ObjectGridException {
    Session session = grid.getSession();
    ObjectMap paymentMap = session.getMap("Payment");

    session.begin();
    Payment payment = (Payment)paymentMap.get(id);
    session.rollback();
    return payment;
}

private void persistPayment(Payment payment)
 throws ObjectGridException {

    Session session = grid.getSession();
```

```
        ObjectMap paymentMap = session.getMap("Payment");

        session.begin();
        paymentMap.put(payment.getId(), payment);
        session.commit();
    }

    private Payment createPayment(String line) {
        String[] tokens = line.split(":");

        Payment payment = new Payment();
        payment.setId(pId++);
        payment.setCardNumber(tokens[0]);
        payment.setAmount(new BigDecimal(tokens[4]));

        return payment;
    }

    private void tearDown() {
        grid.destroy();
    }
}
```

So far, we have created the ObjectGrid instance and BackingMaps in our application
code. This isn't always the best way to do it, and it adds clutter to our code. Only
local ObjectGrid instances are configurable through the programmatic interface.
If we were to continue creating grids like this, we would not be able to take
advantage of many of the features that make WebSphere eXtreme Scale so powerful.
Instead of the programmatic configuration, we can use XML configuration files
to keep information about our ObjectGrid deployment, and then load it when
our application runs. This will eventually allow us to build the linearly scalable
grids which we have discussed in this chapter. Let's take a look at what the XML
configuration for our sample program looks like:

```
<?xml version="1.0" encoding="UTF-8"?>
<objectGridConfig xmlns:xsi="http://www.w3.org/2001/
    XMLSchema-instance"xsi:schemaLocation="http://ibm.com/ws/
    objectgrid/config../objectGrid.xsd"xmlns="http://ibm.com/ws/
    objectgrid/config">
    <objectGrids>
        <objectGrid name="MyGrid">
            <backingMap name="Payment"/>
        </objectGrid>
    </objectGrids>
</objectGridConfig>
```

This is about as simple an XML configuration file we can get. The
`<objectGridConfig>` tag encompasses everything else in the file. In this file,
we can define multiple ObjectGrid instances in the `<objectGrids>`. However, in
this file we define just one. ObjectGrids defined in an XML configuration file, must
have a name set with the `name` attribute. When we load the ObjectGrid from the
`config` file in our code, we must provide a name to the `createObjectGrid(...)`
method so that it can return the correct grid instance. This is a departure from using
anonymous ObjectGrids, which is what we have done in the rest of this chapter.
Our Payment BackingMap is defined in a tag nested under the ObjectGrid instance
to which it belongs. Defining an ObjectGrid instance in an XML configuration file
changes the way we obtain a reference to it in our code:

```
private void initialize() throws ObjectGridException,
   MalformedURLException {
     ObjectGridManager ogm =
              ObjectGridManagerFactory.getObjectGridManager();

     String filename = "c:/objectgrid.xml";
     URL configFile = new URL("file://" + filename);

     grid = ogm.createObjectGrid("MyGrid",configFile);
}
```

The main difference here is that the `createObjectGrid(...)` method has
changed from giving us an anonymous ObjectGrid instance, to requesting the
ObjectGrid instance named `MyGrid` that is defined in the XML file. Notice how the
`grid.defineMap("Payment")` call disappears. We have already defined the `Payment`
BackingMap for the new ObjectGrid instance in the XML file. Once we have a
reference to the ObjectGrid instance, we have everything we need to get to work.

Summary

Data grids give us a great way to better utilize our computing resources. They allow
us to cache objects in memory that could be located on a computer, on the LAN, or in
a data center thousands of miles away. Caching data is one of the core features found
in all data grid products. Understanding how to cache objects with WebSphere
eXtreme Scale is the natural starting point in learning how to use its many other
features to your advantage. Knowledge of where your objects live will help you
create powerful grid topologies that scale linearly and keep up with the demand
of your applications. WebSphere eXtreme Scale will provide your applications
with fast access to remote objects, while giving you a much larger cache to rely on
than you would have without a data grid. It allows us to logically join numerous
computers together, whether the hardware is real or virtual, and create grids that
can store terabytes of live Java objects, all while avoiding costly database hits and
transformations to and from SQL statements.

You should now feel comfortable getting started with WebSphere eXtreme Scale, and creating ObjectGrid instances by using the programmatic API, or by creating a simple XML configuration file. Explore what happens when you examine the ObjectMap instances and BackingMaps with a debugger after puts and transaction commits.

You should be familiar with local ObjectGrid instances. As we explore more features of WebSphere eXtreme Scale, you will be able to tell when using a local instance is right for the situation, and when a distributed grid is more suitable. In Chapter 2, we'll find out more about interacting with data in the grid.

2
The ObjectMap API

Now that we have a general idea of what WebSphere eXtreme Scale can do for us, let's find out how to use it. Putting data into, and retrieving data from the grid is done with four closely related API groups. Each API serves a different purpose, though they all require knowledge of the same foundation topics. Chapter 1 introduced us to the ObjectMap API. The ObjectMap API provides the most basic functionality in WebSphere eXtreme Scale, but that doesn't mean it is the least useful. There are many obvious uses for distributed maps, and a few surprises await us as we progress with ObjectMap. In this chapter, we'll delve deeper into the ObjectMap API.

Through exploring the ObjectMap API, we'll become more familiar with the relationship between an ObjectMap and a BackingMap. We'll also learn how they work together to provide access to and persistence for our objects.

After reading this chapter you will:

- Have a working knowledge of the most commonly used methods in the ObjectMap API
- Programmatically configure local ObjectGrid instances
- Understand what happens when we update objects in distributed ObjectGrid deployments

Different kinds of maps

It's important to distinguish between ObjectMaps and BackingMaps. Though
they are closely related, they perform very different duties in our application.
A BackingMap is the map that stores persistent copies of our objects. All of our
objects that have been committed in a transaction exist inside a BackingMap. This
BackingMap may be in a local ObjectGrid instance, meaning that ObjectGrid is
running inside the same memory space as our application, or in a distributed
ObjectGrid. The distributed ObjectGrid is the one that is made up of at least
one process dedicated to running ObjectGrid instances. Distributed ObjectGrid
instances are typically made up of many processes utilizing the main memory of
many different computers to create a unified logical data store.

We will never directly interact with a BackingMap to insert, update, or remove
objects from it. We will only interact with a BackingMap to configure its behavior.
This configuration is done either programmatically:

```
BackingMap bm = grid.defineMap("payments");
bm.setNullValuesSupported(true);
bm.setTimeToLive(60 * 60 * 24);
bm.setTtlEvictorType(TTLType.CREATION_TIME);
```

Or via an XML configuration file:

```
<?xml version="1.0" encoding="UTF-8"?>
<objectGridConfig xmlns:xsi=...
                  xsi:schemaLocation=...
                  xmlns=...>
    <objectGrids>
       <objectGrid name="PaymentProcessorGrid">
          <backingMap name="payments"
                      nullValuesSupported="true"
                      timeToLive="86400"
                      ttlEvictorType="CREATION_TIME"
       </objectGrid>
    </objectGrids>
</objectGridConfig>
```

Once a BackingMap is initialized, its configuration cannot be changed.

We interact with a BackingMap using an instance of an ObjectMap. An ObjectMap provides all of the insert, update, and remove functionality that we would want to use on a map structure. Many different threads or processes can get an ObjectMap instance that operates on the same BackingMap. This is typically how we use WebSphere eXtreme Scale. We have an ObjectGrid instance which contains many BackingMaps. Our topology also contains many processes, and these processes could be application servers, batch processes, monitoring applications, and so on, where they all need to use objects in the same BackingMaps.

An ObjectMap instance gives us a view into the corresponding BackingMap. It allows us to add new objects to a BackingMap and remove stale objects. In this way, we should look at an ObjectMap as a proxy for a BackingMap. ObjectMap provides all of the client-side details, while the BackingMap itself lives safely away from our application in an ObjectGrid server process. An ObjectMap instance contains all of the functionality we need to get started with WebSphere eXtreme Scale. Depending on our application, the ObjectMap API may provide all of the functionality needed from a data grid. As mentioned in Chapter 1, the ObjectMap acts as a wrapper around a "near cache". Inside the ObjectMap in our ObjectGrid client application is a map that contains key/value pairs obtained from distributed BackingMaps. The near cache doesn't start with any objects in it. Only objects obtained by a `get` or `find` request are stored locally in the near cache. This speeds up access the next time the local client application requests that object.

Get and put

On the surface, ObjectMap looks like a map we would find in the Java standard API with `put` and `get` methods. We would expect an interface similar to `java.util.Map` with a name like ObjectMap. Though it doesn't quite provide all of the methods we've come to expect on a `java.util.Map`, an ObjectMap provides a lot more functionality. We still have methods to `get`, `put`, `update`, and `remove` objects in a BackingMap though, so we'll start with those.

There are three methods for getting data into an ObjectMap. The `put (Object key, Object value)` method does just what you think it would. An object value is placed into the map and is addressable by its key. Individual inserts into an ObjectMap are done using this `put (Object key, Object value)` method. We've seen this a few times in our payment processing example:

```
session.begin();
paymentsMap.put(p.getId(), p);
session.commit();
```

Remember, all of our interactions with the ObjectMap should be done under the context of a transaction. In this example, we just started a transaction with `session.begin()`, and ended it with `session.commit()`. `paymentsMap.put(p.getId(), p)` is placing the payment referenced by `p` into the `paymentsMap` and is giving the payment ID as its key, which is of type `long`. Until `session.commit()` is called, that payment only lives inside the ObjectMap. It has not yet made it to the ObjectMap's corresponding BackingMap inside the ObjectGrid. Invoking the `session.commit()` method pushes all new and changed ObjectMap entries down to the BackingMap.

Creating loops to iterate over Maps and Sets and calling `ObjectMap.put(Object key, Object value)` isn't the best way to get bulk objects into our map. Fortunately, ObjectMap provides us with a `putAll(Map map)` method that accepts our populated Java Map objects. This method takes an instance of a `java.util.Map` and adds all of its key/value pairs to the ObjectMap. We've seen this method before:

```
if (pMap.size() >= 100) {
    session.begin();
    paymentsMap.putAll(pMap);
    session.commit();
    pMap = new HashMap();
}
```

Again, we start a transaction before putting objects in our map. In this example, `pMap` is a `java.util.HashMap` that holds our `Payment` objects until we decide to add them to the ObjectMap. Though this example may be contrived, I'm sure you can think of plenty of cases where an application you have written has objects in an existing `java.util.Map` that would benefit from living inside an ObjectGrid instance. While we work with unpartitioned BackingMaps, the `putAll` method will now work as expected. When we start working with distributed BackingMaps, the `java.util.Map` passed to `putAll` must contain objects that all map to the same partition. This will be covered later, in detail, in the book.

ObjectMap also has several methods to retrieve objects once they are in the grid. The most basic is the `get(Object key)` method. On the surface, `get(Object key)` behaves much like the `get(Object key)` methods on a `java.util.Map` in that it will give you the value object with the key you pass as the argument or null, if that key doesn't exist in the map:

```
public void fraudCheck() throws ObjectGridException {
    session.begin();
    for (long i = 1; i <= totalNumberOfPayments; i++) {
        Payment p = (Payment)paymentsMap.get(i);
        p.fraudCheck();
        paymentsMap.update(p.getId(), p);
    }
    session.commit();
}
```

Just like get (Object key) on java.util.Map, paymentsMap.get(i) returns an object that must be cast to the correct type. Though it's rare, an object of a different type could sneak into a BackingMap and cause a ClassCastException on the cast to Payment in this example. This typically isn't a problem due to the nature of how maps are populated. However, it wouldn't hurt to be prepared for the worst (and prevent it) when casting from object, which is the return type of get (Object key) to your desired data type.

In case we know the keys of multiple Payments we want to get out of the grid, we can call paymentsMap.getAll(List keys). It is simply a list that contains all of the keys for the objects we want to pull from the grid.

```
public void fraudCheck() throws ObjectGridException {
    List keyList = new ArrayList();
    session.begin();
    int totalNumberOfPayments = 10000;
    for (long i = 1; i <= totalNumberOfPayments; i++) {
        keyList.add(i);
        if (keyList.size() == 100) {
            List payments = paymentsMap.getAll(keyList);
            for (Object o : payments) {
                if (!(o instanceof Payment)) continue;
                Payment p = (Payment) o;
                p.fraudCheck();
                paymentsMap.update(p.getId(), p);
            }
            keyList = new ArrayList();
        }
    }
    session.commit();
}
```

This is what fraudCheck() looks like when rewritten to use the getAll(List keys) method. The getAll(List keys) method returns a List of Objects, so they need to be cast into Payment if we are to use the Payment methods. The line that reads if (!(o instanceof Payment)) continue; is not acceptable production code in most cases. However, it should be clear that some action needs to be taken to prevent the previously discussed ClassCastException. Now fraudCheck() pulls Payments out of the ObjectMap in groups of 100 by populating keyList with the keys for the payments to get. Once the list is populated, we call List payments = paymentsMap. getAll(keyList);. From here, we iterate over our new list of payments and perform a fraud check on each one.

Though we've been working with local ObjectGrid instances so far, we need to remember that we will usually deploy to distributed, multi-node WebSphere eXtreme Scale topologies. In this case, we need to remember that ObjectMaps and BackingMaps are distinct. A BackingMap is where objects exist in a persistent state. An ObjectMap only provides an application-side view into a BackingMap.

Updating objects in the grid

Next we'll look at the getForUpdate(Object key) and getAllForUpdate(List keys) methods. These methods present us with the notion that the get(Object key) and getAll(List keys) methods may not get an object that allows updates. This isn't the case. These methods offer different locking semantics than the get methods on the objects they return. On the surface, the getForUpdate(Object key) and getAllForUpdate(List keys) methods behave like their non-ForUpdate counterparts. The getForUpdate(Object key) and getAllForUpdate(List keys) methods return objects managed by a BackingMap.

In a distributed ObjectGrid deployment, many different threads from different processes may try to update an object at about the same time. Updating an object involves three steps: getting the object out of the BackingMap, changing the object, and then committing the change to the BackingMap. When two or more different threads perform this step at about the same time, we could end up overwriting an update with something incorrect. Imagine a situation where two threads try to update a bank account balance. Both threads have an update to add $50.00 to the balance. If both threads read the initial balance as $100.00, and one updates the balance to $150.00 and commits the changes, the other thread is not aware of that change. The second thread still has a balance of $100.00. When the second thread performs the update, the balance is set to $150.00 and the bank account owner just lost $50.00. We can prevent this in eXtreme Scale with a locking strategy.

There are three different locking strategies and three different lock types. Each locking strategy uses the lock types for different purposes. Different lock types will be held for different lengths of time depending on the chosen lock strategy. We will need to build application methods in a way that can handle errors when transactions are rolled back. The granularity of our transactions is influenced by our use of a locking strategy.

Because the getForUpdate(Object key) and getAllForUpdate(List keys) methods differ in semantics compared to their non-ForUpdate counterparts, we need to know about the three different locking strategies available to a BackingMap. A BackingMap is configured with only one LockStrategy. A LockStrategy can be set programmatically, or in the XML configuration file.

Lock strategies

The optimistic lock strategy assumes that objects in a BackingMap are read-mostly, and that one object will not be updated by two threads simultaneously, whether locally or in different client applications. This means that an object modified by thread **1** will not have thread **2** perform concurrent modifications to it. The optimistic lock strategy is just that we optimistically assume that the current thread of execution is the only thread operating on an object at a given time. No one else would want to modify our object, would they?

The pessimistic lock strategy assumes that some other thread is always trying to modify an object already modified by the first thread. In this way, the pessimistic lock strategy goes out of its way to safeguard an object against concurrent changes. This is done by using the lock types to ensure that only one thread can obtain an object with intent to update it at any given time. The pessimistic lock strategy assumes the worst, that other threads are trying to modify our object, and blocks those other threads from writing to that object while we hold an upgradable lock.

The third lock strategy is no-lock. This strategy is the most promiscuous, providing zero locks on objects managed by a BackingMap. The no-lock locking strategy assumes that some other provider will supply locking for objects in the grid. This other provider could be part of our application that is aware of which objects are modified. By piggy-backing locking on this part of our application, we free the BackingMap from managing this, and we obtain better read and write performance, along with the risk of assuming our custom locking is accurate. Typically we'll prefer an optimistic locking strategy over a pessimistic. We don't typically use the no-lock strategy unless we're 100% sure an application can provide better locking for distributed maps.

Lock types

Before we move on, we should have a firm understanding of the three different lock types used by the lock strategies. In order of strength, there is **S** (the *shared lock*), **U** (the *upgradeable lock*), and **X** (the *exclusive lock*). Obviously, the no-lock strategy does not use any of these lock types because the onus is on the application developer to provide an implementation that prevents concurrent updates to an object. Each lock type can block an application from obtaining an object using a different lock type.

The shared lock type is used when reading objects from a BackingMap. This lock type provides assurances that only committed objects are read from a BackingMap. The `get(Object key)` and `getAll(List keys)` methods obtain shared locks on objects. This lock type prevents the application from obtaining an exclusive lock type because it indicates that an object is in use for reading. Writing changes to an object is not possible while a thread holds a shared lock on it. Instead, the thread requesting the exclusive lock will be blocked until the shared lock is released.

Obtaining an upgradeable lock on an object with a shared lock on it is still possible. The upgradeable lock denotes that an object is in use for reading, and that the thread may request an exclusive lock at some later time to write changes to the object. If any thread still has a shared lock on the object, the thread requesting the exclusive lock will be blocked until the shared lock is released. The upgradeable lock mode allows threads to obtain shared locks, but blocks threads requesting upgradeable or exclusive locks. This blocking happens because the upgradeable lock indicates that a thread has the intention of writing to an object. Another upgradeable lock is not obtainable until the first thread with the upgradeable lock either commits the transaction, or the transaction is rolled back, releasing the upgradeable lock.

An upgradeable lock type indicates that at some point, the thread holding the lock on an object intends to write a changed state of the object to the BackingMap. When the thread calls for the transaction to commit, each object with an upgradeable lock has that lock upgraded to exclusive, indicating that no other locks on this object may be obtained. The **U** lock is upgraded to an **X** lock at commit time. When the **X** lock is obtained, other transactions are blocked from getting another **X** lock, or even **U** or **S** locks on the object. The `getForUpdate(Object key)` and `getAllForUpdate(List keys)` methods obtain upgradeable locks on objects. This is in contrast to the shared lock obtained by the `get(Object key)` and `getAll(List keys)` that obtain shared locks on objects. The transaction then writes the object to the BackingMap while holding the exclusive lock, and releases it when the transaction successfully commits. This sequence of locking prevents concurrent updates to an object by ensuring that only one thread at a time holds an upgradeable or exclusive lock on an object.

An exclusive lock is held whenever a thread needs to write an object to a BackingMap. The exclusive lock is the strongest lock type, blocking all other lock requests until the exclusive lock is released. This lock is obtained by both the optimistic and pessimistic lock strategies when writing an object. The write methods include `insert(Object key, Object value)`, `put(Object key)`, `putAll(Map objects)`, `update(Object key, Object value)`, `touch(Object key)`, `remove(Object key)`, and `removeAll(Map objects)`.

Hash map refresher (or crash course)

Locks on objects need to be stored somewhere accessible to different threads. Much like how objects are stored in buckets in the BackingMap, locks are also stored in buckets. This brings us to the `numberOfBuckets` and `numberOfLockBuckets` settings on a BackingMap. These settings are implementation details of a BackingMap, but it's important to know these details in order to assign optimum settings for concurrency and performance. BackingMaps use a hash table data structure to store objects.

Let's review a basic implementation of the hash map data structure so we know what the number of buckets means. Hash maps store objects in buckets. A bucket is a place for a value object keyed with a key object. A good key object is an integer, and as luck would have it, the `hashCode()` method on `java.lang.Object` returns an integer value. Because every object in Java inherits from `java.lang.Object`, we have the `hashCode()` method available to any object we create. We should override the `equals()` and `hashCode()` methods in our objects to provide an appropriate implementation. I will not go into what makes a good hash algorithm here as plenty of papers have been written on the subject. You can use Google, Yahoo!, or the search engine of your choice to find out what goes into making a good hash algorithm. For our purpose, the following implementation suits our needs:

```java
@Override
public int hashCode() {
    final int prime = 31;
    int result = 1;
    result = prime * result + ((amount == null) ?
                0 : amount.hashCode());
    result = prime * result
                + ((ccExpiration == null) ?
                    0 : ccExpiration.hashCode());
    result = prime * result + ((ccName == null) ?
                0 : ccName.hashCode());
    result = prime * result
                + ((ccNumber == null) ?
                    0 : ccNumber.hashCode());
    result = prime * result + ((ccType == null) ?
                0 : ccType.hashCode());
    result = prime * result + (int) (id ^ (id >>> 32));
    result = prime * result + (isApproved ? 1231 : 1237);
    result = prime * result + (isFraudulent ? 1231 : 1237);
    result = prime * result + (isValid ? 1231 : 1237);
    result = prime * result + paymentType;
    return result;
}
```

Ideally, the hashCode() method provides a unique integer for each object instance. It only needs to provide a sufficient distribution of keys that produces the fewest possible collisions across the number of available buckets. This integer value is used by a hash map implementation to determine which bucket will store a reference to the object. A collision occurs when two or more keys map to the same hash code. When this happens, the bucket doesn't store a reference to an object, but a linked list of references to objects that have that hash code. Instead of referencing an object in a bucket by its hash code, a get method on the map with that hash code, the map must perform a key scan on the list of objects with the same hash code. When a few objects occupy the same bucket, we start losing out on the performance benefit of having a hash code in the first place by performing key scans on each bucket with key collisions:

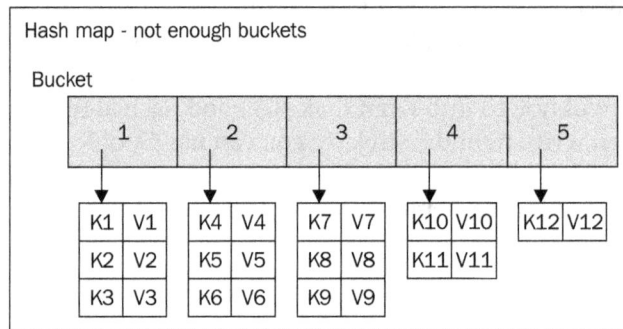

This is why we need to make sure that the number of buckets is set sufficiently high so that each bucket ideally stores one object. In this case, the hash code is the key to one object, and we do not perform a key scan using the object equals() method for each key object in the list. Inserts and lookups to this map of sufficient size are very efficient. At the same time, we do not want to set the number of buckets so large that we allocate far more memory than we will use. The implementation of these maps is an array, meaning that resources are pre-allocated at the time of creation. If you set the number of buckets too high, your application will crash with an OutOfMemoryException while allocating the space for a map. Creating a map that has too many buckets reduces the number of map partitions, or the size of those partitions we can address per JVM. Instead, those maps will need to be spread over more JVMs and possibly more physical computers.

The number of lock buckets is used to track the objects with active locks held on them. This number should be significantly smaller than the number of buckets. Buckets in this lock map are only held for as long as a lock is held on an object. When a lock is requested for an object, the lock map first checks to see if any lock is held on that object. If no lock is held, an entry is made in the map for that object and the requested lock type. When the last lock is removed from the object, the entry is removed from the lock map. The lock map does not need as many buckets as the object map, only as many buckets as you expect to have simultaneous object locks. We shouldn't need to simultaneously obtain a lock on all of the objects in the map. A safe starting number of lock buckets is around 15% of the size of the number of buckets in the object map. If performance is a problem, and you have an appropriate number of buckets for the object map, then the number of buckets on the lock map may be insufficient. Obtaining locks on a large percentage of the total objects simultaneously will cause a linked list of locks to be stored in the lock map, instead of one lock per bucket. Increasing the number of lock buckets will alleviate this performance problem and allow a map to utilize more concurrent locks with acceptable performance.

The lock timeout setting on a BackingMap indicates the length of time a thread should wait before giving up on obtaining a lock for a specified object. If a thread waits longer than the value of this setting, then a LockTimeoutException is thrown. On a grid with reasonable load, a LockTimeoutException should indicate a deadlock. However, if the grid is under heavy load, get requests could queue long enough that LockTimeoutExceptions appear more frequently than deadlock situations. We reduce LockTimeoutExceptions in this case by setting a higher value for the lockTimeout setting on a BackingMap.

```
BackingMap bm = grid.defineMap("payments");
bm.setLockStrategy(LockStrategy.PESSIMISTIC);
bm.setLockTimeout(20);
```

The setLockTimeout(int seconds) method (seen above) takes the number of seconds to wait before a thread throws a LockTimeoutException as its argument. Here, we are explicitly setting the lock strategy to pessimistic and giving a thread 20 seconds to obtain the requested lock. Configured via XML, we get the following:

```
<backingMap name="payments"
            lockStrategy="PESSIMISTIC"
            lockTimeout="20"/>
```

Optimistic collisions

A deadlock is a condition where two or more threads are waiting for a lock promotion on the same object due to the other threads holding a shared lock. Specifically, this happens when two threads hold an **S** lock on an object, and both threads then request an **X** lock to write changes to the object. The general case is that two threads attempt to simultaneously update a shared object resulting in lock contention because neither thread can obtain the higher-level lock it needs to write the changes.

The different locking strategies deal with this situation with some help from the developer. The optimistic locking strategy holds locks for very brief time periods. A lock is only held as long as it takes a thread to read or write an object. When thread 1 calls a `get` method for a payment with a key of 5000, the **S** lock is obtained for key 5000. After obtaining the lock, our payments BackingMap returns the object with that key and releases the **S** lock. This ensures that only objects in a consistent state are read from the BackingMap. If thread 2 holds an **X** lock on the requested object, then thread 1 must wait until that **X** lock is released to obtain the requested **S** lock.

Writing the object to the BackingMap is similar to reading it in the optimistic case. When the transaction commits, an **X** lock is requested for an updated object. This request is blocked, if there are any **S** locks held on the object. Once the **S** lock held by thread 2 is released, thread 1 obtains an **X** lock, and then writes the object to the BackingMap. The transaction releases the **X** lock once the write operation completes.

What happens to the object used by thread 2 though? If its use is read-only, then nothing bad happens to the state of the object in the BackingMap, and our application works as expected. If thread 2 attempts to update the object, then an **X** lock on that object is requested when the transaction commits. Provided that no other threads hold an **S** or **X** lock on the object, thread 2 gets the **X** lock and attempts to write the object to the BackingMap. Before writing the object, the BackingMap performs a check to see if the state of the object in the map matches the original state of the object retrieved from the map. This is to make sure that a thread does not update objects using stale object state. In this case, the object used by thread 2 contains stale a state information because thread 1 already performed an update and committed its transaction. The state of the object in the BackingMap no longer matches the original state of the object used by thread 2. When this happens, an `OptimisticCollisionException` is thrown by the call to `session.commit()`.

What went wrong here? Nothing, actually. The optimistic lock strategy assumes that, for the most part, two threads will never attempt to modify the same object simultaneously. In the event that this happens, the call to commit the transaction throws the OptimisticCollisionException, and the developer must make the appropriate decision on how to deal with it. Throwing the OptimisticCollisionException is the optimistic locking strategy's way of telling us that our assumption of how the application would interact with the object in the BackingMap did not hold true in this instance.

As application developers we should help eXtreme Scale determine when two different threads modify an object concurrently. We do this by implementing the com.ibm.websphere.objectgrid.plugins.OptimisiticCallback interface. This interface provides methods that let eXtreme Scale determine which version of an object was used as the basis for an update. Let's go back to our example of updating a bank account balance. Thread 1 and thread 2 both obtain a copy of an account balance of $100.00. This time the object has a version associated with it, let's say version 500. Thread 1 updates the balance to $150.00 and commits the change. Upon commit, eXtreme Scale uses the OptimisticCallback plugin to compare versions. The version of the object in the map is 500, the version of the object we updated is 500. This shows that another thread did not update this account between the time we got it and the time we updated it. eXtreme Scale then uses the OptimisiticCallback plugin to update the version to 501.

Now when thread 2 commits the update, the versions on the account do not match. Thread 2 has a stale copy of the account object and an OptimisticCollisionException is thrown.

Using an OptimisticCallback plugin with an object is easy. The POJO should have some field that uniquely identifies which version of the object it is. This can be as simple as having a field on the object that keeps track of version number or a time field denoting when the object was last updated. Let's do an example with a version field.

```java
package wxs.sample;

import java.io.Serializable;
import java.math.BigDecimal;

import com.ibm.websphere.projector.annotations.Id;

public class Payment implements Serializable {
    private int id;
    private String cardNumber;
    private BigDecimal amount;

    private long version = 0L;

    public String getCardNumber() {
            return cardNumber;
```

```
        }
        public void setCardNumber(String cardNumber) {
                this.cardNumber = cardNumber;
        }
        public BigDecimal getAmount() {
                return amount;
        }
        public void setAmount(BigDecimal amount) {
                this.amount = amount;
        }
        public long getVersion() {
                return version;
        }
        public void setVersion(long version) {
                this.version = version;
        }
        public int getId() {
                return id;
        }
        public void setId(int id) {
                this.id = id;
        }
}
```

Here we use a Payment object with a version field. This field will be used by our OptimisticCallback plugin.

```
package wxs.sample;

import java.io.IOException;

import java.io.ObjectInputStream;

import java.io.ObjectOutputStream;

import com.ibm.websphere.objectgrid.plugins.OptimisticCallback;

public class PaymentOptimisticCallback implements OptimisticCallback {

    @Override
    public Object getVersionedObjectForValue(Object value) {
            if (value == null) return null;

            Payment payment = (Payment)value;
            return new Long(payment.getVersion());
    }

    @Override
    public Object inflateVersionedValue(ObjectInputStream stream)
                throws IOException, ClassNotFoundException {
            return stream.readObject();
```

```
        }

        @Override
        public void serializeVersionedValue(Object value,
          ObjectOutputStream stream)
          throws IOException {
              stream.writeObject(value);
        }

        @Override
        public void updateVersionedObjectForValue(Object value) {
              if (value == null) return;

              Payment payment = (Payment)value;
              payment.setVersion(payment.getVersion() + 1);
        }

    }
```

The OptimisticCallback interface requires four methods be implemented. The two that we are most concerned with are getVersionedObjectForValue(Object value) and updateVersionedObjectForValue(Object value). The other two methods deal with reading the object from and writing it back to its serialized form. Most of the time it's safe to implement these methods as they are implemented in the example.

The OptimisticCallback#getVersionedObjectForValue(Object value) method take an object that should be a Payment. We will associate this plugin with the Payments BackingMap, and we expect only Payment objects to make it to this method. Based on that expectation, we cast the Object into a Payment and return the version field. We compare the version field from the client-updated copy of the object to the version field from the same Payment in the BackingMap. If they match, then the Payment is safely updated. If they do not match, our Session#commit() call throws an OptimisticCollisionException.

When an update proceeds, the OptimisticCallback#updateVersionedObjectFor Value(Object value) method is called. Again, we expect a Payment object, so we cast the value argument into a Payment. Now we need to update the version field so that any future update does not overwrite this fresh version of the object with stale data. This is as simple as incrementing the value of the version field. If we used the update time as the version field, we would set the version to the current time.

We use the PaymentOptimisticCallback plugin with a BackingMap. We configure the plugin with a BackingMap using the API like this:

```
    private void initializeLocalWithAPI() throws ObjectGridException {
        ObjectGridManager ogm = ObjectGridManagerFactory.
                                                getObjectGridManager();
        grid = ogm.createObjectGrid();
```

```
        BackingMap bm = grid.defineMap("Payment");
        bm.setLockStrategy(LockStrategy.OPTIMISTIC);
        OptimisticCallback poc = new PaymentOptimisticCallback();
        bm.setOptimisticCallback(poc);
}
```

This configuration happens after we define the BackingMap but before it is created.

We can use the `objectgrid.xml` file to insert the same plugin.

```
<?xml version="1.0" encoding="UTF-8" ?>
<objectGridConfig xmlns:xsi="http://www.w3.org/2001/
   XMLSchema-instance" xsi:schemaLocation="http://ibm.com/ws/
   objectgrid/config ../objectGrid.xsd" xmlns="http://ibm.com/ws/
   objectgrid/config">
<objectGrids>
<objectGrid name="MyGrid">
<backingMap name="Payment" lockStrategy="OPTIMISTIC"
            pluginCollectionRef="Payment" />
</objectGrid>
</objectGrids>
<backingMapPluginCollections>
<backingMapPluginCollection id="Payment">
<bean id="OptimisticCallback"
      className="wxs.sample.PaymentOptimisticCallback" />
</backingMapPluginCollection>
</backingMapPluginCollections>
</objectGridConfig>
```

Dealing with OptimisticCollisionExceptions is at the developer's discretion and in most cases is application-specific. The OptimisticCollisionException could be thrown because we tried to make the same update in two different threads. In this case, dealing with the OptimisticCollisionException is as simple as rolling back the transaction. The exception could also be thrown as a result of two threads making changes to different fields on an object. In this case, all of the updates are considered important, and the updated fields do not have collisions. Moreover, we could retrieve the most recent object state with another call to the get method, make our updates, and try to write back to the object in another transaction. A third case sees an object's fields modified by two threads where the updates to the fields are in collision with each other. Either the committed object or the version that caused the OptimisticCollisionException may be the correct version to use, but deciding which version of the object to keep is purely a business decision. Retrieving the current state of the object in the BackingMap, and comparing it to the locally modified version to determine which to keep, should be handled when catching the OptimisticCollisionException.

Deadlocks

We can avoid the OptimisticCollisionException by using the pessimistic lock strategy. The pessimistic strategy assumes that objects can and will be updated simultaneously by multiple threads. By assuming that multiple threads will be writing to objects in a BackingMap, we give up a little concurrency, but we don't need to handle OptimisticCollisionExceptions. Where the optimistic lock strategy only briefly holds **S** or **X** locks, the pessimistic strategy holds locks for the duration of the transaction. The pessimistic lock strategy also makes the **U** lock available for use.

When we use a get method to retrieve an object from a BackingMap, our transaction in thread 1 obtains an **S** lock on that object and holds it for the duration of the transaction. When thread 2 uses a get method to retrieve the same object, the **S** lock held by thread 1 will not block thread 2 from obtaining an **S** lock. Now that both threads have **S** locks, they modify the state of the object and use a put method to push the changed object into the near-cache. Now, when the transaction commits, each thread attempts to get an **X** lock before writing the object to the BackingMap:

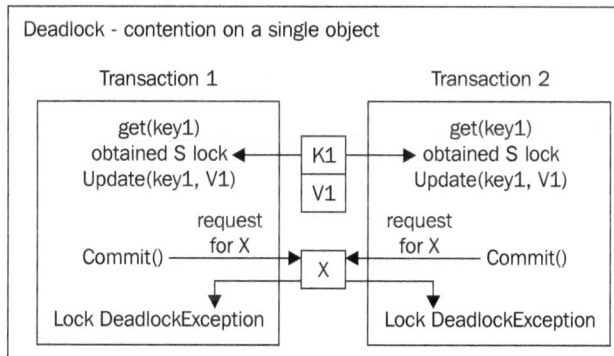

Deadlock - contention on a single object

Transaction 1 | Transaction 2

get(key1)
obtained S lock ← K1 → obtained S lock
Update(key1, V1) | V1 | Update(key1, V1)

Commit() — request for X → X ← request for X — Commit()

Lock DeadlockException | Lock DeadlockException

Each thread holds an **S** lock on the object, and each thread requests an **X** lock. Neither thread will obtain the **X** lock because each holds an **S** lock that must be relinquished in order for the other thread to obtain the **X** lock. WebSphere eXtreme Scale detects this form of deadlock because the contention is on just one object. When this form of deadlock happens, a LockDeadlockException is thrown when the transaction commits. This is in contrast to the LockTimeoutException thrown in other deadlock situations. When handling the LockDeadlockExeption, we should always make sure to rollback the transaction that was in progress when the exception was thrown.

We can prevent the lock promotion deadlock by using the getForUpdate(Object key) and getForUpdate(List keys) methods on an ObjectMap, instead of the get methods. The getForUpdate methods retrieve an object from a BackingMap, but they obtain a **U** lock instead of an **S** lock. This **U** lock blocks other transactions from obtaining either **U** or **X** locks on the same object. However, it does not prevent another transaction from obtaining an **S** lock with a get method. Using the pessimistic lock strategy, we must pay careful attention to the semantics of the ObjectMap methods we call. We must agree that an object obtained via a get method will not be written to the BackingMap in order for our pessimistic agreement to remain valid.

Using the getForUpdate methods to obtain a **U** lock on an object prevents any other transaction(s) from obtaining a **U** or **X** lock on that object. This lock provides serialization to object updates and ensures that only one transaction will modify an object at any given time. Calling getForUpdate methods to obtain a **U** lock in some parts of our code, while calling get methods to obtain an **S** lock for those same objects in other parts of our code, violates that agreement and leads to a deadlock because two transactions that are both waiting to obtain an **X** lock. The **U** lock is not promoted to an **X** lock because **S** locks are held elsewhere. Any of the **S** locks are not promoted to **X** lock because the **U** lock prevents their promotion. Again, we end up with a deadlock. This is why it is very important to agree on the semantics of the get and getForUpdate methods. When using the pessimistic lock strategy, any object obtained by a call to the get methods must be read-only. In order to write an object to a BackingMap, a reference should first be obtained with a getForUpdate method:

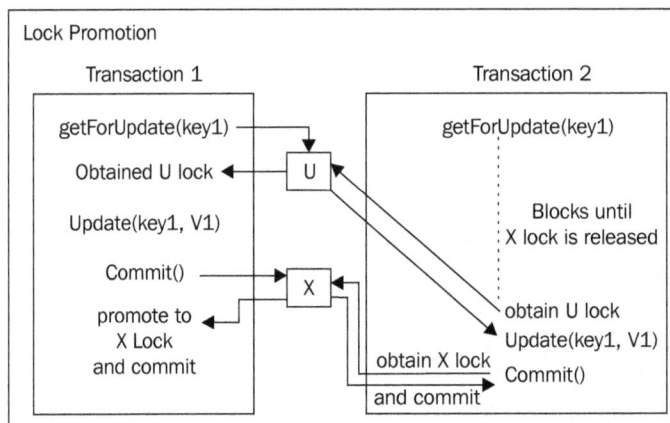

All operations in Transaction 1 take place before any operations in Transaction 2.

So far, we've only dealt with deadlock on one object. In the simplest case, WebSphere eXtreme Scale detects this deadlock and throws a `LockDeadlockException`. When deadlock is not detected, the transactions will wait for the entire lock timeout period before a `LockTimeoutException` is thrown. Another situation we run into `LockTimeoutException` is when there is deadlock caused by lock contention on two or more objects.

Let's assume we're working with a BackingMap in two different threads with their own transactions. Each thread retrieves, changes, and updates objects using a non-deterministic method to obtain the objects. Using a non-deterministic method of object retrieval almost guarantees the order of objects seen by each thread will be different. If thread 1 retrieves an object with `getForUpdate(key1)`, and thread 2 obtains a different object with `getForUpdate(key2)`, then we've not yet caused a deadlock. If those two threads then require the object referenced by the other thread, then each thread would call the `get` method. Thread 1 would call `get(key2)` and thread 2 would call `get(key1)`. The **U** locks held by the threads do not prevent the other from obtaining an **S** lock on the same object. Remember, the **U** lock blocks only requests for **U** locks or **X** locks. Updating the object in the appropriate threads with an update method works as expected, though we get a `LockTimeoutException` when we try to commit the transaction:

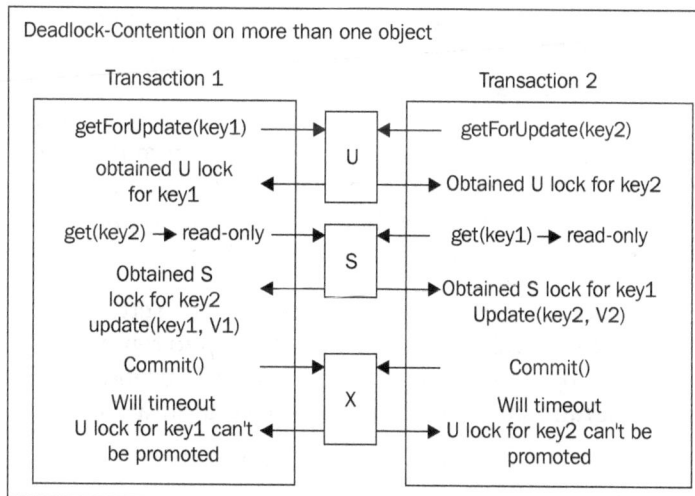

```
Deadlock-Contention on more than one object

        Transaction 1                            Transaction 2

  getForUpdate(key1) ────────►  ┌───┐  ◄────────  getForUpdate(key2)
                                │ U │
     obtained U lock    ◄───────┤   ├────────►  Obtained U lock for key2
        for key1                └───┘

  get(key2) ─► read-only ─────►  ┌───┐  ◄──────  get(key1) ─► read-only
                                 │ S │
      Obtained S        ◄────────┤   ├────────►  Obtained S lock for key1
     lock for key2               └───┘            Update(key2, V2)
     update(key1, V1)

        Commit()       ────────►  ┌───┐  ◄────────   Commit()
                                  │ X │
     Will timeout                 │   │            Will timeout
  U lock for key1 can't ◄─────────┤   ├────────►  U lock for key2 can't be
      be promoted                 └───┘              promoted
```

Because each transaction holds an **S** lock to an object updated by another thread, upgrading the **U** lock to an **X** lock at commit time is impossible. It is likely that both of these transactions will timeout. Using a deterministic method to obtain object keys and their corresponding objects will prevent this problem because the **U** lock is obtained on each object in the same order in each thread. Getting the same locks in the same order will drastically reduce the number of transaction timeouts caused by deadlocks.

If a deterministic method for obtaining keys is not possible, we may want to consider using the optimistic lock strategy. Deadlocks typically won't happen using the optimistic strategy, and handling `OptimisticCollisionException` is at least more predictable than guessing whether a `LockTimeoutException` is due to heavy server load or an actual deadlock caused by faulty application logic. Each locking strategy has its uses. The optimistic strategy assumes a read-mostly map, while the pessimistic strategy assumes that concurrent updates can and will occur with enough frequency that we need to guard against corrupting objects in the BackingMap. Deciding which strategy to use is dependent on the map usage. As we continue, we'll see examples of maps that use the different lock strategies based on their usage.

Removing objects

Until now, we have been dealing primarily with putting, getting, and updating objects in a BackingMap. We can also remove objects in a BackingMap with the ObjectMap `remove(Object key)` and `removeAll(Collection keys)` methods. Removing an object with the `remove(Object key)` method behaves like a remove method on a `java.util.Map` in that the object removed from the map is returned from the method. This method obeys the copy mode specified on the BackingMap. The `removeAll(Collection keys)` method uses the void return value, and does not return the list of objects removed from a BackingMap.

Removing objects from a BackingMap can also be done by setting a time-to-live on each object. The time-to-live value tells the BackingMap to remove any object older than T seconds, or any object that has not been used in T seconds. We can set the time-to-live value programmatically or in the XML configuration file:

```
BackingMap bm = grid.defineMap("payments");
bm.setTimeToLive(60 * 60 * 24);
bm.setTtlEvictorType(TTLType.CREATION_TIME);
```

The argument passed to the setTimeToLive(int ttl) method is given in seconds. In this call, we set the BackingMap to remove objects 24 hours after the object is created. The TTLType is an enumeration of the three TTL eviction types. Here, we chose to remove the object 24 hours after creation time. We can also specify TTLType.LAST_ACCESS_TIME and TTLType.NONE. The TTLType.LAST_ACCESS_TIME tells the BackingMap to remove objects based on the time of their last use. The TTLType.NONE tells the BackingMap that objects are allowed to live inside the map forever, or until they are explicitly removed with a call to one of the ObjectMap remove methods. In XML, the configuration looks like this:

```
<backingMap name="payments"
            ttl="86400"
            ttlEvictorType="LAST_ACCESS_TIME"/>
```

Sometimes, a BackingMap is configured to use the TTLType.LAST_ACCESS_TIME TTL eviction policy, which contains a few objects that are very expensive to create. These objects may not be used within the TTL specified on the BackingMap, but should be kept around due to the cost of constructing them. We could fabricate a method that updates the object with innocuous changes, or we could use the touch(Object key) method to update its last access time. The touch(Object key) method does nothing more than update the last access time of an object. It does not return the object or retrieve a copy of it. This method only updates the last access time, so it is possible to keep an object alive in the BackingMap while other objects are removed due to the TTL and eviction method. This method updates the last access time of the object when the transaction commits, sparing it from eviction by resetting its last access time.

In a naïve implementation of duplicate payment checking, we can use the TTL and TTL evictor type to keep payments in a BackingMap for 24 hours, 36 hours, or whatever our business requirement on duplicate payments happens to be. In this example, we would set the ttlEvictorType setting to be CREATION_TIME and set the ttl setting to be 86400 seconds (24 hours). As each payment comes in, we would first check that it is not in the payments map. If it is in the map, then the payment is a duplicate.

Because this implementation is a bit naïve, we will assume the payment ID field is the same whenever we see a payment that is a duplicate of another. This makes it easy on us because the duplicate check process is as simple as calling the ObjectMap containsKey(Object key) method. Like a java.util.Map the containsKey(Object key) method returns true if the key exists in the BackingMap and false if it does not.

The containsKey(Object key) method is also useful for discerning whether or not a key is actually in a map when the nullValuesSupported setting is true on a BackingMap. Setting the nullValuesSupported value to true allows null value objects for a given key in a BackingMap.

The null value objects still have a key that makes them addressable. Any call to get on that key will return null. This may confuse an application—the key may not exist. When a key does not exist in a map, the ObjectMap get methods return null. By setting nullValuesSupported on a BackingMap, we permit a BackingMap to keep keys with null value objects. Now, the get methods can return null even if a key exists in the map because the value object is null. Using the containsKey(Object key) method helps determine if a null return value is due to the key returning a null reference or if the key does not exist in the map. We can define a BackingMap to support null value objects like this:

```
BackingMap bm = grid.defineMap("payments");
bm.setNullValuesSupported(true);
```

This can be done in the XML configuration by doing the following:

```
<backingMap name="payments"
            nullValuesSupported="true"
            timeToLive="86400"
            ttlEvictorType="CREATION_TIME"/>
```

When a BackingMap is configured this way, null values are allowed for keys. A call to paymentsMap.put(5000, null) is permitted. When the call to paymentsMap.get(5000) is made, the value null is returned. In this case, we may not know if the return value is null because the key is not present, or if the return value is null because the value object is null. Calling the containsKey(Object key) method will determine if the value object is null or the key does not exist. A return value of true indicates the value object is null, and a return value of false indicates the key is not in the map:

```
public void authorize() throws ObjectGridException {
    session.begin();
    for (long i = 1; i <= totalNumberOfPayments; i++) {
    IPayment p = (Ipayment)paymentsMap.get(i);
    if (p == null) {
        boolean ck = paymentsMap.containsKey(i);
        if (!ck) {
            p = new Payment();
            p.setId(createNewPaymentId());
        }
        if (!p.isFraudulent()) {
            p.authCheck();
        }
    }
    session.commit();
}
```

Here, we notice that the Payment with the specified key is null. Because the BackingMap is configured to support null value objects, we don't know if the null return value is because the key is not in the map or if the value object is actually null. By calling the `paymentsMap.containsKey(i)` method, we find out for sure whether the key exists in the map. If it does exist and the Payment object is null, then we create a new Payment and give it a new ID. This implementation could use some improvement though.

This is a naïve implementation because we expect all fields on the payment to be equal, including the payment ID. While this will sometimes be the case, other times the payment ID will be different and the rest of the fields in the object would be the same. As we continue, we will come up with a way to overcome this implementation's shortcomings.

FIFO queues

BackingMaps can act as FIFO (first-in, first-out) queues thanks to the `getNextKey(int timeout)` method. This method retrieves the next key in the map determined by its insertion order. When this method is called, a lock on the object is obtained so that next call to `getNextKey(int timeout)` does not return the same object. In order to iterate over an entire BackingMap, the application must explicitly remove the object with that key when the thread or process is finished with it. Otherwise, the key remains at the front of the queue and the next call to `getNextKey(int timeout)` returns a key that we have already operated upon. Without removing the key, a call to `getNextKey(int timeout)` will return the same key whenever the lock on that object is released. The `getNextKey(int timeout)` method takes a number of milliseconds to wait for an object to become available in the BackingMap. If this timeout is exceeded, then the method gives up and returns null.

We can use the `getNextKey(int timeout)` method to our advantage when processing payments. Let's look at two classes that act as producers and consumers:

```
public class PaymentProducer {
    private long totalNumberOfPayments = 0L;
    private Session session;
    public void loadPayments(String filename)
        throws ObjectGridException,
                FileNotFoundException,
                IOException {

        ObjectMap paymentsMap = session.getMap("payments");
        BufferedReader br = new BufferedReader(
                            new FileReader(filename));
```

```java
            String line = null;
            Map pMap = new HashMap();
            while ((line = br.readLine()) != null) {
                StringTokenizer st = new StringTokenizer(line, ":");
                Payment payment = new Payment();
                payment.setId(Integer.parseInt(st.nextToken()));
                payment.setAmount(new BigDecimal(st.nextToken()));
                payment.setCcNumber(st.nextToken());
                payment.setCcName(st.nextToken());
                payment.setCcExpiration(st.nextToken());
                payment.setCcType(st.nextToken());
                payment.setPaymentType(st.nextToken().charAt(0));

                pMap.put(payment.getId(), payment);
                totalNumberOfPayments++;
                if (pMap.size() >= 100) {
                    session.begin();
                    paymentsMap.putAll(pMap);
                    session.commit();
                    pMap = new HashMap();
                }
                printStatus("loadPayments", totalNumberOfPayments);
            }
        }
        private void printStatus(String method, long i) {
            if (i%1000 == 0) {
                System.out.println(method + " " + i);
            }
        }
        public static void main(String args[]) throws Exception {
            PPObjectGrid.initialize();
            ObjectGrid grid = PPObjectGrid.getGrid();
            PaymentProducer pp = new PaymentProducer();
            pp.setSession(grid.getSession());
            pp.loadPayments(args[0]);
            PPObjectGrid.disconnect();
        }
        public Session getSession() {
            return session;
        }
        public void setSession(Session session) {
            this.session = session;
        }
}
```

Here, we are simply populating a remote BackingMap with the payments in the `payments.txt` file. The producer file does exactly that, and places `Payment` objects in a BackingMap which will act as our FIFO queue. We can have as many producer applications as we want, all putting `Payments` into the BackingMap and they will be removed in FIFO order by applications on the other side of the queue using the `getNextKey(int timeout)` method. The `PaymentProducer` class uses the ObjectMap and BackingMap configurations that we are already familiar with. There should be nothing strange in the `PaymentProducer` class.

Consuming the `Payment` objects is done by taking advantage of the `getNextKey (int timeout)` method. Getting the next key inserted into the BackingMap gives us access to the object associated with that key. Because this method only `gets` us the next key and not the object associated with it, we must call one of the other get methods to get the value object. The `getNextKey(int timeout)` method does not guarantee that the order of keys coming out of the BackingMap is exactly in FIFO order, but it is "close enough." If the exact order of keys is not important, just that a reasonable estimate of FIFO is made, then using the BackingMap as a FIFO queue is not a bad idea. In our case, the exact order in which `Payments` are processed does not matter. We only care that they are processed in a reasonable amount of time:

```
public class PaymentConsumer {
    private Session session;

    public void consumePayments() throws ObjectGridException,
                                         InterruptedException {
        ObjectMap paymentsMap = session.getMap("payments");
        session.begin();
        try {
            long key = 0;
            while ((key =
                    (Long)paymentsMap.getNextKey(15000)) != 0) {
                Payment p = (Payment)paymentsMap.get(key);
                System.out.println("Got payment with key: " + key);
                System.out.println("Payment amount is: " +
                                    p.getAmount().toString());
                p.setAmount(p.getAmount().add(
                            new BigDecimal(Math.random() * 100)));
                System.out.println("Set new payment amount. " +
                            "New payment amount is: " +
                            " " + p.getAmount().toString());
                paymentsMap.remove(p.getId());
            }
            session.commit();
        } finally {
```

```
            PPObjectGrid.disconnect();
        }
    }
    public static void main(String args[]) throws Exception {
        PPObjectGrid.initialize();
        ObjectGrid grid = PPObjectGrid.getGrid();
        PaymentConsumer spc = new PaymentConsumer();
        spc.setSession(grid.getSession());
        spc.consumePayments();
        PPObjectGrid.disconnect();
    }
    public Session getSession() {
        return session;
    }
    public void setSession(Session session) {
        this.session = session;
    }
}
```

The consumePayments() method is what interests us here. This method makes use of the getNextKey(int timout) method to obtain the next key we can use in our process. This class is made so that multiple instances can and should be run simultaneously. By populating the payments BackingMap with the PaymentProducer class, we can have Payments sent to the remote payments BackingMap and consumed by, however, many instances of the PaymentsConsumer class are run. The getNextKey(int timeout) method returns the key, not the value object, next in the BackingMap. After obtaining the key, we call the get method to get the value object corresponding to that key. From there, we increment the payment amount and remove it from the paymentsMap BackingMap. A call to the remove method is very important here. If we commit the transaction without removing the object, then the lock is released on the object and it is still present in the BackingMap.

Not explicitly removing an object from a BackingMap acting as a FIFO queue may be our intent, though sometimes an object should not be removed until certain conditions are met. Keep in mind that once the lock on this object is released, it is immediately visible as the first object in the FIFO queue. The next call to getNextKey(int timeout) will return this same key. While the lock is held, subsequent calls will return the next keys in the queue. As soon as the lock is released, the object is once again visible as the first object in the queue. In order to permanently remove the object from the queue, we must explicitly call the remove(Object key) method, or wait until the configured eviction policy removes the object on our behalf.

This example used the PPObjectGrid helper class. This class is responsible for setting up a connection to a distributed ObjectGrid instance with a static configuration:

```
public class PPObjectGrid {
    private static ObjectGridManager ogm;
    private static ClientClusterContext context;
    private static ObjectGrid grid;

    public static void initialize()
        throws ObjectGridException {
        HostPortConnectionAttributes[] ogHosts =
            { new HostPortConnectionAttributes("localhost",
                "6601") };
        ogm = ObjectGridManagerFactory
                .getObjectGridManager();
        context = ogm.connect("ppCluster", ogHosts,
                                null, null);
        grid = ogm.getObjectGrid(context,
                                    "PaymentProcessorGrid");
    }
    public static ObjectGrid getGrid() {
        return grid;
    }
    public static void disconnect() {
        ogm.disconnect(context);
    }
}
```

This class simply provides some methods to connect to, and disconnect from, an ObjectGrid instance. All of the setup is done in the initialize method to connect to the PaymentProcessorGrid running in a container on the localhost. The rest of the application should call the getGrid() method when a reference to the ObjectGrid is needed. The ObjectGrid reference is used to obtain an ObjectMap. Anytime an ObjectMap is needed, the application should call getGrid() to get the ObjectGrid that contains the corresponding BackingMap.

Unsupported methods

You may have noticed that we are using the awkward convention of keeping track of the keys we use for payments in a BackingMap and using sequential integers as keys. We've use this convention up to now because the ObjectMap API does not include several methods implemented on java.util.Map. We can obtain a java.util.Map representation of an ObjectMap by calling the getJavaMap() method on an ObjectMap:

```
Map map = paymentsMap.getJavaMap();
```

This `java.util.Map` does not implement all of the methods specified by the `java.util.Map` interface. Most notably, this map does not have an implementation of the `keySet()`, `entrySet()`, or `values()` methods. In a typical Java application, a developer might get an entry set for a map and iterate over those entries with a `for` for each loop. The body of the loop would contain any business logic required of the objects in the map. This is a great approach for maps that fit in the main memory, but it does not scale to the size of maps that can be held in an ObjectGrid instance.

The `keySet()`, `entrySet()`, and `values()` methods work because when the entirety of the map is in the main memory. For large maps, the entries will not fit in the main memory. That's one of the reasons why we're using WebSphere eXtreme Scale in the first place. We need to work with maps with large entry sets that span multiple computers' main memory. Implementing these methods on ObjectMap would be disastrous for our application because calling any of them would pollute our heap space with hundreds, thousands, or millions of objects until an `OutOfMemoryException` is thrown. These methods are not implemented because it is so easy to forget the size of the data in a BackingMap and use the methods because they are there. Whenever we get a `java.util.Map` reference to an ObjectMap through a call to the `getJavaMap()` method, we will get an `UnsupportedOperationException` when these methods are called. These are not the only unsupported methods when using the `getJavaMap()` method, but they are the most notable.

Wrapping up

There are two more methods that we need to cover before wrapping up this chapter. They are the `insert(Object key, Object value)` and `update(Object key, Object value)` methods.

The `insert(Object key, Object value)` method will attempt to insert a new value into a BackingMap. This method will never update an object with its key that already exists in the BackingMap. If the key already exists in the BackingMap, then a `DuplicateKeyException` is thrown. A call to the `insert(Object key, Object value)` method is telling a BackingMap that we expect to put a new key/value pair in, or do nothing if that key already exists. Insert means insert a new key/value pair, not update a key/value pair.

The `update(Object key, Object value)` method requires that a key already exists in the map to be considered a success. This method updates the object with the specified key, meaning that the key must already exist in the map. If the key is not in the BackingMap, a `KeyNotFoundException` is thrown. Update means update an existing key/value pair, not insert a new key/value pair.

Summary

We've covered a lot of ground in this chapter. Though the size of the API we've covered is relatively small, the knowledge of the semantics behind these methods is important to get the most out of WebSphere eXtreme Scale. We covered the main ObjectMap API methods in detail, while examining the BackingMap configuration options that are all used to make certain agreements in exchange for performance and scalability enhancements.

We also looked at the different lock strategies and what they provide in terms of concurrency and application design. Our methods will look different depending on if a map has an optimistic lock strategy than if it has a pessimistic lock strategy. We learned about the semantics of the `get` and `getForUpdate` methods and how to apply them to avoid deadlock. A brief example of using a `BackingMap` as an "almost"-FIFO queue showed us the `getNextKey` method which brought us to the unsupported methods. An ObjectMap can be represented as a `java.util.Map` backed by that ObjectMap, but it does not have all of the functionality of a `java.util.Map` for good reason. There are some map operations that should not be used on extremely large data sets.

The topics in this chapter will keep coming up as we continue to explore the features of WebSphere eXtreme Scale, and keeping a working knowledge of them will benefit you for as long as you work with data grids in general, and not just the IBM implementation of a data grid. It's important to know the foundation topics before moving on to the APIs that build on them. In the next chapter, we will look at the Entity API.

3
Entities and Queries

So far, we've looked at caching objects through WebSphere eXtreme Scale using the ObjectMap API. ObjectMap provides a useful caching API for simple POJOs that do not have relationships between classes. This works well for simple object models, but sometimes we need to work with classes that have relationships between them. WebSphere eXtreme Scale provides the Entity API for the times we need to work with more complex object models. This allows us to group objects together in the grid by using their relationships to group them in a meaningful way. Related objects are stored together in the grid. Though this may not seem important working with a local ObjectGrid instance, it becomes extremely important when we work with distributed ObjectGrids.

The Entity API lets us define relationships between classes so that ObjectGrid can manage those relationships when caching objects. It lets us work with POJOs instead of making us write boilerplate code to manage relationships. Defining an Entity can be done with annotations on a POJO class or through XML configuration.

Relationships and schema may conjure images of SQL queries and relational databases. In addition to making it easy to cache objects, the Entity API opens the doorway to the Query API. The Query API works like SQL where we can write queries to run against the classes defined as Entities in our BackingMaps. Querying our cached objects lets us work with them when we don't know the primary keys of the objects we want to work with. Like SQL, Query lets us search for objects meeting the criteria we define in the query. As the query language looks like SQL, learning it takes very little time for developers who are already familiar with SQL. By the end of this chapter, you'll be able to:

- Define a POJO as an Entity and understand the relationship between Entity classes and BackingMaps
- Be able to use the EntityManager methods to find, insert, update, and delete objects from a BackingMap

- Use the Query API to search for cached objects and apply criteria to the query

- Understand the use of indexes maintained by ObjectGrid and how to create an index statically and at runtime

Entities

Conceptually, a persistent entity is an object that can be saved to some data store. EJB 1.0 introduced us to entity beans, though they were difficult to use. Since then, several different flavors of object persistence frameworks have evolved. Although eXtreme Scale Entities have no technical relation to other object persistence frameworks, the concept remains the same. We define a class as an Entity, and then store instances of that class in a data store.

Defining a class as an Entity is done using either Java Annotations or XML configuration in Java 5.0 or higher. Pre-Java 5.0 environments can only use XML configuration. The Java Annotations we use to define Entities are in the `com.ibm.websphere.projector.annotations` package.

Defining Entities

Let's see how we define an Entity using annotations:

```
public class Payment implements Serializable {
    private String cardNumber;
    private String street;
    private String city;
    private String state;
    private BigDecimal amount;
  // getters and setters omitted for brevity
}
```

The Payment class is just a POJO. It can be turned into an Entity with the `@Entity` annotation:

```
@Entity
public class Payment implements Serializable {
    @Id private String cardNumber;
    private String street;
    private String city;
    private String state;
    private BigDecimal amount;
  // getters and setters omitted for brevity
}
```

Classes annotated with `@Entity` are passed as arguments to EntityManager instance methods. EntityManager is the class used to perform all of our caching operations with an ObjectGrid instance.

Defining an object as an `@Entity` indicates an ObjectGrid instance that a BackingMap with the entity name should be created after a class is registered with an ObjectGrid instance when the ObjectGrid instance starts. The `@Entity` annotation has four optional attributes; the following two are interesting to us: `name` and `schemaRoot`. We'll cover the `name` attribute now and the `schemaRoot` attribute when we get into class relationships.

By default, the `name` attribute is the unqualified class name of the class defined as an `@Entity`. The name is used by the Query language when referring to objects of this class:

```
@Entity(name="Payment")
public class Payment implements Serializable {
    @Id private String cardNumber;
    private String street;
    private String city;
    private String state;
    private BigDecimal amount;
 // getters and setters omitted for brevity
}
```

Setting the `name="Payment"` does the same as the default behavior. If we want to refer to objects in queries as MyPayment, then we would set `name="MyPayment"`. This will make more sense when we get in to the Query API.

Defining the Payment class as an `@Entity` also introduced the `@Id` annotation. An entity must have at least one field defined as an `@Id`. It acts as a primary key for the entity and is most conspicuously used by the `EntityManager#find(clazz, id)` method. With our `@Entity` and a primary key `@Id` defined, let's look at how to use it with an ObjectGrid instance. First, we need an instance of EntityManager:

```
public class PaymentLoader {

    EntityManager em;

    StringBuffer fileContents = new StringBuffer();

    public static void main(String[] args) {
        PaymentLoader pl = new PaymentLoader();

        try {
            pl.initialize();
            pl.loadPayments(args[0]);
```

```
        } catch (ObjectGridException e) {
            e.printStackTrace();
        } catch (IOException e) {
            e.printStackTrace();
        }

        System.out.println("All done!");
    }

    private void initialize() throws ObjectGridException {
        ObjectGridManager ogm =
            ObjectGridManagerFactory.getObjectGridManager();
        ObjectGrid grid = ogm.createObjectGrid();
        grid.registerEntities(new Class[] {Payment.class});
        em = grid.getSession().getEntityManager();
    }

    // .. more methods omitted for brevity
}
```

The `initialize()` method uses an instance of ObjectGridManager to create an instance of ObjectGrid. This ObjectGrid instance is not yet aware of the `@Entity` class Payment. We set up this grid programmatically, so we need to programmatically tell the ObjectGrid instance what classes to inspect for entity annotations. We do this with the `ObjectGrid#registerEntities(Class[] classes)` method. We create a new `Class[]` with the Payment class as its only element.

Persisting Entities

When the grid instance is initialized (called by the `getSession()` method because we do not explicitly initialize it), it inspects the Payment class for annotations. Finding the `@Entity` annotation, a BackingMap named "Payment" is created. The `@Id` annotation uses the cardNumber field as its primary key. We obtain an EntityManager reference by calling the `Session#getEntityManager()` method.

Now, with an EntityManager instance, we can cache objects. Here are the remaining methods from PaymentLoader:

```
    private void loadPayments(String filename) throws IOException {
        BufferedReader br = null;
        try {
            br = new BufferedReader(new FileReader(filename));
            String line;
            while ((line = br.readLine()) != null) {
                Payment payment = createPayment(line);
                persistPayment(payment);
```

```
            }
        } finally {
            if (br != null) {
                br.close();
            }
        }
    }

    private void persistPayment(Payment payment) {
        em.getTransaction().begin();
        em.persist(payment);
        em.getTransaction().commit();
        System.out.println("Persisted payment with card number: " +
            payment.getCardNumber());
    }

    private Payment createPayment(String line) {
        Payment payment = new Payment();
        String[] tokens = line.split(":");
        payment.setCardNumber(tokens[0]);
        payment.setStreet(tokens[1]);
        payment.setCity(tokens[2]);
        payment.setState(tokens[3]);
        payment.setAmount(new BigDecimal(tokens[4]));

        return payment;
    }
```

Most interesting among these methods is the persistPayment(payment) method. This is where we use the EntityManager to interact with the ObjectGrid instance. Interacting with an ObjectGrid through an EntityManager follows the same rule as interacting with it through the Session methods. We must conduct all cache operations within the scope of a transaction.

The EntityManager equivalent to a transaction started by a Session is the EntityTransaction. Typically, we begin and commit transactions like we do in the sample code: em.getTransaction().begin() and em.getTransaction().commit(). We can use the Session transaction and EntityTransaction methods interchangeably, though it's better to pick one and stick to it.

Once we have an active transaction, we can use the EntityManager methods to interact with the grid. Those methods are find(Class clazz, Object primaryKey), findForUpdate(Class clazz, Object primaryKey), merge(Object entity), persist(Object entity), and remove(Object entity).

As we have an empty Payment BackingMap, we first use the `persist(Object entity)` method to put objects into the cache. In this case, we persist each payment in its own transaction.

Composition versus Inheritance

One more thing about Entities and their relationship with BackingMaps. A BackingMap named Payment is created when the ObjectGrid instance starts. The relationship between entities and BackingMaps is one-to-one. Every Entity class is bound to one BackingMap with the specified name. You may notice this means that classes and their subclasses are stored in different BackingMaps, instead of a class and all of its descendants using the same BackingMap. That is to say, eXtreme Scale does not offer an equivalent of single-table inheritance. Though this may seem like a deal-breaker, designing a schema that favors object composition instead of class inheritance may alleviate this problem (and probably many others in the application).

Let's take a quick look at an example. If we have a few different types of payment, say an auth, deposit, and refund, and we implement them as a class hierarchy, we end up with four classes. We have an abstract Payment class and a class for auth, deposit, and refund which extend Payment. Using inheritance, we have three different BackingMaps, one for each concrete subclass. This makes querying the grid more difficult. Instead of querying one BackingMap, we query three and then combine the results. Instead of subclassing, we implement the Payment class as-is and give it a field for PaymentType. This PaymentType is a simple Java Enum with the three different types of payments our application supports. The Payment class is composed with a PaymentType. Additional fields on the payment types are added by creating a one-to-one relationship with an addendum class. We'll look at this in more detail shortly. Using composition, we have a cleaner implementation where using one `find` method or query on the Payment BackingMap takes care of everything.

The Find methods

There are two methods used to find objects with the Entity API: `find(Class clazz, Object primaryKey)` and `findForUpdate(Class clazz, Object primaryKey)`. Both of these methods return an Object instance, which must be cast into the class passed as the first argument to the method.

Both methods return an instance of the object we're looking for. The difference is the lock placed on each object in the far-cache in a distributed deployment is based on the lock strategy defined on the BackingMap. Under the optimistic lock strategy, both `find` and `findForUpdate` obtain an 'S' lock for the duration of the read operation. Using the optimistic locking strategy requires an implementation of OptimisticCallback to check for differences in the object if it is saved again. By checking for differences at commit time, the transaction can try to obtain an 'X' lock if differences exist. Many threads can obtain a reference to an object in this manner, and potentially all of them could update the object as long as an OptimisticCallback is implemented.

With a pessimistic lock strategy, the `findForUpdate` method obtains a 'U' lock for the duration of the transaction, and then upgrades to an 'X' lock at commit time, should the object change during the transaction. A 'U' lock indicates that a transaction intends to update an object, and that no other threads should be given a reference to that object *for an update* until the current transaction no longer has a 'U' lock.

Obtaining a reference to an object with `findForUpdate` places a 'U' lock on the entry in the BackingMap. Calls to find the same object place an 'S' lock on the entry during the read transaction. The 'S' lock does not block other lock types on the same BackingMap entry. The 'U' lock blocks any other `findForUpdate` calls on that same BackingMap entry. In this way, only one thread at a time may update an object obtained through `findForUpdate`.

This section will make more sense when we start working with distributed environments.

Entity life-cycle states

Using the `find` and `findForUpdate` methods may seem a little strange because we don't call another EntityManager method to explicitly save our changes. Entity objects are managed by eXtreme Scale. eXtreme Scale takes care of tracking changes to an object, and saving those changes when a transaction commits, or discarding them upon rollback. Entity objects exist in one of three life-cycle states: `new`, `managed`, or `detached`.

An object in the new state is one that has not yet persisted to the cache. An ObjectGrid instance does not know about this particular object. Take a look at the persistPayment method again:

```
private void persistPayment(Payment payment) {
        em.getTransaction().begin();
        em.persist(payment);
        em.getTransaction().commit();
}
```

Before the call to `em.persist(payment)`, payment is in the `new` state. The ObjectGrid instance knows nothing about this entity because it is a new object, which was just created and not yet persistent in a BackingMap. Calling `em.persist(payment)` saves the object in the cache and puts it in the `managed` state where it remains until the transaction ends.

Let's get back to objects returned from the find methods. Those objects are also in the `managed` state *during the scope of the transaction*. Once the transaction ends, any objects returned by the find methods, or even entities cached with the persist(object) method, enter the `detached` state.

How does the life-cycle apply to the find methods? Let's look at some code, where we want to find the payment we just persisted:

```
em.getTransaction().begin();
em.persist(payment);
em.getTransaction().commit();

em.getTransaction().begin();
Payment p = (Payment)em.findForUpdate(Payment.class,
                                      payment.getCardNumber());
p.setAmount(p.getAmount().add(new BigDecimal("10.00")));
em.getTransaction().commit();

p = null;

em.getTransaction().begin();
p = (Payment)em.find(Payment.class, payment.getCardNumber());
em.getTransaction().rollback();
```

Persisting of the payment is done in the same way as before. The second transaction uses the `findForUpdate` method, passing the class Payment and the primary key of the payment, which is the credit card number (obviously, this isn't a good way to assign a primary key to the payment in a production application). After obtaining the Payment, we then add $10.00 to the amount and commit the transaction.

Why didn't we call `EntityManager#persist(p)`? eXtreme Scale manages the entity for us. Once in a managed state, eXtreme Scale tracks changes to an entity and applies those changes to the cache when the transaction commits. With the Entity API, we don't need to explicitly save a changed object, as that's done for us.

Just to prove that the Payment amount is $10.00 greater than the original amount, we start a third transaction and call `find` with the same primary key to get the same payment. We inspect the payment amount and it is in fact $10.00 more than before. Instead of committing the transaction, we roll it back because we only performed a read operation.

Merge, remove, and the detached state

In the previous code, we set p = null. If we hadn't set p = null, then the Payment referenced by p would be in the detached state. The detached state means that an Entity is not associated with an ObjectGrid transaction. It exists outside the scope of a transaction. Any changes to that object are not saved in the cache while it is detached:

```
em.getTransaction().begin();
em.persist(payment);
em.getTransaction().commit();

em.getTransaction().begin();
Payment p = (Payment)em.findForUpdate(Payment.class,
                                payment.getCardNumber());
p.setAmount(p.getAmount().add(new BigDecimal("10.00")));
em.getTransaction().commit();

// p is detached - any changes that take place in this
// method will not be saved to the cache!
doLongRunningTask(p);
```

If we use an Entity outside of a transaction and change its state, we may want to save those changes to the cache again. We do that in the context of another ObjectGrid transaction. After starting a transaction, we call the EntityManager#merge(Object object) method:

```
em.getTransaction().begin();
p = (Payment)em.find(Payment.class, payment.getCardNumber());
em.getTransaction().rollback();

p.setAmount(new BigDecimal("1.00"));

em.getTransaction().begin();
Payment managedPayment = (Payment)em.merge(p);
em.getTransaction().commit();
```

EntityManager#merge(Object object) associates the object with the ObjectGrid cache again. The important point to remember is that EntityManager#merge returns a managed instance of the object. The EntityManager#merge(Object object) method does not put the object passed as an argument back in the managed state. The object referenced by p remains in the detached state. Instead, EntityManager#merge (Object object) returns a new object which is in the managed state.

Once we have a managed object, any changes to the object while it was in the
`detached` state are recorded and made permanent in the cache when the transaction
commits. If the transaction rolls back, then the changes are discarded. While in the
transaction scope, any changes made to the object after it is merged are also tracked
and persisted when the transaction commits.

In the previous code, we changed the amount of the payment to $1.00, giving a
pretty steep discount to whoever bought something expensive. Because we set the
amount outside the scope of a transaction, the change does not persist to the cache.
In order to make our change durable, we start a new transaction and merge the
payment object. Committing this transaction saves the change.

Finally, we come to the `EntityManager#remove(Object object)` method. The
`remove` method takes an Entity out of the cache. Any calls to find this entity with the
removed Entity's primary key will return null references. The `remove` method is our
way to delete objects we don't want in the cache.

The `remove` method takes an Entity object in the `managed` state as its argument. This
is important to remember, otherwise you may find yourself trying to delete objects
that are in the unmanaged or detached states, and wondering why they are still
found by the find methods.

```
em.getTransaction().begin();
managedPayment = (Payment)em.merge(p);
em.remove(managedPayment);
em.getTransaction().commit();

em.getTransaction().begin();
System.out.println("looking for payment...");
p = (Payment)em.find(Payment.class, payment.getCardNumber());
if (p == null) {
    System.out.println("No payment with card number: " +
                        payment.getCardNumber());
} else {
    System.out.println("Found the payment!");
}
em.getTransaction().rollback();
```

In the code above, we should never reach the code in the `else` block. At the
start, we make sure we have a managed Payment object and pass it to the
`remove` method. If the object is not an Entity, or is in the `detached` state, an
`IllegalArgumentException` is thrown.

Entity relationships

The Payment class holds a little too much information. Namely, it holds address information and that address data should exist in its own class. Each payment has address data associated with it. This is where we discover Entity relationships.

If you're familiar with object-relational mapping, you may recall that there are at least four types of relationship between classes. In eXtreme Scale terms, the relationships are defined by annotations in the com.ibm.websphere.projector. annotations package. Those relationships are @OneToOne, @OneToMany, @ManyToOne, and @ManyToMany. At first, we'll model the Payment-Address relationship as one-to-one.

First, we'll define the Address class:

```
@Entity
public class Address {
    @Id
    private int id;

    @OneToOne
    private Payment payment;

    private String street;
    private String city;
    private String state;
    private String zip;

    // getters and setters omitted
}
```

The @Entity and @Id annotations are familiar. We add the @OneToOne annotation on the Payment field. This corresponds to the @OneToOne annotation we placed on the address field in Payment. If an Entity class has a field that is defined as an Entity, but a relationship to that Entity is not defined, then a com.ibm.websphere.projector. MetadataException is thrown.

```
@Entity
public class Payment implements Serializable {
    @Id private String cardNumber;
    private BigDecimal amount;

    @OneToOne(cascade=CascadeType.ALL)
    private Address address;

    // getters and setters omitted
}
```

The @OneToOne annotation on the Address has an additional attribute set. The cascade type is the setting that controls the EntityManager methods that apply to the far-side of a relationship. This means that we control which EntityManager methods apply to relationships. The possible options are of the CascadeType enum: PERSIST, REFRESH, MERGE, REMOVE, REFRESH, INVALIDATE, and ALL. Of those, we are most familiar with the first four now.

Setting CascadeType.PERSIST means persisting a new Payment object also persists the Address object on the other end of the @OneToOne relationship. Likewise, setting CascadeType.MERGE causes the EntityManager#merge(Object object) method to return a managed Payment with a managed Address, and merges any changes to those objects into the current transaction. We want all EntityManager operations applied to a Payment to also apply to the Address, so we set the relationship to cascade=CascadeType.ALL. Any EntityManager method that is passed a Payment will perform the same operation on the Address referenced by the Payment.

Using our new Address is easy. We only change the createPayment method:

```
private Payment createPayment(String line) {
        String[] tokens = line.split(":");

        Address address = new Address();
        address.setStreet(tokens[1]);
        address.setCity(tokens[2]);
        address.setState(tokens[3]);

        Payment payment = new Payment();
        payment.setCardNumber(tokens[0]);
        payment.setAddress(address);
        address.setPayment(payment);
        payment.setAmount(new BigDecimal(tokens[4]));

        return payment;
    }
```

Instead of setting the address fields on the Payment, we create an instance of Address and set that on Payment. We also set the reverse on the Address object. Saving addresses to the Address BackingMap happens when we call em.persist(payment). The persist operation cascades to the Address, persisting the address, because we set cascade=CascadeType.ALL on the @OneToOne relationship in the Payment.

@OneToMany, @ManyToOne

Now that we have a way to associate a Payment with an Address, it might be nice to have a way to group the Payments that come in the same file. We create a Batch class that contains a reference to a Collection of Payment objects:

```
@Entity(schemaRoot = true)
public class Batch {
    @Id String name;

    @OneToMany(cascade=CascadeType.ALL)
    Collection<Payment> payments = new ArrayList<Payment>();

    // getters and setters omitted
}
```

The `@OneToMany` annotation creates a relationship between one Batch and many instances of Payment. Those Payment objects in the payments collection are associated with one instance of Batch. We use generics to let eXtreme Scale know which class is on the other side of the relationship. If we do not use generics and leave the `@OneToMany` annotation as it is, eXtreme Scale would not know which class is on the other side of the relationship. There are no hints for it to look at other Entity classes.

If our code doesn't use generics to tell eXtreme Scale about the Entity on the other side of the relationship, we can specify the Entity class in the annotation:

```
@OneToMany(cascade=CascadeType.ALL,
           targetEntity=Payment.class)
Collection payments = new ArrayList();
```

The `targetEntity` attribute sets the class of the Entity object on the other side of the relationship, if generics are not used or are not available for use such as a pre-Java SE 5.0 environment.

We can specify the inverse relationship on the Payment class. There are many Payment objects per Batch object to specify the `@ManyToOne` relationship:

```
@Entity
public class Payment implements Serializable {
    @Id private String cardNumber;
    private BigDecimal amount;

    @OneToOne(cascade=CascadeType.ALL)
    private Address address;

    @ManyToOne
    private Batch batch;

    // getters and setters omitted
}
```

We don't need to specify the `targetEntity` here because it is inferred by the type declaration. The target Entity of this relationship is a Batch. The BatchEntity cascades all EntityManager operations to its relationships. Persisting a Batch persists all of the Payments in the Collection marked `@OneToMany`. Instead of persisting Payment objects directly, we can add them to the payments collection on a Batch:

```
private void loadPayments(String filename)
  throws IOException {
    BufferedReader br = null;
    try {
        br = new BufferedReader(new FileReader(filename));
        String line;

        Batch batch = new Batch();
        batch.setName("The first batch");

        while ((line = br.readLine()) != null) {
            Payment payment = createPayment(line);
            payment.setBatch(batch);
            batch.getPayments().add(payment);
        }
        persistBatch(batch);
    } finally {
        if (br != null) {
            br.close();
        }
    }
}
```

We call `persistBatch(batch)` after reading the file and creating (but not persisting) all of the Payment objects. We add each payment to the payments collection on Batch. Persisting the Batch object persists all of the Payment objects too. Each Payment has an Address associated with it, and those are also persisted thanks to the `cascade=CascadeType.ALL` on the `@OneToOne` relationship between Payment and Address. In persist call on the Batch, we save the Batch, all of its Payment objects, and all of the Address objects to the grid as we cascade the `EntityManager#persist (Object object)` action to the far side of the defined relationships.

```
private void persistBatch(Batch batch) {
    em.getTransaction().begin();
    em.persist(batch);
    em.getTransaction().commit();
}
```

That's it! `em.persist(batch)` saves everything when the transaction commits.

schemaRoot

You may have noticed the `schemaRoot` attribute in the `@Entity` annotation on Batch:

```
@Entity(schemaRoot = true)
public class Batch {
    @Id String name;

    @OneToMany(cascade=CascadeType.ALL, targetEntity=Payment.class)
    Collection payments = new ArrayList();

    // getters and setters omitted
}
```

The `schemaRoot` attribute is used in distributed environments. There can be only one Entity per schema marked as `schemaRoot`. Distributed eXtreme Scale environments are partitioned. A partitioned BackingMap does not contain all entries in the logical map. Each partition only contains a subset of the total objects in the map. When we have many partitions, the EntityManager uses the Entity marked as the `schemaRoot` to route related objects to the same partition.

In our example, the Batch is marked as `schemaRoot`. All Payment objects related to the Batch, and all Address objects related to each Payment, are cached in the same partition. The EntityManager finds the partition to cache the objects based on the `hashCode()` value of the Batch object. This means that all Payment and Address objects are stored in the same partition as the Batch object that is the root Entity of an object model. If this is unclear, it will make more sense when we start working with distributed eXtreme Scale environments.

The Query API

Storing Entity objects with the EntityManager API gives us a convenient way to store objects with relationships. You may have noticed that we are somewhat limited in how we find Entities if we rely on the EntityManager interface. The find method only accepts a primary key to search for in our objects. What if we don't know the primary key of the object or objects we want to find? We turn to the Query interface. The Query interface gives us a way to search an ObjectGrid instance using an SQL-like language to find managed entities that meet certain criteria.

Our first work with Query will be very simple:

```
private void queryBatch() {
    Query query = em.createQuery("select b.name from Batch b");
    String batchName = (String)query.getSingleResult();
    System.out.println("Batch name is: " + batchName);
}
```

We start working with the Query interface by creating a Query from the
`EntityManager#createQuery(String queryStr)` method. The `queryStr`
argument is an ObjectGrid Query Language query that outlines the kind of
objects we're interested in getting when the query runs.

The Query Language looks like SQL. It is made up of a `select` statement, `from`
clause, and optional `where`, `having`, and `group by` clauses. The `select` statement can
select certain fields from objects or the Entity objects specified in the `from` clause. The
`from` clause specifies the Entity or Entities where the selected fields come from. In
our example, we select the name field from a Batch object.

There are two basic methods to get results from a Query. They are
`Query#getSingleResult()` and `Query#getResultIterator()`. The
`GetSingleResult()` method runs a Query which returns just one result. If the
Query returns more than one result, it throws `NonUniqueResultException`. If there
is an empty result set, it throws `NoResultException`. Fortunately, our Query returns
the name of the single Batch entity we persisted. The Query does not run until one of
the methods that get the results is called. The Query in our sample did not run when
we called `createQuery`. It runs when `getSingleResult` is called. We also need to
cast the result into the expected type.

In the code above, we run the query with `getSingleResult()`. When we have
more than one persistent Batch, which should be most of the time, we call
`Query#getResultIterator()`:

```
em.getTransaction().begin();
Query query = em.createQuery("select b.name from Batch b");
Iterator batchIterator = query.getResultIterator();

while (batchIterator.hasNext()) {
    Batch batch = (Batch)batchIterator.next();
    processBatch(batch);
}
em.getTransaction().commit();
```

The `Query#getResultIterator()` method is used when there is more than one
expected result, though it still works when the query returns just one result. Within
the transaction scope, we can use this iterator to work with the objects returned by
the Query. Our query is pretty indiscriminate now. It returns the names for all Batch
objects in the partition.

We need a way to narrow the scope of results returned by a query. We do this with query parameters. A query parameter is a named or numbered placeholder for a value we want in a query. Let's say we want to find a batch with a particular ID (and ignore the fact that we can call the `EntityManager#find(Batch.class, id)` method):

```
Query query = em.createQuery(
            "select b from Batch b where b.id = ?1");
query.setParameter(1, 1234567890);
Iterator batchIterator = query.getResultIterator();
```

First, we create a Query with the query language. We include a `where` clause that accesses a field on the Entity objects in the BackingMap. We can access fields on Entity objects in the query as if we were accessing them on the Entity object in Java code. We alias a Batch object as `b`, and compare its ID to the placeholder set by `?1`.

We test `b.id` for equality to a parameter which we will set at runtime. We don't know which Batch ID we want to use, when we build and deploy our application. This query could run frequently with a different Batch ID passed in each time. We pass in the Batch ID we want to search for by calling the `Query#setParameter (int paramIndex, Object paramValue)` method. We pass in the numeric value of the placeholder, along with the value that should be used in the query. Here, we pass Batch ID 1234567890 as the first parameter in the query. When the query runs, it will return the Batch with that ID.

We could have used a named parameter instead of a numbered parameter:

```
em.getTransaction().begin();
Query query = em.createQuery(
            "select b from Batch b where b.id = :batchId");
query.setParameter("batchId", 1234567890);
Iterator batchIterator = query.getResultIterator();

while (batchIterator.hasNext()) {
    Batch batch = (Batch)batchIterator.next();
    processBatch(batch);
}
em.getTransaction().commit();
```

Instead of a question mark followed by a number, a named parameter is a colon followed by the parameter name. This parameter name corresponds to the parameter name passed into the `Query#setParameter(String paramName, Object paramValue)` method.

Joins and aggregate functions

We can perform joins on related Entities using the `from` clause. Let's take a look at finding Batches which contain more than 1000 Payments. The Query Language lets us examine an object's fields as part of a query, but we cannot call methods on that object. This prevents us from writing a query like this:

```
query = em.createQuery("select object(b) from Batch b " +
                       "where b.payments.size() > 1000)");
```

Instead, we perform a join on Batch and Payment objects:

```
query = em.createQuery("select object(b) " +
                       "from Payment p, Batch b " +
                       "where p.batch = b " +
                       "group by b " +
                       "having (count(p) > 1000)");
```

This looks complicated. However, if we break it down, we'll get it. The first line asks for Batch objects, which are aliased as 'b' in this query. That alias is defined in the `from` clause. The `from` clause aliases Payment objects as 'p', and Batch objects as 'b'. We can refer to these aliases anywhere else in the query, like in the `select` clause.

The Payment and Batch objects in their BackingMaps are Cartesian joined in the `from` clause because we specify the Payment and Batch entities. A Cartesian join creates all possible combinations of objects in both BackingMaps. This can be a very expensive operation based on the number of objects in a BackingMap.

As we perform a Cartesian join, we must narrow down the scope of the results with the `where` clause. The `where` clause instructs the query to return only those combinations where the Batch referenced by the Payment 'p' is the same Batch object the Payment is paired up with in the Cartesian join. This reduces the potential number of results to the Batch rows that are paired up with their Payment objects.

Performing a Cartesian join on a large number of Batches and Payments may not be the best decision. Right away, we can narrow down the number of combinations generated by performing a more intelligent join operation:

```
query = em.createQuery("select object(b) " +
                       "from Batch b, IN(b.payments) p " +
                       "group by b " +
                       "having (count(p) > 1000)");
```

The `from` clause in this query is different from the previous example. We use an *in* collection declaration. This provides functionality like a right outer join, if you're familiar with SQL. Instead of generating all possible combinations of Batch-Payment, the query only starts with the Batch-Payment combinations where the Batch referenced by a Payment is the Batch it is paired up with for the query. This makes the previous query's `where` clause redundant, so we remove it.

The `group by` clause instructs the query to sort rows based on the Batch in the combination. This groups all rows with Batch ID 1234567890 together as all Batch-Payment combinations that have Batch ID 1234567890 belong to one group. Grouping rows lets us apply aggregate functions to their rows.

The first aggregate function we meet is the count function. The count function works on any data type except Collections. It doesn't count the number of items in a collection; it counts the number of *somethings* in a group though. Here, our *something* is Payment objects. We build a query to create a group that contains Payment objects, and then we count those objects. The count function returns a Java long primitive type.

Two more aggregate functions are min and max. These functions accept most numeric data types, and return the same data type that was passed in to them. They also accept String, `java.util.Data`, and `java.sql.Date` data types.

The final two aggregate functions are avg and sum. These functions take numeric input. The return type of avg is a Java double primitive. Primitive int input to sum returns an int. Primitive double input to sum returns a double. BigInteger and BigDecimal input return BigInteger and BigDecimal output respectively.

IDs and Indexes

Look back to the Entity class definitions we have. There are two annotations on them that we have not gone over yet. The ID field has the `@Id` annotation. The `@Id` specifies an entity's primary key. It can be used on one or more fields. When it is used on one field like in the Payment class, then that single field is the primary key for the entity. When used on multiple fields, those fields make up a composite key for the entity. All entities must have a primary key. The primary key uniquely identifies an entity object, and no other object of that class can have the same primary key. If another entity with the same primary key is inserted into a BackingMap, then the persist method throws an `EntityExistsException`. If we are working with an object and change its primary key, then it is considered a new entity and is persisted with the new primary key. In this example, our classes use a single field primary key.

The @Index annotation is also on the ID field. The @Index annotation instructs ObjectGrid to build a database-like index on the ID field. By creating an index on a field, we optimize read queries that use the index. This read optimization comes at the slight cost of write performance. Inserting an entity with an index causes additional housekeeping to take place in ObjectGrid when the transaction commits. Too many indexes on an entity will cause writes to be unnecessarily impeded. An improperly indexed entity will be slow to query. Finding the right balance of indexed fields is important.

```
@Entity
public class Address implements Serializable {
    @Index String streetLine1;
    @Index String streetLine2;
    @Index String city;
    @Index String state;
    @Index String country;
    @Index String zipCode;
    @OneToMany(cascade=CascadeType.ALL)
        List<Card> cards = new ArrayList<Card>();
    @Id @Index int id;
    ... other methods omitted for brevity...
}
```

The Address class has indexes on six String fields (as seen above). These indexes are defined *statically*. They are defined on the class either by annotation in our example, or by XML configuration. Persisting an Address requires ObjectGrid to update the index for each of these six fields. When we query for Addresses, we can expect our query to run reasonably fast, if we use the equals operator for each indexed field:

```
String queryString = "select object(addr) from Address addr " +
                     "where addr.streetLine1 = ?1 " +
                     "and addr.city = ?2 " +
                     "and addr.state = ?3 " +
                     "and addr.zipCode = ?4";
Query query = entityManager.createQuery(queryString);
query.setParameter(1, street);
query.setParameter(2, city);
query.setParameter(3, state);
query.setParameter(4, zip);
```

We know that the query uses the indexes because the `query.getPlan()` method tells us that it does. The `query.getPlan()` method only runs on local ObjectGrid instances. Running it on a distributed ObjectGrid instance will give the same result, as if there were no indexes defined:

```
for q2 in  ( ( (Address ObjectMap using INDEX on streetLine1 = ( ?1)
AND_Collection Address ObjectMap using INDEX on city = ( ?2))
AND_Collection Address ObjectMap using INDEX on state = ( ?3))
AND_Collection Address ObjectMap using INDEX on zipCode = ( ?4))
    returning new Tuple( q2  )
```

If we did not have any indexes defined, our query plan would perform sequential scans over each attribute until the correct string is found. The plan for attribute scans looks like this:

```
for q2 in Address ObjectMap using INDEX SCAN
filter (((( q2.c[3] =  ?1 ) AND ( q2.c[0] =  ?2 ) )
AND ( q2.c[2] =  ?3 ) ) AND ( q2.c[5] =  ?4 ) )
returning new Tuple( q2  )
```

Each attribute is scanned until the desired string is found. Then, the query moves on to the next attribute until the correct Address object is located (or not). Obviously, using the indexes improves the read performance of the query. But, what if there are some fields that don't always need an index. We might not query these fields often, and the class may be overloaded with indexes to begin with. The indexes we have used so far are statically defined. ObjectGrid allows us to dynamically define indexes on a BackingMap too.

Defining an index dynamically gives us the freedom to add an index to a BackingMap after the ObjectGrid instance is started. We can also remove the dynamically defined index while the ObjectGrid is running. In a reporting application that only runs once per day, we can define indexes that are helpful to that application, run the queries that utilize those indexes, and remove them when the application is finished. The drawback of using dynamically defined indexes is that they are not immediately ready for use. ObjectGrid needs time to create the index on the specified attribute. Rather than waiting for index building to complete, we create a class that implements the `DynamicIndexCallback` interface. This interface provides methods that are called when certain index life-cycle events occur. Once we provide an implementation of these methods, we register our class with the `createDynamicIndex(...)` method on BackingMap. Let's look at the DynamicIndexCallback interface first:

```
public interface DynamicIndexCallback {
    void destroy(String idxName);
    void error(String idxName, Throwable t);
    void ready(String idxName);
}
```

This doesn't look so bad. There are only three methods to implement, each corresponding to a life-cycle event of a MapIndex. We are more interested in the `ready(...)` and `error(...)` methods for our example. We have removed the `@Index` annotation from the state field on Addresses. This means that a query, in which the state attribute is in the `where` clause, will perform a scan of the state attribute on all of the addresses in the BackingMap to find the needed addresses. On a large data set, this will be slow because we expect to have millions of addresses in the BackingMap. What if we only query using the state attribute at 8 a.m. every morning during the reporting application? We would like the query to run in a reasonable amount of time so the rest of the ObjectGrid isn't affected by its slow performance. But, we also don't want to pay the price of indexing the state on every address.

We can build an index on the state attribute, while the ObjectGrid is running, to speed up reporting. Once the index is built, we can use it to query the Address BackingMap very quickly. Let's say we want a report that contains the number of credit cards and payments per address for a selected group of states:

```
PaymentReporter pr = new PaymentReporter();
pr.setGrid(pp.getGrid());
pr.reportStates();
```

We'll start by making a PaymentReporter class that requires an ObjectGrid instance:

```
public void reportStates() {
    StateReportRunner data = new StateReportRunner();
    data.setStates(
            new String[] { "MA", "CA", "NY", "NM", "FL", "ME" });
    StateReportIndex sri = new StateReportIndex();
    sri.setData(data);
    sri.setGrid(grid);
    BackingMap addressMap = grid.getMap("Address");
    try {
        addressMap.createDynamicIndex(
                "stateIndex", false, "state",sri);
    } catch(IndexAlreadyDefinedException iade) {
        throw new RuntimeException(iade);
    }
}
```

The `reportStates()` method creates a report for six states. It does this by defining a `DynamicIndexCallback` and then by creating a dynamic index on the Address BackingMap. The `StateReportIndex` class implements the `DynamicIndexCallback`, and it's important to see what that class looks like in its entirety:

```
public class StateReportIndex implements DynamicIndexCallback {
    private StateReportRunner data;
    private ObjectGrid grid;
    @Override
    public void destroy(String idxName) {
        System.out.println("Destroy called on index: " + idxName);
    }
    @Override
    public void error(String idxName, Throwable t) {
        System.out.println(
                    "Error using dynamic index named: " + idxName);
        t.printStackTrace();
        throw new RuntimeException(t);
    }
    @Override
    public void ready(String idxName) {
        System.out.println(
                "The index named " + idxName + " is ready for use!");
        try {
            Session session = grid.getSession();
            ObjectMap addressMap = session.getMap("Address");
            MapIndex idx =
                (MapIndex)addressMap.getIndex("stateIndex");
            session.begin();
            data.runReport(session.getEntityManager(), idx);
            session.commit();
        } catch(ObjectGridException oge) {
            throw new RuntimeException(oge);
        }
    }
    public StateReportRunner getData() {
        return data;
    }
    public void setData(StateReportRunner data) {
        this.data = data;
    }
    public ObjectGrid getGrid() {
        return grid;
    }
    public void setGrid(ObjectGrid grid) {
        this.grid = grid;
    }
}
```

The `StateReportIndex` has getters and setters for an ObjectGrid and a `StateReportRunner`. A `StateReportRunner` encapsulates all of the data and behavior needed when the index is ready. The purpose of `StateReportRunner` is to be completely self-sufficient, once it is set on the `StateReportIndex`. A `StateReportIndex` should be on its own, once set as the callback on the Address BackingMap. The index is created on the fly. It will not be finished in a predetermined amount of time where the application can just wait for it. Using a dynamic index in a meaningful way requires creating a `DynamicIndexCallback`:

```
public class StateReportRunner {
    String[] states;
    public void runReport(EntityManager em, MapIndex idx) {
    for(int i = 0; i < states.length; i++) {
            System.out.println("Report for state: " + states[i]);
            try {
                Iterator iter = idx.findAll(states[i]);
                while(iter.hasNext()) {
                    Tuple tuple = (Tuple)iter.next();
                    int addrKey = (Integer)tuple.getAttribute(0);
                    Address address = (Address)em.find(
                                        Address.class, addrKey);
                    System.out.println("      " + address);
                    System.out.println(
                        "      --- Number of credit cards:" +
                        address.getCards().size());
                    int numberOfPayments = 0;
                    Iterator cardIter =
                      address.getCards().iterator();
                    while(cardIter.hasNext()) {
                        Card card = (Card)cardIter.next();
                        numberOfPayments += card.getPayments().size();
                    }
                    System.out.println(
                        "      --- Number of payments:" +
                        numberOfPayments);
                }
            } catch(Exception e) {
                throw new RuntimeException(e);
            }
        }
    }
    public String[] getStates() {
        return states;
    }
    public void setStates(String[] states) {
        this.states = states;
    }
}
```

`StateReportRunner` encapsulates the data and behavior for this report. If we were to create another report that used different data, and had different behavior, we would create another class that implemented the `runReport(EntityManager em, MapIndex idx)` method and pass it to the `StateReportIndex`. The `runReport(EntityManager em, MapIndex idx)` method takes a MapIndex as a parameter. We haven't seen it before, though we know it must come from the `StateReportIndex`.

In the `reportStates()` method, we have:

```
BackingMap addressMap = grid.getMap("Address");
try {
    addressMap.createDynamicIndex(
            "stateIndex", false, "state", sri);
} catch(IndexAlreadyDefinedException iade) {
    throw new RuntimeException(iade);
}
```

Here, we work directly with the Address BackingMap, not an ObjectMap as we have done most often in the past. We are making a change to the way data is stored, and therefore, operate on the BackingMap. Remember, ObjectMap is for interacting with data inside of a BackingMap, not the BackingMap itself. The `addressMap.createDynamicIndex(String idxName, isRangeMap isRange, String attr, DynamicIndexCallback callback)` does the job of creating the index for us. There is no telling when the index will be created and ready for use. The `DynamicIndexCallback` we have supplied as a parameter will help us use the index. When the index is ready, surprisingly, the `DynamicIndexCallback.ready(String idxName, MapIndex idx)` is called. In our example, this is where our `StateReportIndex.ready()` method is called:

```
Session session = grid.getSession();
ObjectMap addressMap = session.getMap("Address");
MapIndex idx = (MapIndex)addressMap.getIndex("stateIndex");
session.begin();
data.runReport(session.getEntityManager(), idx);
session.commit();
```

By ignoring the try/catch block, we have the interesting stuff. We now operate on an ObjectMap, instead of a BackingMap. The index is on the objects, and we use the ObjectMap `getIndex(String name)` method to obtain a MapIndex by name. In this case, we called it `stateIndex` when we called the `createDynamicIndex(...)` method, and that is how we will refer to it going forward.

MapIndex is a small class containing only one method that we find interesting. We cast a MapIndex because the getIndex(...) method could also return a MapRangeIndex object. In our case, we know a MapIndex object is returned, and cast to it without testing its instance because we passed false to the createMapIndex(...) method, where we specified whether or not we wanted a MapRangeIndex. With a reference to an EntityManager and a MapIndex, the ready(...) method calls StateReportRunner.runReports():

```java
public void runReport(EntityManager em, MapIndex idx) {
    for(int i = 0; i < states.length; i++) {
        System.out.println("Report for state: " + states[i]);
        try {
            Iterator iter = idx.findAll(states[i]);
            while(iter.hasNext()) {
                Tuple tuple = (Tuple)iter.next();
                int addrKey = (Integer)tuple.getAttribute(0);
                Address address = (Address)em.find(
                                    Address.class, addrKey);
                System.out.println("      " + address);
                System.out.println(
                        "         --- Number of credit cards:" +
                        address.getCards().size());
                int numberOfPayments = 0;
                Iterator cardIter = address.getCards().iterator();
                while(cardIter.hasNext()) {
                    Card card = (Card)cardIter.next();
                    numberOfPayments += card.getPayments().size();
                }
                System.out.println(
                        "         --- Number of payments:" +
                        numberOfPayments);
            }
        } catch(Exception e) {
            throw new RuntimeException(e);
        }
    }
}
```

The MapIndex method we're interested in is the findAll(Object value) method. This method finds all entities that match the values passed to this method. We are iterating over the states in the array, and passing each one to the idx.findAll(attr) method to get all of the addresses that are in that state. Once we have all of the addresses in the state, we print some output that tells us how many credit cards are active at that address, and the total number of payments that have been made by those credit cards to the merchants we process.

The important things to remember when using a dynamic index are:

- The index class `ready(...)` method needs to get a reference to a MapIndex
- The runner encapsulates the behavior and the data needed, once the index is created

Summary

We've covered a lot of ground in this chapter. We've seen parts of the Entity and Query APIs that should give us an idea of how they are used, rather than a boring trip down the API documentation. Working with Entities gives us a few advantages over the ObjectMap API. Our applications don't need to keep track of the relationships between objects, like we would need to do, if we stick to the ObjectMap API. We have the convenience of working with relationships between objects, and not IDs for foreign keys like we have with databases. Registering Entity classes is easy. As we'll see in the next few chapters, we can also perform the same registering and configuration by using XML, in case we need to leave out the annotations. We learned about the query API and about some of the aggregate functions available to us. The Query API provides an SQL-like view into an ObjectGrid which allows us to find objects that meet whatever criteria we define, either fuzzy or exact. We saw how to get objects resulting from a query and how to use transaction scope to our advantage. Keeping transactions short for data that needs to be available for other transactions is a priority. Longer transactions aren't a problem though, as long as they aren't so large as to consume all network and ObjectGrid server resources. Finally, we got a glimpse of creating indexes on the fly. This is useful for keeping performance and throughput high, while giving us the flexibility to run queries on indexed fields when needed.

This chapter was just a start in using these APIs. We will continue to expand our Entity and Query repertoire, as we explore more features in WebSphere eXtreme Scale.

4
Database Integration

The previous chapters have been exclusively concerned with Websphere eXtreme Scale and its use as a cache and persistent data store. By using the partitioning and replication functions, which we'll look at in the next few chapters, we can build a production-worthy application with persistent, reliable, and durable data storage, without ever touching a disk. However, there are a few key features that data grids lack.

There are three compelling reasons to integrate with a database backend. First, reporting tools do not have good data grid integration. Using CrystalReports and other reporting tools, don't work with data grids right now. Loading data from a data grid into a data warehouse with existing tools isn't possible either.

The second reason we want to use a database with a data grid is when we have an extremely large data set. A data grid stores data in memory. Though much cheaper than in the past, system memory is still much more expensive than a typical magnetic hard disk. When dealing with extremely large data sets, we want to structure our data so that the most frequently used data is in the cache and less frequently used data is on the disk.

The third compelling reason to use a database with a data grid is that our application may need to work with legacy applications that have been using relational databases for years. Our application may need to provide more data to them, or operate on data already in the legacy database in order to stay ahead of a processing load. In this chapter, we will explore some of the good and not-so-good uses of an in-memory data grid. We'll also look at integrating Websphere eXtreme Scale with relational databases.

You're going where?

Somewhere along the way, we all learned that software consists of algorithms and data. CPUs load instructions from our compiled algorithms, and those instructions operate on bits representing our data. The closer our data lives to the CPU, the faster our algorithm can use it. On the x86 CPU, the registers are the closest we can store data to the instructions executed by the CPU.

CPU registers are also the smallest and most expensive data storage location. The amount of data storable in registers is fixed because the number and size of CPU registers is fixed. Typically, we don't directly interact with registers because their correct usage is important to our application performance. We let the compiler writers handle translating our algorithms into machine code. The machine code knows better than we do, and will use register storage far more effectively than we will *most of the time*.

Less expensive, and about an order of magnitude slower, we have the Level 1 cache on a CPU (see below). The Level 1 cache holds significantly more data than the combined storage capacity of the CPU registers. Reading data from the Level 1 cache, and copying it to a register, is still very fast. The Level 1 cache on my laptop has two 32K instruction caches, and two 32K data caches.

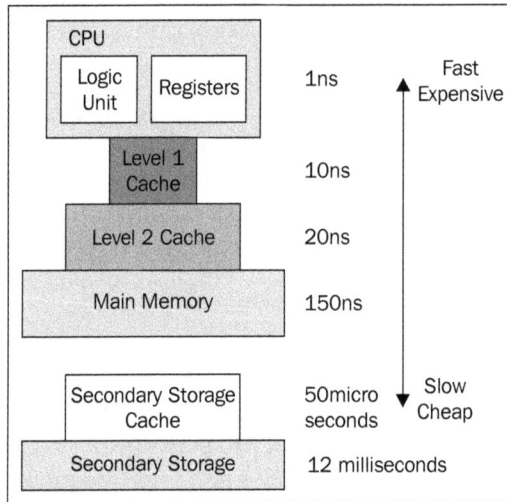

Still less expensive, and another order of magnitude slower, is the Level 2 cache. The Level 2 cache is typically much larger than Level 1 cache. I have 4MB of the Level 2 cache on my laptop. It still won't fit the contents of the Library of Congress into that 4MB, but that 4MB isn't a bad amount of data to keep near the CPU.

Up another level, we come to the main system memory. Consumer level PCs come with 4GB RAM. A low-end server won't have any less than 8GB. At this point, we can safely store a large chunk of data, if not all of the data, used by an application. Once the application exits, its data is unloaded from the main memory, and all of the data is lost. In fact, once our data is evicted from any storage at or below this level, it is lost. Our data is ephemeral unless it is put onto some secondary storage. The unit of measurement for accessing data in a register, either Level 1 or 2 cache and main memory, is a nanosecond.

Getting to secondary storage, we jump up an SI-prefix to a microsecond. Accessing data in the secondary storage cache is on the order of microseconds. If the data is not in cache, the access time is on the order of milliseconds. Accessing data on a hard drive platter is *one million times slower* than accessing that same data in main memory, and *one billion times slower* than accessing that data in a register. However, secondary storage is very cheap and holds millions of times more than primary storage. Data stored in secondary storage is durable. It doesn't disappear when the computer is reset after a crash.

Our operation teams comfortably build secondary storage silos to store petabytes of data. We typically build our applications so the application server interacts with some relational database management system that sits in front of that storage silo. The network hop to communicate with the RDBMS is in the order of microseconds on a fast network, and milliseconds otherwise.

Sharing data between applications has been done with the disk + network + database approach for a long time. It's become the traditional way to build applications. Load balancer in front, application servers or batch processes constantly communicating with a database to store data for the next process that needs it.

As we see with computer architecture, we insert data where it fits. We squeeze it as close to the CPU as possible for better performance. If a data segment doesn't fit in one level, keep squeezing what fits into each higher storage level. That leaves us with a lot of unused memory and disk space in an application deployment. Storing data in the memory is preferable to storing it on a hard drive. Memory segmentation in a deployment has made it difficult to store useful amounts of data at a few milliseconds distance. We just use a massive, but slow, database instead.

Where does an IMDG fit?

We've used ObjectGrid to store all of our data so far. This diagram should look pretty familiar by now:

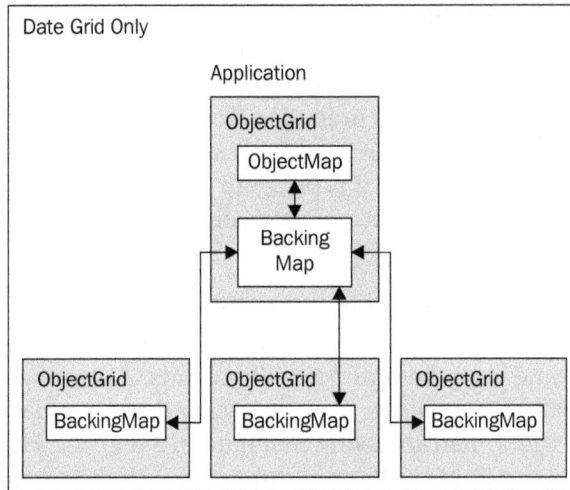

Because we're only using the ObjectGrid APIs, our data is stored in-memory. It is not persisted to disk. If our ObjectGrid servers crash, then our data is in jeopardy (we haven't covered replication yet). One way to get our data into a persistent store is to mark up our classes with some ORM framework like JPA. We can use the JPA API to persist, update, and remove our objects from a database after we perform the same operations on them using the ObjectMap or Entity APIs. The onus is on the application developer to keep both cache and database in sync:

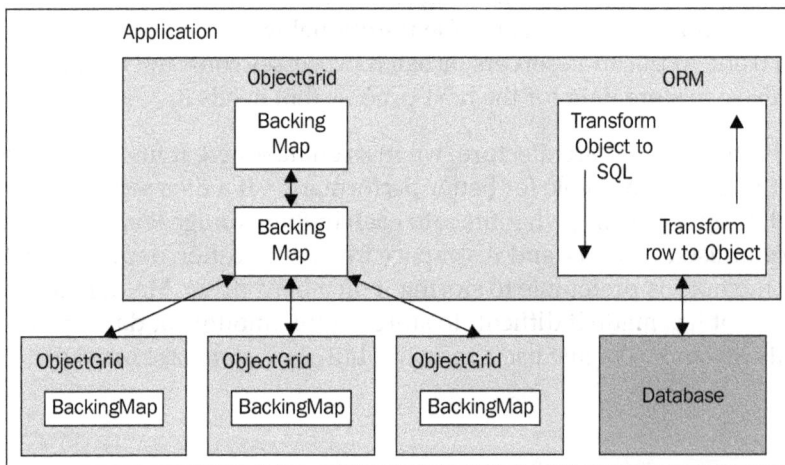

If you take this approach, then all of the effort would be for naught. Websphere eXtreme Scale provides functionality to integrate with an ORM framework, or any data store, through Loaders. A Loader is a BackingMap plugin that tells ObjectGrid how to transform an object into the desired output form. Typically, we'll use a Loader with an ORM specification like JPA. Websphere eXtreme Scale comes with a few different Loaders out of the box, but we can always write our own.

A Loader works in the background, transforming operations on objects into some output, whether it's file output or SQL queries. A Loader plugs into a BackingMap in an ObjectGrid server instance, or in a local ObjectGrid instance. A Loader does not plug into a client-side BackingMap, though we can override Loader settings on a client-side BackingMap.

While the Loader runs in the background, we interact with an ObjectGrid instance just the same as we have in the previous chapters. We use the ObjectMap API for objects with zero or simple relationships, and the Entity API for objects with more complex relationships. The Loader handles all of the details in transforming an object into something that can integrate with external data stores:

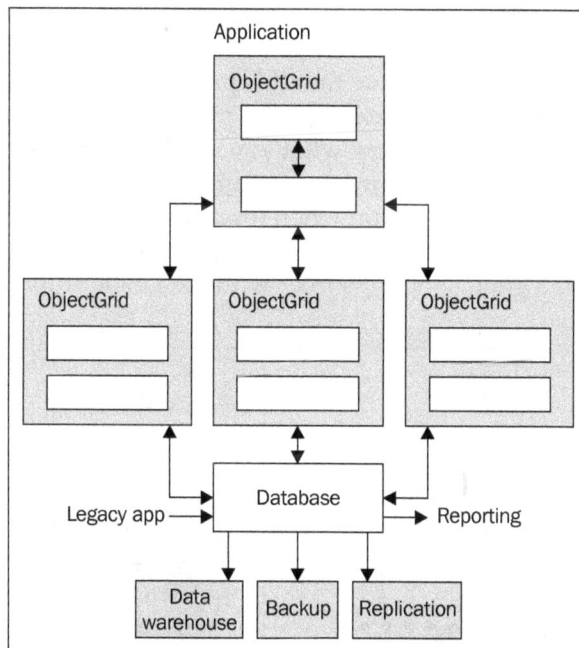

Why is storing our data in a database so important? Haven't we seen how much faster Websphere eXtreme Scale is than an RDBMS? Shouldn't all of our data be stored in in-memory? An in-memory data grid is good for certain things. There are plenty of things that a traditional RDBMS is good at that any IMDG just doesn't support.

An obvious issue is that memory is significantly more expensive than hard drives. 8GB of server grade memory costs thousands of dollars. 8GB of server grade disk space costs pennies. Even though the disk is slower than memory, we can store a lot more data on it.

An IMDG shines where a sizeable portion of frequently-changing data can be cached so that all clients see the same data. The IMDG provides orders of magnitude with better latency, read, and write speeds than any RDBMS. But we need to be aware that, for large data sets, an entire data set may not fit in a typical IMDG. If we focus on the frequently-changing data that must be available to all clients, then using the IMDG makes sense.

Imagine a deployment with 10 servers, each with 64GB of memory. Let's say that of the 64GB, we can use 50GB for ObjectGrid. For a 1TB data set, we can store 50% of it in cache. That's great! As the data set grows to 5TB, we can fit 10% in cache. That's not as good as 50%, but if it is the 10% of the data that is accessed most frequently, then we come out ahead. If that 10% of data has a lot of writes to it, then we come out ahead.

Websphere eXtreme Scale gives us predictable, dynamic, and linear scalability. When our data set grows to 100TB, and the IMDG holds only 0.5% of the total data set, we can add more nodes to the IMDG and increase the total percentage of cacheable data (see below). It's important to note that this predictable scalability is immensely valuable. Predictable scalability makes capacity planning easier. It makes hardware procurement easier because you know what you need. Linear scalability provides a graceful way to grow a deployment as usage and data grow. You can rest easy knowing the limits of your application when it's using an IMDG. The IMDG also acts as a shock absorber in front of a database. We're going to explore some of the reasons why an IMDG makes a good shock absorber with the Loader functionality.

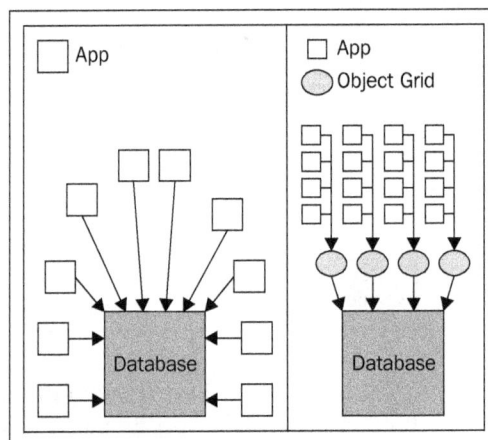

There are plenty of other situations, some that we have already covered, where an IMDG is the correct tool for the job. There are also plenty of situations where an IMDG just doesn't fit.

A traditional RDBMS has thousands of man-years of research, implementation tuning, and bug fixing already put into it. An RDBMS is well-understood and is easy to use in application development. There are standard APIs for interacting with them in almost any language:

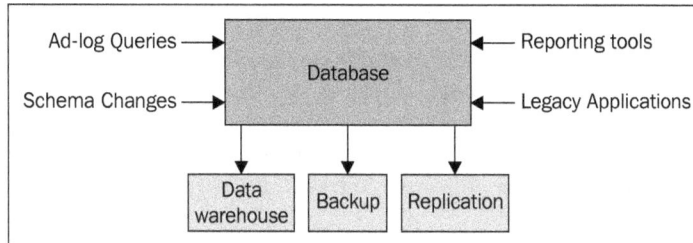

In-memory data grids don't have the supporting tools built around them that RDBMSs have. We can't plug CrystalReports into an ObjectGrid instance to get daily reports out of the data in the grid. Querying the grid is useful when we run simple queries, but fails when we need to run the query over the entire data set, or run a complex query. The query engine in Websphere eXtreme Scale is not as sophisticated as the query engine in an RDBMS. This also means the data we get from ad hoc queries is limited. Running ad hoc queries in the first place is more difficult. Even building an ad hoc query runner that interacts with an IMDG is of limited usefulness.

An RDBMS is a wonderful cross-platform data store. Websphere eXtreme Scale is written in Java and only deals with Java objects. A simple way for an organization to share data between applications is in a plaintext database. We have standard APIs for database access in nearly every programming language. As long as we use the supported database driver and API, we will get the results as we expect, including ORM frameworks from other platforms like .NET and Rails. We could go on and on about why an RDBMS needs to be in place, but I think the point is clear. It's something we still need to make our software as useful as possible.

JPALoader and JPAEntityLoader

One of the most common ways for a Java application to interact with a database is with some JPA implementation. We'll use the Hibernate implementation for these examples, though any JPA implementation will work. The JPA spec, and the ObjectGrid APIs, contain many parallels, which make learning the integration concepts much easier. The JPA spec most closely matches the EntityManager API in terms of interacting with persistent data. In fact, both classes used for interacting with persistent data are EntityManagers, though they are in different packages. Due to similarities in class and method names, we'll configure JPA and ObjectGrid differently. We'll use the ObjectGrid annotations and the JPA XML configuration when the class and annotation names overlap.

We need to configure our application models to use JPA. This means we create our `persistence.xml` and `orm.xml` files as we normally would for JPA:

```
File: persistence.xml
<?xml version="1.0" encoding="UTF-8"?>
<persistence xmlns="http://java.sun.com/xml/ns/persistence"
             xmlns:xsi="http://www.w3.org/2001/XMLSchema-instance"
          xsi:schemaLocation="http://java.sun.com/xml/ns/persistence
          http://java.sun.com/xml/ns/persistence/persistence_1_0.xsd"
             version="1.0">
   <persistence-unit name="PaymentProcessor"
                    transaction-type="RESOURCE_LOCAL">
     <provider>org.hibernate.ejb.HibernatePersistence</provider>
     <class>wxs.sample.models.Payment</class>
     <class>wxs.sample.models.Address</class>
     <class>wxs.sample.models.Batch</class>
     <class>wxs.sample.models.Card</class>

     <properties>
        <property name="hibernate.connection.url"
           value="jdbc:mysql://galvatron:3306/payment_processor" />
        <property name="hibernate.connection.driver_class"
                 value="com.mysql.jdbc.Driver" />
        <property name="hibernate.connection.password"
                 value="pp_password" />
        <property name="hibernate.connection.username"
                 value="pp_user" />
        <!-- <property name="hibernate.hbm2ddl.auto"
                    value="create" />-->
        <property name="hibernate.show_sql" value="false" />
     </properties>
   </persistence-unit>
</persistence>
```

We specify our four classes to use as JPA entities and set the Hibernate connection properties. In this example, I'm using a MySQL database named payment_processor. I'm also asking Hibernate to generate my schema based on the XML configuration I provide for the JPA entity mappings:

```xml
File: orm.xml
<?xml version="1.0" encoding="UTF-8"?>
<entity-mappings xmlns="http://java.sun.com/xml/ns/persistence/orm"
            xmlns:xsi="http://www.w3.org/2001/XMLSchema-instance"
      xsi:schemaLocation="http://java.sun.com/xml/ns/persistence/orm
                      orm_1_0.xsd" version="1.0">
    <entity class="wxs.sample.models.Payment" access="FIELD">
        <attributes>
            <id name="id"/>
            <basic name="paymentType">
                <enumerated>STRING</enumerated>
            </basic>
            <many-to-one name="batch"
                        target-entity="wxs.sample.models.Batch"
                        fetch="LAZY"/>
            <many-to-one name="card"
                        target-entity="wxs.sample.models.Card"
                        fetch="LAZY"/>
        </attributes>
    </entity>

    <entity class="wxs.sample.models.Batch" access="FIELD">
        <attributes>
            <id name="id"/>
            <basic name="status">
                <enumerated>STRING</enumerated>
            </basic>
        </attributes>
    </entity>

    <entity class="wxs.sample.models.Card" access="FIELD">
        <attributes>
            <id name="id"/>
            <basic name="cardType">
```

```
                    <enumerated>STRING</enumerated>
            </basic>
            <many-to-one name="address"
                        target-entity="wxs.sample.models.Address"
                        fetch="LAZY">
                <!-- <cascade>
                <cascade-persist/>
                <cascade-merge/>
                </cascade> -->
            </many-to-one>
        </attributes>
    </entity>

    <entity class="wxs.sample.models.Address" access="FIELD">
        <attributes>
            <id name="id"/>
        </attributes>
    </entity>
</entity-mappings>
```

Again, there is nothing out of the ordinary here, just a normal `orm.xml` file. Our
models now pull double-duty, working for both ObjectGrid and JPA. Because of this,
we need to annotate them with a bit of JPA information. First we'll look at Payment:

```
File: Payment.java
@Entity @javax.persistence.Entity
public class Payment implements Serializable {
    @Id @Index @javax.persistence.Id
    int id;

    @ManyToOne
    Batch batch;

    @ManyToOne
    Card card;

    PaymentType paymentType;
    BigDecimal amount;
}
```

We need to include the `@javax.persistence.Entity` and `@javax.persistence.Id`
annotations in the class file. If we don't, an ObjectGridException is thrown when the
class is examined by ObjectGrid:

```
com.ibm.websphere.objectgrid.ObjectGridRuntimeException: The
class class wxs.sample.models.Payment in the persistence unit
PaymentProcessor does not contain JPA key metadata.
```

We need to include these two annotations in each of our model classes, and leave the rest of the JPA configuration to the `orm.xml` file.

Now, we need to tell ObjectGrid about our JPA configuration. Of course, this happens in the `objectgrid.xml` file:

```
File: objectgrid.xml
<?xml version="1.0" encoding="UTF-8"?>
<objectGridConfig xmlns:xsi="http://www.w3.org/2001/
                            XMLSchema-instance"
            xsi:schemaLocation=http://ibm.com/ws/objectgrid/config
                            ../objectGrid.xsd
                xmlns="http://ibm.com/ws/objectgrid/config">
    <objectGrids>
        <objectGrid name="PaymentProcessorGrid"
                    entityMetadataXMLFile="ppEntities.xml">

            <bean id="TransactionCallback"
            className="com.ibm.websphere.objectgrid.jpa.JPATxCallback">
                <property name="persistenceUnitName"
                        type="java.lang.String"
                        value="PaymentProcessor" />
            </bean>

            <backingMap name="Payment" pluginCollectionRef="Payment" />
            <backingMap name="Batch" pluginCollectionRef="Batch" />
            <backingMap name="Card" pluginCollectionRef="Card" />
            <backingMap name="Address" pluginCollectionRef="Address" />
            <backingMap name="idGeneratorMap" />

        </objectGrid>
    </objectGrids>

    <backingMapPluginCollections>

        <backingMapPluginCollection id="Payment">
            <bean id="Loader"
        className="com.ibm.websphere.objectgrid.jpa.JPAEntityLoader" />
        </backingMapPluginCollection>
        <backingMapPluginCollection id="Batch">
            <bean id="Loader"
        className="com.ibm.websphere.objectgrid.jpa.JPAEntityLoader" />
        </backingMapPluginCollection>

        <backingMapPluginCollection id="Card">
            <bean id="Loader"
```

```
            className="com.ibm.websphere.objectgrid.jpa.JPAEntityLoader" />
        </backingMapPluginCollection>

        <backingMapPluginCollection id="Address">
            <bean id="Loader"
        className="com.ibm.websphere.objectgrid.jpa.JPAEntityLoader" />
        </backingMapPluginCollection>
    </backingMapPluginCollections>
</objectGridConfig>
```

The first thing that should stick out is the slightly different format we're using for this file. By specifying backingMapPluginCollection, we can define BackingMapPlugins, and associate them with our BackingMaps. This keeps the BackingMap definition simpler by limiting it to the BackingMap name and BackingMap attributes. The plugins can safely go in their own section. They are associated with the BackingMap by name and ID. The pluginCollectionRef attribute names the ID of the backingMapPluginCollection to be used with a BackingMap.

The second thing that should stick out about this file is the TransactionCallback bean configuration:

```
<bean id="TransactionCallback"
      className="com.ibm.websphere.objectgrid.jpa.JPATxCallback">
    <property name="persistenceUnitName"
              type="java.lang.String"
              value="PaymentProcessor" />
</bean>
```

This transaction callback coordinates JPA transactions, which are separate from ObjectGrid transactions. The TransactionCallback bean is required to use the JPALoader or JPAEntityLoader. We set one property on it, the name of the persistence unit we specified in persistence.xml. We do not specify the location of that file because it is assumed to be on the classpath.

The backingMapPluginCollection specifies a JPAEntityLoader for each BackingMap we've defined:

```
<backingMapPluginCollection id="Payment">
    <bean id="Loader"
      className="com.ibm.websphere.objectgrid.jpa.JPAEntityLoader"/>
</backingMapPluginCollection>
```

The Loader's job

What does the JPAEntityLoader do? It plugs into the BackingMap and interacts with the JPA implementation on our behalf. An action on the contents of a BackingMap generates an equivalent action on the database used by the Loader. Whenever the BackingMap is changed through persist, merge, or remove, that action applies to the corresponding data in the database as well. Inserting an object with `entityManager. persist(address)` notifies the Loader to execute the SQL insert into `address (id, streetLine1, streetLine2, city, state, zipCode)`. Removing an object from a BackingMap by calling `entityManager.remove(address)` triggers the Loader, which executes the SQL equivalent to delete from `address where id = ?` with the corresponding address ID.

However, we defined relationships on our ObjectGrid Entities, and we define those same relationships in the JPA configuration. This allows us to maintain referential integrity in the database through the JPAEntityLoader. Because this is a new application, we can ask the JPA implementation to generate a schema based on our JPA entity definitions. By using the definitions in `orm.xml`, we should get a schema that has these tables:

```
mysql> show tables;
+---------------------------+
| Tables_in_payment_processor |
+---------------------------+
| address                   |
| batch                     |
| card                      |
| payment                   |
+---------------------------+
4 rows in set (0.02 sec)
```

The table definitions should look like this:

```
mysql> describe address;
+-------------+--------------+------+-----+---------+-------+
| Field       | Type         | Null | Key | Default | Extra |
+-------------+--------------+------+-----+---------+-------+
| id          | int(11)      | NO   | PRI |         |       |
| streetLine1 | varchar(255) | YES  |     | NULL    |       |
| streetLine2 | varchar(255) | YES  |     | NULL    |       |
| city        | varchar(255) | YES  |     | NULL    |       |
| state       | varchar(255) | YES  |     | NULL    |       |
| country     | varchar(255) | YES  |     | NULL    |       |
| zipCode     | varchar(255) | YES  |     | NULL    |       |
+-------------+--------------+------+-----+---------+-------+
```

```
mysql> describe card;
+----------------+--------------+------+-----+---------+-------+
| Field          | Type         | Null | Key | Default | Extra |
+----------------+--------------+------+-----+---------+-------+
| id             | int(11)      | NO   | PRI |         |       |
| cardNumber     | varchar(255) | YES  |     | NULL    |       |
| cardType       | varchar(255) | YES  |     | NULL    |       |
| name           | varchar(255) | YES  |     | NULL    |       |
| expirationDate | varchar(255) | YES  |     | NULL    |       |
| address_id     | int(11)      | YES  | MUL | NULL    |       |
+----------------+--------------+------+-----+---------+-------+

mysql> describe payment;
+-------------+--------------+------+-----+---------+-------+
| Field       | Type         | Null | Key | Default | Extra |
+-------------+--------------+------+-----+---------+-------+
| id          | int(11)      | NO   | PRI |         |       |
| paymentType | varchar(255) | YES  |     | NULL    |       |
| amount      | decimal(19,2)| YES  |     | NULL    |       |
| batch_id    | int(11)      | YES  | MUL | NULL    |       |
| card_id     | int(11)      | YES  | MUL | NULL    |       |
+-------------+--------------+------+-----+---------+-------+

mysql> describe batch;
+------------------+--------------+------+-----+---------+-------+
| Field            | Type         | Null | Key | Default | Extra |
+------------------+--------------+------+-----+---------+-------+
| id               | int(11)      | NO   | PRI |         |       |
| status           | varchar(255) | YES  |     | NULL    |       |
| originalFileName | varchar(255) | YES  |     | NULL    |       |
+------------------+--------------+------+-----+---------+-------+
```

Let's run our example in a local ObjectGrid instance first. It's easy to set up the BackingMaps to use a JPAEntityLoader programmatically. We'll set up the local instance in the useLocalObjectGrid method:

```
JPATxCallback jpaTxCallback = new JPATxCallback();
jpaTxCallback.setPersistenceUnitName("PaymentProcessor");
grid.setTransactionCallback(jpaTxCallback);

BackingMap batchMap = grid.getMap("Batch");
batchMap.setLoader(new JPAEntityLoader());
```

ObjectGrid needs a `jpaTxCallback` object configured in order to use a JPA Loader. We set the persistence unit name to be what we specified in the `persistence.xml` file. The local ObjectGrid instance works with the same JPA files on the classpath as a distributed ObjectGrid instance. Next, we get a reference to the BackingMap used to store Batch objects, and set its Loader to a JPALoader instance. No further configuration is required right now. Batch objects become durable in the database after the ObjectGrid transaction and JPA transaction are complete. Let's do the same for the rest of our models:

```
BackingMap paymentMap = grid.getMap("Payment");
paymentMap.setLoader(new JPAEntityLoader());

BackingMap addressMap = grid.getMap("Address");
addressMap.setLoader(new JPAEntityLoader());

BackingMap cardMap = grid.getMap("Card");
cardMap.setLoader(new JPAEntityLoader());
```

We're ready to run it and see what happens! The programming model does not change even though we're using a `JPAEntityLoader` now. We interact with the ObjectGrid instance as we have in previous chapters. Running the `PaymentProcessor` program now yields the same results as before, though it may run a bit slower.

Using these examples with a JPA Loader requires that all of the classes the JPA implementation normally uses be on the classpath. My classpath looks like this:

```
c:\wxs\workspace\PaymentProcessor\bin\;
c:\jboss-4.2.2.GA\server\default\lib\*;
c:\jboss-4.2.2.GA\lib\*;
c:\wxs\ObjectGrid\lib\*
```

This picks up all of the classes used by the Hibernate JPA implementation, the ObjectGrid libraries, and the classes in our example. Of course, creating a JAR file for our classes is a better idea for production use, but this is fine for development and local ObjectGrid instances.

Performance and referential integrity

If you run the `PaymentProcessor` as it stands now, you should notice that the performance is way down and your hard drives are spinning a lot. Because we stopped the configuration of the BackingMap after adding the JPAEntityLoader, we get the default write-behind behavior. Let's talk about read-through, write-through, and write-behind behavior so that we understand why our application suddenly slowed to a crawl.

These three behaviors dictate the performance of our application when it uses an inline cache. They specify when a Loader goes to the database to fetch or write an object to its SQL equivalent. Our goal is reducing the number of times the Loader goes to the database for any reason. Accessing an object in the database is orders of magnitude slower than accessing it in the cache. We want to maximize the cache hit rate while minimizing the database write rate. The read-through, write-through, and write-behind behaviors influence the entity relationships we define on our model classes.

A Loader used with an inline cache offers read-through behavior out of the box. Read-through means a Loader goes to the database and performs a select operation when the object is not found in the inline cache.

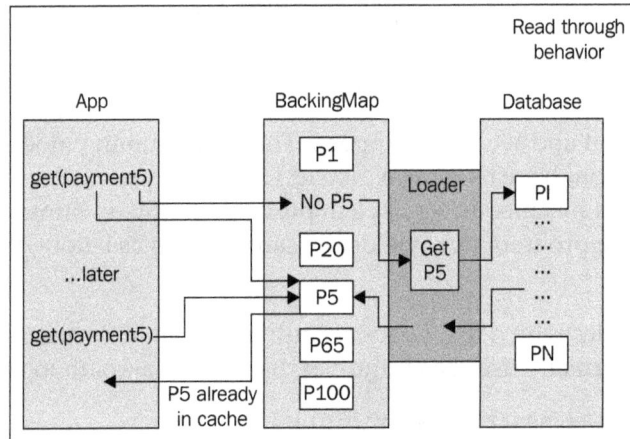

Our PaymentProcessor application makes a request for a payment with ID 5 (seen above). This payment does not exist in the cache, so the BackingMap requests the Loader to find that payment in the database. If found, that payment is returned to the application, and it lives in the cache until removed or evicted. All of this happens transparently during our application call to find the payment. To our application, we read *through* the cache to the database. Our application does not call any JPA API to achieve this.

Removal versus eviction

Setting an eviction policy on a BackingMap makes more sense now that we're using a Loader. Imagine that our cache holds only a fraction of the total data stored in the database. Under heavy load, the cache is constantly asked to hold more and more data, but it operates at capacity. What happens when we ask the cache to hold on to one more payment? The BackingMap needs to remove some payments in order to make room for more.

BackingMaps have three basic eviction policies: LRU (least-recently used), LFU (least-frequently used), and TTL (time-to-live). Each policy tells the BackingMap which objects should be removed in order to make room for more. In the event that an object is evicted from the cache, its status in the database is not changed. With eviction, objects enter and leave the cache due to cache misses and evictions innumerable times, and their presence in the database remains unchanged.

The only thing that affects an object in the database is an explicit call to change (either persist or merge) or remove it as per our application. Removal means the object is removed from the cache, and the Loader executes the delete from SQL to delete the corresponding row(s) from the database. Your data is safe when using evictions. The cache simply provides a window into your data. A remove operation explicitly tells both ObjectGrid and the database to delete an object.

Write-through and write-behind

Getting back to the slow down due to the Loader configuration, by default, the Loader uses write-through behavior:

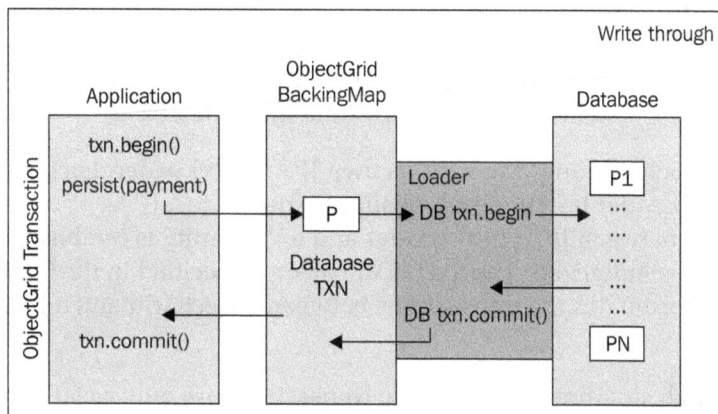

Now we know the problem. Write-through behavior wraps a database transaction for every write! For every ObjectGrid transaction, we execute one database transaction. On the up side, every object assuredly reaches the database, provided it doesn't violate any relational constraints. Despite this harsh reaction to write-through behavior, it is essential for objects that absolutely must get to the database as fast as possible. The problem is that we hit the database for *every* write operation on every BackingMap. It would be nice *not* to incur the cost of a database transaction every time we write to the cache.

Write-behind behavior gives us the help we need. Write-behind gives us the speed of an ObjectGrid transaction and the flexibility that comes with storing data in a database:

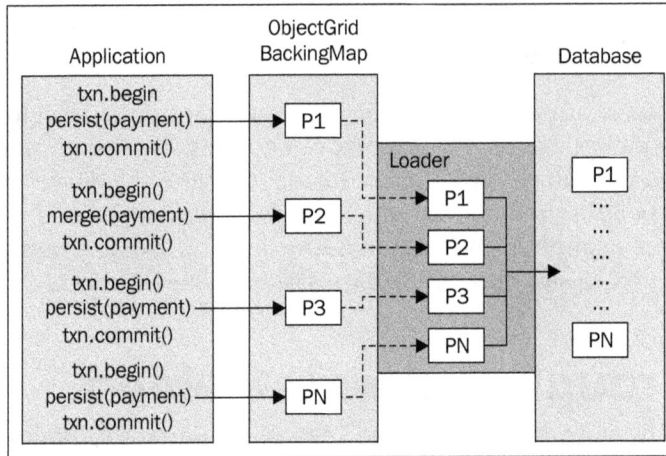

Each ObjectGrid transaction is now separate from a database transaction. BackingMap now has two jobs. The first job is to store our objects as it always does. The second job is to send those objects to the JPAEntityLoader. The JPAEntityLoader then generates SQL statements to insert the data into a database.

We configured each BackingMap with its own JPAEntityLoader. Each BackingMap requires its own Loader because each Loader is specific to a JPA entity class. The relationship between JPAEntityLoader and a JPA entity is established when the BackingMap is initialized. The jpaTxCallback we specified in the ObjectGrid configuration coordinates the transactions between ObjectGrid and a JPA EntityManager.

In a write-through situation, our database transactions are only as large as our ObjectGrid transactions. Update one object in the BackingMap and one object is written to the database. With write-behind, our ObjectGrid transaction is complete, and our objects are put in a write-behind queue map. That queue map does not immediately synchronize with the database. It waits for some specified time or for some number of updates, to write out its contents to the database:

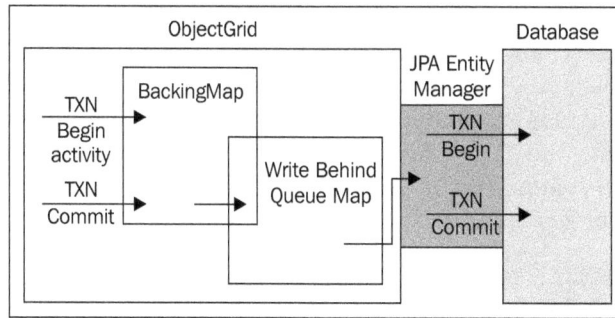

We configure the database synchronization conditions with the `setWriteBehind` (`"time;conditions"`) method on a BackingMap instance. Programmatically the `setWriteBehind` method looks like this:

```
BackingMap paymentMap = grid.getMap("Payment");
paymentMap.setLoader(new JPAEntityLoader());
paymentMap.setWriteBehind("T120;C5001");
```

The same configuration in XML looks like this:

```
<backingMap name="Payment" writeBehind="T120;C5001"
            pluginCollectionRef="Payment" />
```

Enabling write-behind is as simple as that. The `setWriteBehind` method takes one string parameter, but it is actually a two-in-one. At first, the `T` part is the time in seconds between syncing with the database. Here, we set the payment BackingMap to wait two minutes between syncs. The `C` part indicates the number (count) of changes made to the BackingMap that triggers a database sync.

Between these two parameters, the sync occurs on a *whichever comes first* basis. If two minutes elapse between syncs, and only 400 changes (persists, merges, or removals) have been put in the write-behind queue map, then those 400 changes are written out to the database. If only 30 seconds elapse, but we reach 5001 changes, then those changes will be written to the database.

ObjectGrid does not guarantee that the sync will take place exactly when either of those conditions is met. The sync may happen a little bit before (116 seconds or 4998 changes) or a little bit later (123 seconds or 5005 changes). The sync will happen as close to those conditions as ObjectGrid can reasonably do it.

The default value is "T300;C1000". This syncs a BackingMap to the database every five minutes, or 1000 changes to the BackingMap. This default is specified either with the string "T300;C1000" or with an empty string (" "). Omitting either part of the sync parameters is acceptable. The missing part will use the default value. Calling setWriteBehind("T60") has the BackingMap sync to the database every 60 seconds, or 1000 changes. Calling setWriteBehind("C500") syncs every five minutes, or 500 changes.

Write-behind behavior is enabled if the setWriteBehind method is called with an empty string. If you do not want write-behind behavior on a BackingMap, then do not call the setWriteBehind method at all.

A great feature of the write-behind behavior is that an object changed multiple times in the cache is only written in its final form to the database. If a payment object is changed in three different ObjectGrid transactions, the SQL produced by the JPAEntityLoader will reflect the object's final state before the sync. For example:

```
entityManager.getTransaction().begin();
Payment payment = createPayment(line, batch);
entityManager.getTransaction().commit();
some time later...
entityManager.getTransaction().begin();
payment.setAmount(new BigDecimal("44.95"));
entityManager.getTransaction().commit();
some time later...
entityManager.getTransaction().begin();
payment.setPaymentType(PaymentType.REAUTH);
entityManager.getTransaction().commit();
```

With write-through behavior, this would produce the following SQL:

```
insert into payment (id, amount, batch_id, card_id, payment_type)
values (12345, 75.00, 31, 6087, 'AUTH');

update payment set (id, amount, batch_id, card_id, payment_type)
values (12345, 44.95, 31, 6087, 'AUTH')
   where id = 12345;

update payment set (id, amount, batch_id, card_id, payment_type)
values (12345, 44.95, 31, 6087, 'REAUTH')
   where id = 12345;
```

Now that we're using write-behind, that same application behavior produces just one SQL statement:

```
insert into payment (id, amount, batch_id, card_id, payment_type)
values (12345, 44.95, 31, 6087, 'REAUTH');
```

BackingMap and Loader

The following problem does not exist in WebSphere eXtreme Scale version 7.0 and later. eXtreme Scale 7.0 solved the problem of writing data to a database out of order. The problem applies only to eXtreme Scale pre-7.0. The solution to this problem is left in as an example of using "soft references" to other objects and it remains a useful technique. We've seen that each BackingMap has its own instance of a Loader. Because each BackingMap uses the Loader to sync with the database according to its own conditions, we end up with different BackingMaps syncing at different times. Most of the time, we expect this to be a good thing. There are only four BackingMaps in our application that sync with the database (as seen below), but a larger application can have many more. Letting the BackingMaps sync on their own schedules reduces peak database load from an ObjectGrid instance.

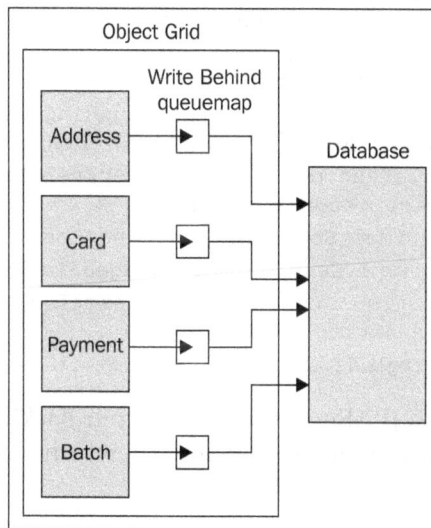

Our PaymentProcessor application should be pretty fast again after enabling write-behind on the BackingMaps. Each ObjectGrid transaction is no longer encumbered by a database transaction. By letting the application run for a bit, we see the output speed on the console. Part of that output includes this:

```
An exception occurred: javax.persistence.RollbackException: Error
while commiting the transaction
    at org.hibernate.ejb.TransactionImpl.commit(TransactionImpl.java:71)
    at com.ibm.websphere.objectgrid.jpa.JPATxCallback.
    commit(JPATxCallback.java:158)
```

```
    at com.ibm.ws.objectgrid.SessionImpl.commit(SessionImpl.java:1242)
    at com.ibm.ws.objectgrid.writebehind.WriteBehindLoader.pushChanges
      (WriteBehindLoader.java:1147)
    at com.ibm.ws.objectgrid.writebehind.WriteBehindLoader.pushChanges
      (WriteBehindLoader.java:1058)
    at com.ibm.ws.objectgrid.writebehind.WriteBehindLoader.
      run(WriteBehindLoader.java:768)
    at java.lang.Thread.run(Thread.java:735)
Caused by: org.hibernate.TransientObjectException: object references
an unsaved transient instance - save the transient instance before
flushing: wxs.sample.models.Payment.card -> wxs.sample.models.Card
    at org.hibernate.engine.CascadingAction$9.noCascade(
      CascadingAction.java:353)
    at org.hibernate.engine.Cascade.cascade(Cascade.java:139)
    at org.hibernate.event.def.AbstractFlushingEventListener.cascadeOn
      Flush(AbstractFlushingEventListener.java:131)
    at org.hibernate.event.def.AbstractFlushingEventListener.prepareEn
      tityFlushes(AbstractFlushingEventListener.java:122)
    at org.hibernate.event.def.AbstractFlushingEventListener.flushEver
      ythingToExecutions(AbstractFlushingEventListener.java:65)
    at org.hibernate.event.def.DefaultFlushEventListener.onFlush(
      DefaultFlushEventListener.java:26)
    at org.hibernate.impl.SessionImpl.flush(SessionImpl.java:1000)
    at org.hibernate.impl.SessionImpl.managedFlush(SessionImpl.java:338)
    at org.hibernate.transaction.JDBCTransaction.
      commit(JDBCTransaction.java:106)
    at org.hibernate.ejb.TransactionImpl.commit(TransactionImpl.java:54)
```

This is an artifact of using a JPAEntityLoader with our BackingMaps. The problem is the org.hibernate.TransientObjectException, which indicates that something is wrong with our ORM:

```
save the transient instance before flushing: wxs.sample.models.
Payment.card -> wxs.sample.models.Card
```

Our objects are JPA entities. A JPA entity manager enforces referential integrity through the ORM mapping files specified in persistence.xml. When we persist a payment instance, the instances of card and batch that it references must already be in the database due to foreign key constraints on the payment object and payment table:

```
<entity class="wxs.sample.models.Payment" access="FIELD">
  <attributes>
    <id name="id"/>
      <basic name="paymentType">
        <enumerated>STRING</enumerated>
      </basic>
```

```
                <many-to-one name="batch"
                        target-entity="wxs.sample.models.Batch"
                        fetch="LAZY"/>
                <many-to-one name="card"
                        target-entity="wxs.sample.models.Card"
                        fetch="LAZY"/>
        </attributes>
    </entity>
```

In the ORM definition, we notify the entity manager that a payment references an instance of a Card, and an instance of a Batch. A row for each of these objects must exist in the database before the JPA entity manager persists the payment. If that's not enough, then the database schema should enforce these constraints:

```
mysql> show create table payment\G
*************************** 1. row ***************************
        Table: payment
Create Table: CREATE TABLE `payment` (
  `id` int(11) NOT NULL,
  `paymentType` varchar(255) default NULL,
  `amount` decimal(19,2) default NULL,
  `batch_id` int(11) default NULL,
  `card_id` int(11) default NULL,
  PRIMARY KEY  (`id`),
  KEY `FK3454C9E6E0571E5E` (`batch_id`),
  KEY `FK3454C9E6E130BC56` (`card_id`),
  CONSTRAINT `FK3454C9E6E130BC56` FOREIGN KEY (`card_id`) REFERENCES
`card` (`id`),
  CONSTRAINT `FK3454C9E6E0571E5E` FOREIGN KEY (`batch_id`) REFERENCES
`batch` (`id`)
) ENGINE=InnoDB DEFAULT CHARSET=utf8
```

Whether the JPA entity manager allows it or not, the payment table definition clearly sets foreign key constraints on the batch and card tables. What's going wrong here?

Remember, each BackingMap has its own Loader, and each Loader syncs with the database according to its own rules. Because the Loaders do not sync at the same time, in the same order, or in the correct order according to the relationships set up by our ORM mappings, we run into referential integrity constraints.

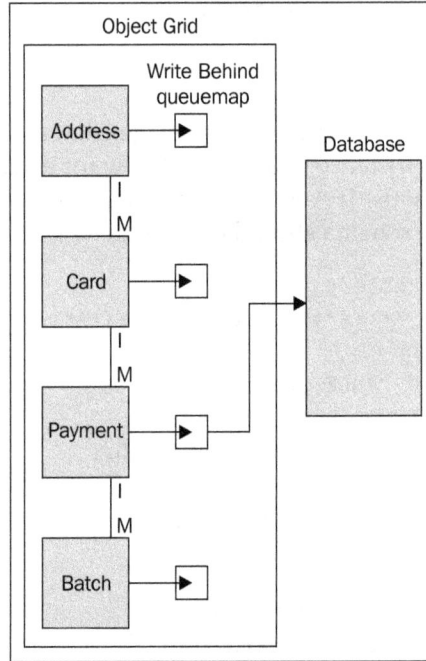

We're getting this exception because the BackingMap holding our payment objects syncs to the grid before the BackingMap that holds a card one of the payment objects references (as seen above). Because we can't specify the order in which BackingMap objects write to the database, we face a few difficult decisions.

Picking battles

The first thing we can do is disable write-behind on the card BackingMap. Each time we create a card and persist it to the BackingMap, the JPAEntityLoader will immediately write it to the database before the ObjectGrid transaction commits:

```
BackingMap batchMap = grid.getMap("Batch");
batchMap.setLoader(new JPAEntityLoader());
batchMap.setLockStrategy(LockStrategy.PESSIMISTIC);

BackingMap paymentMap = grid.getMap("Payment");
paymentMap.setLoader(new JPAEntityLoader());
paymentMap.setWriteBehind("T120;C5001");
```

```
BackingMap addressMap = grid.getMap("Address");
addressMap.setLoader(new JPAEntityLoader());
addressMap.setWriteBehind("T60;C11");

BackingMap cardMap = grid.getMap("Card");
cardMap.setLoader(new JPAEntityLoader());
```

Can you guess what happens when we run the program now:

```
org.hibernate.TransientObjectException: object references an unsaved
transient instance - save the transient instance before flushing: wxs.
sample.models.Card.address -> wxs.sample.models.Address
```

Same problem, different relationship! This time the problem is between `Address` and `Card`. In fact, we could have encountered this exception before we encountered the `TransientObjectException` between `Payment` and `Card`. Now what? Disable write-behind on Address too? Sure, why not:

```
BackingMap batchMap = grid.getMap("Batch");
batchMap.setLoader(new JPAEntityLoader());
batchMap.setLockStrategy(LockStrategy.PESSIMISTIC);

BackingMap paymentMap = grid.getMap("Payment");
paymentMap.setLoader(new JPAEntityLoader());
paymentMap.setWriteBehind("T120;C5001");

BackingMap addressMap = grid.getMap("Address");
addressMap.setLoader(new JPAEntityLoader());

BackingMap cardMap = grid.getMap("Card");
cardMap.setLoader(new JPAEntityLoader());
```

Potentially, we now have two database writes before we create a payment. One write for the address commit, and one write for the card commit. We're losing out on some write-behind benefits very quickly. Only one of our entities now has write-behind enabled for it. One of the goals we had in using ObjectGrid was to reduce the volume of database write transactions. This is still faster than a database-only approach, but it is significantly slower than having write-behind enabled on the address and card BackingMaps.

If strict referential integrity is a high priority and unchangeable in the current schema, then we are stuck with what we've got. This is nothing to scoff at. Read requests are significantly faster for objects in the cache. The BackingMap for payments still has write-behind enabled, and the creation of payments is still the highest-volume processing we do. Because of the huge number of payments we create and modify, inserting ObjectGrid between the database and our application is worth it for this alone.

However, if you're willing to loosen up the database schema requirements a little bit, and throw ORM relationships out of the window, then we can do much better than what we've got.

JPALoader

We're having problems because the BackingMaps do not sync with regard to JPA entity relationships. The order of insertion is important in a database, and we cannot specify an order for BackingMaps to load their objects. Rather than fighting that, we can embrace it and dumb down our ObjectGrid and JPA entities. Decoupling entities removes the insertion order requirement between the two. As long as we don't mind having a payment with a `card_id` that doesn't yet exist in the card table, we can get some work done with this approach. Besides, that card will be in the table in the next five minutes, or 1000 BackingMap changes, if we're using the default write-behind values:

```
<entity class="wxs.sample.models.Payment" access="FIELD">
    <attributes>
        <id name="id"/>
        <basic name="paymentType">
            <enumerated>STRING</enumerated>
        </basic>
    </attributes>
</entity>

<entity class="wxs.sample.models.Batch" access="FIELD">
    <attributes>
        <id name="id"/>
        <basic name="status">
            <enumerated>STRING</enumerated>
        </basic>
    </attributes>
</entity>

<entity class="wxs.sample.models.Card" access="FIELD">
    <attributes>
        <id name="id"/>
        <basic name="cardType">
            <enumerated>STRING</enumerated>
        </basic>
    </attributes>
</entity>
```

```
<entity class="wxs.sample.models.Address" access="FIELD">
    <attributes>
        <id name="id"/>
    </attributes>
</entity>
```

The new `orm.xml` file removes all of the relationship metadata. That takes care of the JPA part. We now need to pull the ObjectGrid entity metadata out of our model classes:

```
@javax.persistence.Entity
public class Batch implements Serializable {
    @javax.persistence.Id int id;
    BatchStatus status;
    String originalFileName;
}
```

Note that we keep the JPA entity metadata in the class while removing the ObjectGrid entity metadata. The JPA entity metadata stays because we're still using JPA to map the entity to a database table. The ObjectGrid entity metadata goes away because we need to get a little "closer to the metal" as the saying goes:

```
@javax.persistence.Entity
public class Payment implements Serializable {
    @Id @Index @javax.persistence.Id
    int id;
    int batchId;
    int cardId;

    PaymentType paymentType;
    BigDecimal amount;
}
```

We've removed the ObjectGrid entity annotations. We can no longer use the ORM features of entities to define relationships between our models. It's back to the ObjectMap API, including defining the map in our `useLocalObjectGrid()` method:

```
grid.defineMap("Payment");
BackingMap paymentMap = grid.getMap("Payment");
paymentMap.setLoader(new JPALoader());
paymentMap.setWriteBehind("");
```

Because we're not using the ORM of ObjectGrid entities, we must remove the references to Batch and Card from the Payment class. We replace them with their respective IDs. When the JPALoader generates SQL from payment objects, it now has the batch ID that the payment references. This technique works because we're generating object IDs within our application. The combination of application-generated object IDs, and backing off from ORM, allows us to insert objects "out of order":

```
mysql> show create table payment\G
*************************** 1. row ********
        Table: payment
Create Table: CREATE TABLE `payment` (
  `id` int(11) NOT NULL,
  `batchId` int(11) NOT NULL,
  `cardId` int(11) NOT NULL,
  `paymentType` varchar(255) default NULL,
  `amount` decimal(19,2) default NULL,
  PRIMARY KEY  (`id`)
) ENGINE=InnoDB DEFAULT CHARSET=utf8
```

Without the Foreign key constraints on the payment table, we can insert payments with non-existent `cardId` and `batchId`. Additionally, we need to rework our application to use ObjectMap and Session, in place of the EntityManager API.

Changing all our classes to use the ObjectMap and the Session APIs removes some functionality that is useful. The query functionality we gain with ObjectGrid entities is too good to pass up in some situations. Particularly when we query for addresses and cards that already exist, we'd like to preserve this functionality. There is nothing to stop us from taking a hybrid approach to using ObjectGrid entities where it works and is helpful, and then dropping down to the lower level APIs for ObjectMap and Session where we need it. In this case, we're going to leave the ObjectGrid entity annotations on Address and Card.

Running the `PaymentProcessor` program with the hybrid approach gives us all of the advantages of read-through/write-behind behavior. We only gain this error-free functionality by losing our grip on the database schema and allowing our classes to have a little more knowledge of the database schema.

Summary

As usual, we covered a lot of ground in this chapter. This was a good opportunity to discuss what in-memory data grids do well. We also got to see some effects of their relative immaturity. Data grids don't yet have the widespread use held by relational databases. As such, there is a lack of tool support when integrating with an IMDG. The IMDG is also inherently platform-specific now. WebSphere eXtreme Scale caches Java objects themselves, not an interoperable representation. Where interoperability is an issue, relational databases shine.

Fortunately, we've seen how we can integrate our IMDG with our relational database. We can now build new applications using the data grid as a cache, and integrate it with a database for durability, data capacity, and reporting uses.

Configuring an ObjectGrid instance to use a JPALoader of JPAEntityLoader is easy. Starting the flow of objects to SQL to database rows is like turning on a switch. The most important thing to remember when using Loaders is that referential integrity will come back to haunt you if write-behind is enabled. There are a few ways to look at that problem. Is referential integrity the most important requirement in an application? Perhaps write-behind isn't the right behavior for that application. More realistically, a hybrid approach of write-through for critical referential integrity objects, and write-behind for high-volume or change-heavy objects works well. If write-speed is important, then relaxing the relational constraints in the database schema and in the ORM file makes sense.

Among WebSphere eXtreme Scale, a relational database, and a JPA provider, we can now achieve very high performance with increased durability and interoperability. Now that we know our way around WebSphere eXtreme Scale, and have covered the legacy issues, we can focus on building highly-scalable, highly-available deployments in the upcoming chapters.

5

Handling Increased Load

This chapter and the next chapter go hand-in-hand. There is an overlap in the topics covered in each chapter, though we'll explore different uses for each topic in different chapters. These chapters cover the building blocks we'll use most frequently while deploying WebSphere eXtreme Scale.

The previous chapters mostly used one kind of eXtreme Scale instance: the local instance. A local eXtreme Scale instance exists in its client program's address space. Most of the client APIs are available and work with a local eXtreme Scale instance. This chapter introduces the client/server, or distributed, eXtreme Scale instance.

In a distributed eXtreme Scale instance, the client process and server process are separate. Separating the client and server processes lets us configure more interesting topologies on the server side. eXtreme Scale server topologies let us group memory and CPU resources to build a data grid more capable than any single-process or single-server deployment.

An eXtreme Scale deployment can include many server or container processes. Using many server processes lets us store data sets that are larger in size than the memory of one JVM heap. Containers spread across multiple servers give us even more memory for large data sets. Other areas where multiple container processes are helpful include making more bandwidth to the data set available, and more CPU cycles for DataGrid clients.

By the end of this chapter, we'll be able to:

- Understand the advantages of a distributed eXtreme Scale deployment
- Configure eXtreme Scale to use multiple container processes with the `objectgrid.xml` configuration file
- Learn how to partition our data sets

The building blocks

The point of building out an eXtreme Scale deployment is to make more memory, CPU, and network bandwidth available. More memory means we can store more objects. More CPU cycles gives us lower latency in servicing client requests and running grid agents which will be introduced in Chapter 7. More network bandwidth allows more clients to simultaneously connect to the grid by spreading our data across more physical computers. We'll do a brief overview of the topics here, and get into more detail as we progress.

A distributed eXtreme Scale deployment is made up of at least one catalog server process and at least one container server process. The catalog server coordinates the efforts of the container processes. A common scenario is to have a few catalog servers managing many container servers in a deployment.

In a distributed deployment, a container process is where our objects live after a client commits a transaction with put or insert operations. Catalog and container processes are started on the command line with the startOgServer.bat or startOgServer.sh scripts. The location of these processes is determined by the system administrator (or whoever is responsible for the deployment). We control the computers on which the catalog and container processes run.

On a smaller scale, a container process logically contains partitions. A partition is a subset of the objects put in a BackingMap. The partition in which an object is placed is determined by that object's hashCode() method. By partitioning our objects, we immediately realize the gains of having many container processes. A larger number of partitions lets us throw more computers at a deployment. If we divide our objects into 10 partitions, and have 10 computers each with 16GB of memory, then we can store 160GB of objects in that deployment (ignoring overhead).

A partition is made of even smaller pieces called **shards**. Shards can take one of the three different roles, and their placement is determined by the catalog server process. Partitions are not placed directly in the grid because they're made from shards. Instead, the shards are placed into container processes based on rules we set in the objectgrid.xml and deployment.xml configuration files.

Shards and partitions

A shard is the smallest unit of a partition. Many shards can live in one container. In each shard there is a MapSet. A **MapSet** is a set of BackingMaps that are *partitioned* using a common key. The common key scheme is used mainly by the Entity API because we have class hierarchies where placement of parents and children in the same shard matters. It gives us much closer locality of reference. We don't worry about common keys so much with the ObjectMap API because each map is assumed to stand alone.

An easy way to think about a common key is with an object hierarchy of two classes, Parent and Child. Parent has many Children through the Entity `@OneToMany` annotation and it cascades persistent operations. Let's say we always access a child through its parent. A parent with a child set on it is persisted using the `EntityManager#persist(parent)` method.

Persisting the parent object cascades the operation to the child. Both parent and child are serialized to the partition that the parent is placed in. The parent and child object both exist in the partition obtained by finding the partition of the parent object. The Parent and Child classes share a partition key, which is the partition key of the Parent. This concept can be applied all the way down an Entity class hierarchy.

Using a common partition key is a way of ensuring that the data that is accessed together, stays together. A call to `EntityManager.find(Parent.class, id)` returns all children for that parent in one RPC. If the Parent and Child did not use a common partition key, we would need at least two RPCs, one to find the parent, and the other to find the children.

The BackingMaps in a MapSet are partitioned and replicated together. In the deployment policy file, which we will create below, we define one MapSet which holds all of the BackingMaps. We specify only the number of partitions to use with the MapSet, though we will add more options later.

A partition is logically the next step up from a shard. Shards can take on one of three roles: primary shard, synchronous replica, and asynchronous replica. The combination of a primary shard and its replicas make up a partition.

A partition holds a subset of the objects in the BackingMaps referenced in the MapSet. The BackingMaps in the MapSet do not hold the complete set of objects stored in the BackingMap. Instead, the BackingMaps contain only the objects whose `hashCode()` method returns a value that places it in that partition.

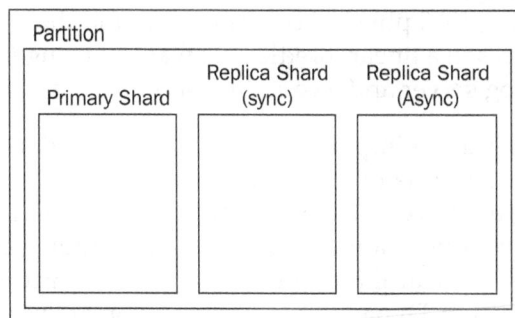

A container holds shards that make up each partition. In our deployment policy file, we have defined a partition as having zero replicas. Therefore, the partition consists of only one shard. Each partition logically contains a MapSet. We don't work directly with MapSets. They are just a way to group BackingMaps to use the same partitioning and replication configuration.

A BackingMap in a partition contains only a subset of the total objects stored in the logical BackingMap. Let's think of a partition as a folder, and a BackingMap as a filing cabinet. Logically, the set of records is the total of all of the records in each folder. Each folder being a partition allows us to store some records. We're not obligated to store every record in one folder. Instead, we spread them out based on some organizational scheme: maybe alphabetically, maybe numerically. No matter which way they are organized, there is a systematic approach to our filing.

A logical BackingMap is made up of many BackingMaps spread across many partitions. When making a `put` or `update` call on a BackingMap, the ObjectGrid client is able to correctly place the object into the right partition based on the object's hash code.

A client is responsible for placing objects in the correct partition and connecting to the right container process to ask for an object. The client does this by using the `ClientClusterContext` which is obtained when we first connect to an ObjectGrid instance. The number of partitions in a deployment is known at server start time. By keeping track of which container process holds a particular shard, the catalog server can pass this information on to the client at connect time. The `ClientClusterContext` object contains data about the current grid topology.

Client/Server ObjectGrid

A distributed eXtreme Scale deployment is made up of many JVMs. These JVMs can be located on one physical computer, or span many data centers. There are some deployments using 1500 physical computers around the world. eXtreme Scale uses additional resources in a linear, predictable way, by using two different server process types—a **catalog server** and a **container server**.

A catalog server controls a few important services in an eXtreme Scale deployment. The two services we're concerned with right now are the grouping service and shard balancing service. These services let us build dynamic ObjectGrid deployments, without doing a lot of configuration up front. Dynamic topologies are the preferred way to use eXtreme Scale because we only need an `objectgrid.xml` file and a `deploymentpolicy.xml` file. Dynamic deployments don't require us to know the final topology before we start the container processes. We can add container processes to a dynamic deployment at any time.

A static deployment requires a description of each ObjectGrid container, and the host on which it runs in an XML configuration file. This file is then used to start each ObjectGrid server instance. While this may be acceptable for small deployments, the dynamic deployment is much easier to work with, and scales to handle much higher load with minimal administration.

The grouping service and shard balancing service work with resources provided by ObjectGrid container processes. A container process is where objects are stored while the catalog service handles the administrative functions for the grid. The container process provides its heap space to store cached objects and its CPU cycles to serve client requests.

The simplest dynamic deployment has one catalog server and one container server. Let's look at what we need to do to create this deployment. Let's also look at one client process using the dynamic deployment.

A basic deployment

Starting a catalog service is straightforward. We use the `startOgServer` script in the `ObjectGrid/bin` directory. Let's see what we need to provide to the script when we invoke it:

C:\wxs\ObjectGrid\bin>startOgServer

Running this script without any arguments gives a lot of output describing the options used to start the different ObjectGrid processes. Let's look at the general startup options:

```
To start a ObjectGrid catalog server:
    <server> [options]
To start an ObjectGrid container server:
    <server> -objectgridFile <xml file> [options]
    <server> -objectgridUrl <xml URL> [options]
```

Here are some of the catalog server-specific options:

```
Catalog server options:
    -catalogServiceEndPoints <server:host:port:port,server:host:port:port>
    -quorum true|false
    -heartbeat 0|1|-1
    -clusterFile <xml file>
    -clusterUrl <xml URL>
    -clusterSecurityFile <cluster security xml file>
```

```
-clusterSecurityUrl <cluster security xml URL>

-domain <domain name>

-listenerHost <hostname>

-listenerPort <port>
```

Simply providing a name for the catalog server is enough to start the catalog server process. None of these options are required for development use, though it might be useful to set the listener host. By default, the catalog server listens for IIOP requests on localhost port 2809. It would be helpful if it listened on the host name of the computer, rather than localhost, or else it would not be able to accept connections. Port 2809 is fine for our purposes (unless it is already in use on that computer).

Catalog services can run in standalone or clustered configurations. For now, we will use standalone, which is why we can get away without providing any additional catalog server settings.

Let's start our catalog server:

```
C:\wxs\ObjectGrid\bin>startOgServer.bat catalog0 -listenerHost galvatron
```

This starts an instance of the catalog server as a background process. Here, I told it to listen for connections to the host galvatron, which is the host name of my catalog server box. The catalog server process does not take control of your shell. Stopping the catalog service is easy:

```
C:\wxs\ObjectGrid\bin>stopOgServer.bat catalog0 -catalogServiceEndPoints
galvatron:2809
```

Stopping the catalog server required the catalog service end points argument. This shows us that the catalog server listens to client requests on port 2809 on the host galvatron. We can replace the host name with whatever your computer host name is.

Starting a container

A catalog server is the administrative control center for an ObjectGrid deployment. It is useless for storing objects though. For that, we need to start an ObjectGrid container. Starting a container requires a little more information than starting a catalog server:

```
To start an ObjectGrid container server:

   <server> -objectgridFile <xml file> [options]

   <server> -objectgridUrl <xml URL> [options]
```

Container server options:

   -catalogServiceEndPoints <host:port,host:port>

   -deploymentPolicyFile <deployment policy xml file>

   -deploymentPolicyUrl <deployment policy xml URL>

   -listenerHost <hostname>

   -listenerPort <port>

   -haManagerPort <port>

   -serverProps <server properties file>

   -zone <zoneName>

At the bare minimum, starting a container process requires an ObjectGrid configuration XML file. We've seen this file before in previous chapters when we explored configuring ObjectGrid instances and BackingMaps through XML. This is the file we pass to the startOgServer script:

```
<objectGrids>
    <objectGrid name="PaymentProcessorGrid"
                entityMetadataXMLFile="ppEntities.xml">

        <bean id="TransactionCallback"
    className="com.ibm.websphere.objectgrid.jpa.JPATxCallback">
            <property name="persistenceUnitName"
                    type="java.lang.String"
                    value="PaymentProcessor" />
        </bean>

        <backingMap name="Payment"
                    writeBehind="T120;C5001"
                    pluginCollectionRef="Payment" />
        <backingMap name="Batch"
                    lockStrategy="PESSIMISTIC"
                    pluginCollectionRef="Batch" />
        <backingMap name="Card"
                    writeBehind="T60;C1001"
                    pluginCollectionRef="Card" />
        <backingMap name="Address"
                    writeBehind="T60;C1001"
                    pluginCollectionRef="Address" />
        <backingMap name="idGeneratorMap" />

    </objectGrid>
</objectGrids>

<backingMapPluginCollections>
```

```xml
<backingMapPluginCollection id="Payment">
    <bean id="Loader"
      className="com.ibm.websphere.objectgrid.jpa.JPALoader">
        <property name="entityClassName"
                  type="java.lang.String"
                  value="wxs.sample.models.Payment"/>

    </bean>
</backingMapPluginCollection>

<backingMapPluginCollection id="Batch">
    <bean id="Loader"
      className="com.ibm.websphere.objectgrid.jpa.JPALoader">
        <property name="entityClassName"
                  type="java.lang.String"
                  value="wxs.sample.models.Batch"/>
    </bean>
</backingMapPluginCollection>

<backingMapPluginCollection id="Card">
    <bean id="Loader"
        className=
        "com.ibm.websphere.objectgrid.jpa.JPAEntityLoader">
        <property name="entityClassName"
                  type="java.lang.String"
                  value="wxs.sample.models.Card"/>
    </bean>
</backingMapPluginCollection>

<backingMapPluginCollection id="Address">
    <bean id="Loader"
        className=
        "com.ibm.websphere.objectgrid.jpa.JPAEntityLoader">
        <property name="entityClassName"
                  type="java.lang.String"
                  value="wxs.sample.models.Address"/>
    </bean>
</backingMapPluginCollection>
        </backingMapPluginCollections>
    </objectGridConfig>
```

This is the full XML configuration of the ObjectGrid deployment, which we built in the previous chapters. This configuration file is required because we no longer have programmatic access to create and initialize an ObjectGrid instance. The client app is no longer responsible for setting up the grid.

As we're working in a dynamic, distributed deployment, we should also provide a deployment policy file. The deployment file provides suggestions about the topology created by the catalog server. That's right! The catalog server decides where our objects are stored in the grid. It creates this topology based on the deployment file. While the ObjectGrid configuration contains information on what is stored in the grid, the deployment policy file contains information about what the grid should look like:

```
<deploymentPolicy>

    <objectgridDeployment objectgridName="PaymentProcessorGrid">
      <mapSet name="ppMapSet"
              numberOfPartitions="5">
        <map ref="Payment"/>
        <map ref="Batch"/>
        <map ref="Card"/>
        <map ref="Address"/>
        <map ref="idGeneratorMap"/>
      </mapSet>
    </objectgridDeployment>
</deploymentPolicy>
```

The last thing we need to start the container is the catalog service end point. This allows the container to notify the catalog server that is available for use. We'll get to that in just a second.

First, we need to pass in some JVM arguments, like the classpath and any other JVM args you want. Any arguments to the startOgServer script after -jvmArgs are passed to the JVM. Type them out just as you would start a standalone Java application:

```
C:\wxs\ObjectGrid\bin>startOgServer.bat server0 -objectgridFile c:\wxs\
workspace\PaymentProcessor\bin\jpa-objectgrid.xml -deploymentPolicyFile
c:\wxs\workspace\PaymentProcessor\bin\ogdeployment.xml

-catalogServiceEndPoints galvatron:2809 -jvmArgs -cp c:\jboss-4.2.2.GA\
server\default\lib\*;c:\wxs\wor

kspace\PaymentProcessor\bin;c:\jboss-4.2.2.GA\lib\*
```

It is important to note that the classpath argument contains the classes (or JAR files) that make up our data model. All classes cached by the grid must be included in the classpath. We need our application POJOs on the classpath, since they are the classes of the objects that we will cache in the grid.

Additionally, our Loaders need the JPA classes on the classpath. I'm using Hibernate as my JPA provider to show that we can mix and match different components, as long as they support standard interfaces.

After starting the two processes, we have a deployment that looks like the following figure:

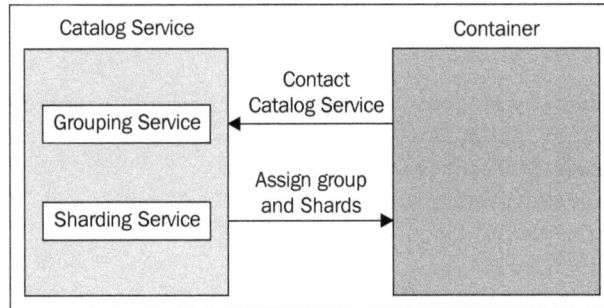

At startup, the container is empty. The container contacts the catalog server at the specified host and port, and the catalog server assigns it to a core group. Once it is part of a group, the catalog server assigns *shards* to the container.

Connecting to a distributed grid

Making a connection to an ObjectGrid server is a little more work than using a local instance. We can do away with the programmatic BackingMap configuration, but we need to do a little more work to locate the grid.

First, we need an ObjectGrid client configuration file. The client configuration file should contain similar information to the ObjectGrid configuration file we passed to the server. ObjectGrid client and server processes both work with BackingMaps. In order to be used on the client, a BackingMap must be defined in the client configuration file. This means the BackingMaps that we defined in the ObjectGrid configuration file passed to the server must be defined on the client as well.

A client application uses the ObjectMap, or Entity APIs, to interact with a BackingMap on the client side if the "near cache" is enabled. The client-side BackingMap contains objects from all partitions and functions as a local cache. It is synchronized with the server-side BackingMap when a transaction commits.

Because we need to define our BackingMaps on the client side, we can simply use the same ObjectGrid configuration file that we passed to the server. Or, we can simplify it to include only the BackingMap definitions and omit the plugins and additional configuration settings:

```
<objectGridConfig>
    <objectGrids>
        <objectGrid name="PaymentProcessorGrid">
            <backingMap name="Payment" />
            <backingMap name="Batch" />
            <backingMap name="Card" />
            <backingMap name="Address" />
        </objectGrid>
    </objectGrids>
</objectGridConfig>
```

Any settings defined in the client-side configuration file **override** the settings specified in the server-side file.

Now that we have an `objectgridClient.xml` file, and we know the host name and port the catalog server is listening on, we can connect to the distributed ObjectGrid instance:

```
private void connectToObjectGrid() {
    ogm = ObjectGridManagerFactory.getObjectGridManager();
    String clusterHost = ogHost + ":" + ogPort;
    try {
        context = ogm.connect(clusterHost, null, clientConfig);
    } catch(ConnectException e) {
        rethrowAsRuntimeException(e);
    }
    grid = ogm.getObjectGrid(context, "PaymentProcessorGrid");
}
```

This is a fairly generic method for connecting to an ObjectGrid instance. First, we connect to the catalog server to retrieve a ClientClusterContext. This context provides a detailed definition of the deployment topology. This includes the host and port location of each partition, as well as the total number of partitions. As we know the total number of partitions, the ObjectGrid client can determine which partition an object belongs in.

Determining the partition, client-side is beneficial in two ways. First, it reduces the load on the ObjectGrid server. Second, the server processes do not need to determine which partition millions of objects belong in. A central partitioning process would bottleneck scalability. Offloading this work to the client frees us from having every client contact a partition-finding service and the associated network hops in order to then place the object in the correct partition.

Instead of determining which partition an object belongs in on the client side, the client can connect directly to the JVM hosting that partition, and then put the object in the correct BackingMap directly. This reduces network traffic to one hop for any GET or PUT operation. The ObjectGrid client obtains the location of each partition when it obtains the ClientClusterContext. An ObjectGrid client can directly place objects on the correct host and partition because it has detailed information about the ObjectGrid topology and our objects define a consistent hash code.

The context variable holds a reference to a ClientClusterContext instance. The ClientClusterContext provides the client everything it needs to know about the location of partitions and hosts participating in the ObjectGrid deployment. We get this context from one of the `ObjectGridManager.connect()` methods. This is different than using a local ObjectGrid instance. When we used a local instance, we called the `ObjectGridManager.createObjectGrid()` method. The first argument is the location of a catalog server responsible for managing the cluster. We pass the host name in to the payment processor application as a command line argument. By default, we attempt to connect to the catalog server on port 2809. This can be overridden as a command line argument.

We're also passing the name of the client configuration XML file on the command line. This file is used to tell the catalog server which ObjectGrid instances to include in the ClientClusterContext. A catalog server can manage many ObjectGrid instances. For now, we define just one ObjectGrid instance per cluster. For simple deployments, it's easy to copy the configuration file used to start the container servers as the client configuration file too. Larger deployments should favor a more targeted approach. The container configuration should contain all of the ObjectGrid definitions, and the client configuration file should contain only the ObjectGrid names the client actually needs.

Once we have a ClientClusterContext, we can obtain a reference to the grid we want to interact with by calling the `ObjectGridManager.getObjectGrid(...)` method. We pass in the ClientClusterContext, which has all of the information about any grid, and the name of the grid we want to connect to.

At this point, we have an ObjectGrid reference, and the programming model is identical to that of a local instance. Our code does not change. This makes it easy to develop and unit test our app using a local instance, and perform integration testing, nightly builds, and go to production on a distributed grid.

Adding more containers

Running one container allows several clients to use the same grid, but doesn't offer much more than that. We are still limited to one JVM heap, one computer's CPU resources, and bandwidth. Starting additional containers is easy:

```
C:\wxs\ObjectGrid\bin>startOgServer.bat server1 -objectgridFile c:\wxs\
workspace\PaymentProcessor\bin\jpa-objectgrid.xml -deploymentPolicyFile
c:\wxs\workspace\PaymentProcessor\bin\ogdeployment.xml

-catalogServiceEndPoints galvatron:2809 -jvmArgs -cp c:\jboss-4.2.2.GA\
server\default\lib\*;c:\wxs\wor

kspace\PaymentProcessor\bin;c:\jboss-4.2.2.GA\lib\*
```

This is almost the same line used to start `server0`. This gives us a second container to store objects in. We can start as many servers as we want with this command line by changing the server name each time we use it.

Remember that containers hold shards. A shard is the smallest unit of placement in the ObjectGrid, which means that a grid configured to use just one shard won't get any benefit out of running in a grid with multiple containers. The shard can't be broken down any further, and we are limited to just one shard running in one container. In order to take advantage of the huge number of containers we deploy, we need to increase the number of partitions, along with their building block shards running in the grid.

We configure the number of partitions used in a grid by setting the number on the MapSet:

```
<objectgridDeployment objectgridName="PaymentProcessorGrid">
    <mapSet name="ppMapSet"
            numberOfPartitions="1"
            minSyncReplicas="0"
            maxSyncReplicas="0"
            maxAsyncReplicas="0">
    <map ref="Payment"/>
    <map ref="Batch"/>
    <map ref="idGeneratorMap"/>
    </mapSet>
```

Starting more containers with only one partition is useless. Those additional containers will be empty. In order to get ObjectGrid to use those containers, we need to increase the number of partitions. Let's say we want to start five containers. Let's see what happens when we deploy with ten partitions. We should have two partitions per container when we're done. Set the `numberOfPartitions` on the `ppMapSet` to `10` in the deployment policy file.

Once we set the number of partitions, we start up a catalog server and five container servers. These can run locally, or on different computers if you have them. Amazon's EC2 is a great way to get cheap computing resources if you want to go down that route. We start the catalog server and container servers using the same `startOgServer` script and options described a few pages earlier.

When everything is up and running, I have a catalog server named `catalog0`, and five containers named `server0` through `server4`. I can take a look at my server topology using the `xsadmin` tool included with WebSphere eXtremeScale. `xsadmin` is not a supported tool for interacting with ObjectGrid instances. It is actually a sample application to get familiar with using JMX to interact with the grid.

Running `xsadmin` without any options gives us the help output. Let's look at the required options:

```
Only one of these must be specified:
 -containers 'Show all containers'
 -primaries 'Show all primaries'
 -unassigned 'Show all unassigned shards'
 -mapsizes 'Show all map sizes'
 -hosts 'Show all hosts'
 -mbeanservers 'Show all MBean server end points'
```

Let's see what the output tells us. We'll look at the containers first:

```
C:\wxs\ObjectGrid\bin>xsadmin -containers

Connecting to Catalog service at localhost:1099

*** Show all online containers for grid - PaymentProcessorGrid & mapset
- ppMapSet
Host: 192.168.1.203
  Container: server0_C-0, Server:server0, Zone:DefaultZone
    P:3 Primary
    P:9 Primary
  Container: server1_C-0, Server:server1, Zone:DefaultZone

    P:0 Primary

    P:8 Primary

  Container: server2_C-0, Server:server2, Zone:DefaultZone
```

```
   P:1 Primary
   P:4 Primary
Container: server3_C-0, Server:server3, Zone:DefaultZone
   P:5 Primary
   P:7 Primary
Container: server4_C-0, Server:server4, Zone:DefaultZone
   P:2 Primary
   P:6 Primary


Num containers matching = 5
Total known containers = 5
Total known hosts = 1
```

This output gives us a host-by-host breakdown of each container. I've started five containers on my development box. Those containers correspond to `server0` through `server4` that I started on the command line. Under each container is the partition information. It is formated as **P:N** Type. We can see that the `server0_C-0` container holds partitions 3 and 9, and they are both primary partitions.

What happens when we add additional resources to the cluster? Let's say we start more EC2 AMIs, or have additional servers added to our rack. We can start additional containers, and the catalog server will migrate a few partitions to these new containers:

```
Container: server0_C-0, Server:server0, Zone:DefaultZone
   P:3 Primary
   P:9 Primary
Container: server1_C-0, Server:server1, Zone:DefaultZone
   P:0 Primary
Container: server2_C-0, Server:server2, Zone:DefaultZone
   P:1 Primary
   P:4 Primary
Container: server3_C-0, Server:server3, Zone:DefaultZone
   P:5 Primary
Container: server4_C-0, Server:server4, Zone:DefaultZone
   P:2 Primary

   P:6 Primary
Container: server5_C-0, Server:server5, Zone:DefaultZone
   P:7 Primary
Container: server6_C-0, Server:server6, Zone:DefaultZone
   P:8 Primary
```

Now, we have four containers with one partition, and three containers with two partitions. When we run a few instances of the payment processor application using this grid, we quickly see that there are a few problems.

From the screenshot above, we can see the containers with two partitions are using about 50 percent more CPU and memory than the containers with one partition. We could start additional containers until each one has only one partition. At that point, we cannot scale out anymore. Ten containers are as good as we can do with ten partitions. Rather than immediately placing one partition per container, we should aim to reduce the difference in resource consumption.

Partition placement

Let's talk a little bit about what happens when a new container becomes available. On start up, the container process notifies the catalog server that an additional container is available for use:

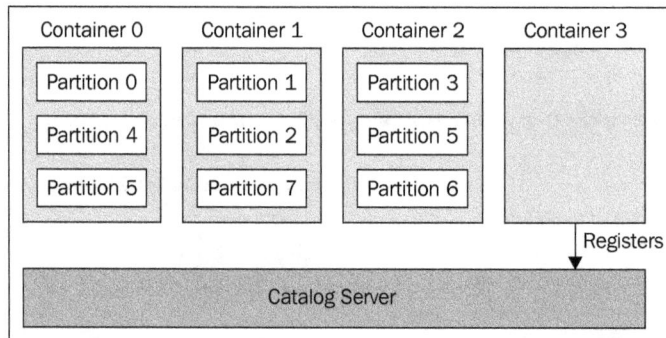

Once the catalog server knows about the new container, it assigns several partitions to it using a waterfall algorithm. As more containers become available, partitions are migrated from the containers that contain the most partitions, to the containers that contain the fewest partitions. In the previous figure, each of the three existing containers holds three partitions.

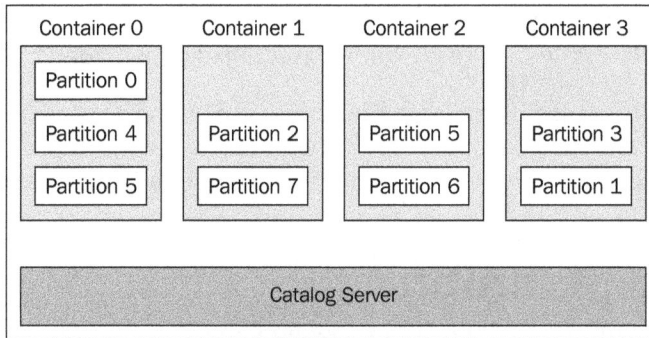

When the fourth container starts, the catalog server assigns two shards to it (as seen above). This is done to keep the distribution as even as possible. In this situation, we end up with container0 holding one more shard than the other containers. As it contains an extra shard, it must do 50 percent more work than the other containers.

In order to reduce the disparity in container workload, we must make each partition hold a smaller amount of data. We do this by increasing the number of partitions in the deployment:

```
<objectgridDeployment objectgridName="PaymentProcessorGrid">
  <mapSet name="ppMapSet"
          numberOfPartitions="101"
          minSyncReplicas="0"
          maxSyncReplicas="0"
          maxAsyncReplicas="0">
    <map ref="Payment"/>
    <map ref="Batch"/>
    <map ref="idGeneratorMap"/>
    <map ref="IBM_SYSTEM_MAP_defaultMapSet"/>
  </mapSet>
```

Now with 101 partitions, each partition is worth only 1.01 percent of memory, CPU, and network bandwidth, instead of 11.11 percent. In the previous example, containers assumed either 33.33 percent, or 22.22 percent, of the total load when we had four containers. Starting with three containers and 101 partitions, two containers assume 34 percent of the load, and one container assumes 33 percent of the load. Moving up to four containers, one container gets 26 percent of the load, and each of the other three get 25 percent of the load. Now, there is only a 4 percent difference between the most heavily loaded container, and the evenly loaded containers.

From this exercise, we see that a large number of partitions are beneficial in keeping container load even. The WebSphere eXtreme Scale lab recommends a minimum of 10 partitions per container when scaled out to the end of a deployment.

Capacity planning

Now, for the difficult part. We need to know how many partitions, shards, and containers we need to hold a set of data. As we expect the volume of data and clients to grow, we need to support our current load, as well as our load 3-5 years down the road. We just mentioned the **end of a deployment**. A WebSphere eXtreme Scale deployment can remain active for months and years without a restart. As we would like the grid to remain active for such long periods of time, we need to have the ability to add capacity to it as our needs grow.

We know how to add additional containers to an already running grid. As we have a suggested lower limit of 10 shards per container, and a lower limit of one shard per container, we know the number of partitions we set determines the maximum number of containers our deployment uses:

```
<objectgridDeployment objectgridName="PaymentProcessorGrid">
    <mapSet name="ppMapSet"
            numberOfPartitions="101"
            minSyncReplicas="0"
            maxSyncReplicas="0"
            maxAsyncReplicas="0">
    <map ref="Payment"/>
    <map ref="Batch"/>
    <map ref="idGeneratorMap"/>
    <map ref="IBM_SYSTEM_MAP_defaultMapSet"/>
</mapSet>
```

As our payment processing business grows, we need to scale out. As we saw in the figure of running processes, each container can support only so many clients. Each container can only hold so many payment objects. We need to start the capacity planning process by carefully measuring the CPU utilization and memory usage for a single container. By obtaining measurements for a single container, we know how many clients a container supports, and how many objects fit in the heap.

Again, the WebSphere eXtreme Scale team has recommendations for targeted resource utilization. We should aim for less than 60 percent JVM heap utilization, and less than 60 percent CPU utilization.

In order to find out the maximum suggested object number per JVM, we need to load our payment processing data into a single container, and note how many objects are in the grid when the JVM heap is 60 percent full. We should use real data rather than estimating object size.

In order to get the object count, I like to pass the -Xrunhprof option to the container start script:

```
C:\wxs\ObjectGrid\bin>startOgServer.bat server0 -objectgridFile c:\wxs\
workspace\PaymentProcessor\bin\jpa-objectgrid.xml -deploymentPolicyFile
c:\wxs\workspace\PaymentProcessor\bin\ogdeployment.xml -c

atalogServiceEndPoints galvatron:2809 -jvmArgs -cp c:\jboss-4.2.2.GA\
server\default\lib\*;c:\wxs\wor

kspace\PaymentProcessor\bin;c:\jboss-4.2.2.GA\lib\* -Xrunhprof:file=dump.
hprof,format=b -ms1536M -Xmx1536M
```

I've also passed in the -ms and -Xmx options to set the heap size to 1.5GB. Now, I will run the payment processor application against a one container deployment, and stop the container process when the heap utilization reaches 920MB. As I've enabled the heap profiler, this can take a long time. Once I have my output file, dump.hprof, I can run it through my favorite heap analyzer. I use jhat or the Eclipse Memory Analyzer (http://www.eclipse.org/mat/). From here, we can add up the total number of Payments, Batches, Cards, and Addresses to find out the maximum number of objects we should put in one container. In my test, I got about 1.3 million objects into one JVM heap at 60 percent utilization.

Assuming we have 50 customers, each sending 200,000 payments per day, we should support 10,000,000 payments in the grid at any particular time to start with. In addition to our current needs, we should have some idea of what our needs will be 3-5 years in the future. Assuming 25 percent volume growth per year, we should expect to store about 30,000,000 objects in the grid at any given time, five years from now.

This estimate assumes we're only dealing with primary partitions. Even though we haven't had a discussion about replication yet, we should consider that in to our calculations. If we have one synchronous replica, then we now duplicate each object. Additional replicas duplicate those objects again. Let's say we have one primary shard, one synchronous replica, and two asynchronous replicas. Now, we need to store 40,000,000 objects in the grid right now, and up to 120,000,000 in five years. At 1.3 million objects per JVM, we'll need to start with 31 JVMs with a 1.5GB heap, and scale up to 93 JVMs in five years.

Now that we know the number of JVMs we need, we can multiply that number by ten, which is the minimum recommended number of shards per container. In five years time, we will need 10 shards for each of our 93 JVMs for 930 shards. Since each partition is made up of four shards, that give us 232.5 partitions, the WebSphere eXtreme Scale team recommends we round this up to the nearest prime number and we get 233 partitions.

```
<mapSet name="ppMapSet"
        numberOfPartitions="233"
        minSyncReplicas="1"
        maxSyncReplicas="1"
        maxAsyncReplicas="2">
  <map ref="Payment"/>
  <map ref="Batch"/>
  <map ref="idGeneratorMap"/>
</mapSet>
```

Above is the MapSet definition we would include in our `ogdeployment.xml` file. This configuration will give us ample room to grow our data set over five years.

CPU utilization should also remain at less than 60 percent. We can determine the number of clients a container supports by starting a catalog server and two container servers. In this exercise, we want to ensure that the network isn't saturated, artificially limiting the CPU load. If we run several instances of the payment processor application, we should be able to get the CPU usage on both container servers to 100 percent.

As we don't want to run at 100 percent CPU utilization all of the time, we reduce the number of clients using the grid until the container server CPU utilization is at roughly 60 percent. This is the number of clients two containers support. This exercise also shows us our expected throughput for two containers. Since WebSphere eXtreme Scale scales up linearly, the throughput and number of supported clients increases at the same rate per two container servers added to the grid.

If your hardware was able to support 20 clients on two containers at 60 percent CPU, you should expect 100 clients at 10 containers and 1000 clients at 100 containers. For our payment processor grid, we should expect to support about 310 clients on day one, and over 900 clients at the end of five years.

Hitting the wall

IBM recommends no less than 10 shards per container. If we have less than 10 shards per container, the difference in load starts on a noticeable increase. Hopefully, this situation happens only at or near the end of the planned grid lifetime. If each container holds just one shard, then we have reached the end of the road for scalability. Should you need to grow the grid beyond the planned number of JVMs, an outage is unavoidable.

Avoid this situation with realistic planning up front to determine how many JVMs are required. Despite good planning, we can always reach the point where we have too few shards per JVM. If the planning stage used accurate data for determining the number of JVMs required, and shards/JVM is dropping, then you're experiencing faster-than-expected growth.

If you reach the point where five years of expected resources are simply not enough, then you have an enviable problem. Popularity to the point of burning through five years of data grid capacity is a wonderful problem to have! At this point, your application is so popular and heavily used that there are probably other problems besides the shard/JVM ratio. In this case, the outage required to add more partitions to the deployment policy file is less of an issue because a new release of your application is right around the corner anyway. A new application release accompanied by a grid outage is acceptable. Once restarted, the grid can preload data from a database. The new version of the application should have a large number of additional partitions to ensure plenty of growth in the future.

Adding additional capacity to the grid while it is running is done by adding more capable computers to the deployment. We maintain the same number of JVMs during the cycle by first taking existing servers offline. We replace them with more powerful computers by giving them the same configuration files, and then pointing them to the same catalog server as the rest of the grid. When the first server is taken offline, the catalog server migrates the shards from that container to containers that have room for them. When the new server comes online, and the container contacts the catalog server, it is assigned some shards.

Though we have replaced one JVM with another, the new JVM is running on a computer where it has a larger heap size and more CPU to handle transactions and application logic. These new computers should be measured in the same way the originals were measured, by objects in the heap at 60 percent utilization and the number of clients at 100 percent and 60 percent CPU utilization. By bringing the older hardware offline and replacing it with more capable hardware, we can scale a grid up before we need to stop the world to scale it out.

Summary

This chapter covered a lot of concepts that apply to working with any data grid product. We now know how to build a distributed ObjectGrid deployment and connect to the grid in our application.

We looked at two different configuration files required to define an ObjectGrid deployment. We saw the ObjectGrid configuration file in previous chapters. Now, we rely on this configuration file to run a server deployment. A copy, or variation, of this file is used on the client side. The client configuration file helps the client find out about the grid it works with and the maps defined in it.

We also introduced the ObjectGrid deployment policy file. This file determines what happens when additional container servers are added to the deployment. After examining this file, we looked at correctly sizing the number of shards, partitions, and JVMs required in a deployment, based on measurable factors.

We wrapped up by describing some options when the grid grows to its planned capacity. In Chapter 6, we'll continue looking at ObjectGrid deployments by adding replication and high-availability to our knowledge.

6

Keeping Data Available

By continuing our exploration of the building blocks that make up a WebSphere eXtreme Scale deployment, we delve further into shards, partitions, and replication in this chapter. Our focus this time is data availability. In Chapter 5, we learned how to create a scale-out deployment emphasizing total capacity. We'll now look at building redundancy into our deployment with replication. We'll look at reasons to add replication to a deployment and at the two different replica types.

Before we proceed, you should have a firm understanding of the relationship between shards and partitions. We use the xsadmin tool and container log files to get a better idea of how shard placement and startup works. As we use xsadmin, we find out that shards can move around a deployment at runtime. This is known as shard migration.

Shard migration plays an important role in WebSphere eXtreme Scale's flexibility. As shards can migrate from container to container, we find that it is easy to make up for the lost shards, should a container fail. While shards have the freedom to move, we can restrict them to certain physical locations by defining zones. Zones enable us to place shards on specific boxes in specific data centers, depending on their role.

This is also a good time to find out how to pre-load data in a grid. Starting an empty ObjectGrid deployment is fine, but there will be a zero percent cache hit rate at the beginning. Pre-loading data from a database gives us a way to improve our cache hit percentage right from the start. There are several ways to pre-load data, and we'll look at the pros and cons of each.

At the end of this chapter, we'll be able to:

- Configure an ObjectGrid deployment to use replication
- Understand the advantages of using replication
- Place shards onto machines in specific locations
- Pre-load data to improve cache hit rate
- Configure a client to use preferred zones

Containers, shards, partitions, and replicas

Before we get into replication specifically, let's make sure we have a solid understanding of the ObjectGrid terminology introduced so far. A firm grasp of the terms already introduced, along with their relationships, eases us into the replication topics.

The foundation

The foundation of an ObjectGrid deployment is the ObjectGrid container process. This process runs either in a standalone mode, or as part of a WebSphere Application Server deployment. We're mostly concerned with the standalone mode. In the previous chapters, we started container processes using a command line:

```
./startOgServer.sh server0 \
    -catalogServiceEndpoints domU-12-31-39-00-C5-C7:2809 \
    -objectgridFile ~/PaymentProcessor/src/jpa-objectgrid.xml \
    -deploymentPolicyFile ~/PaymentProcessor/src/ogdeployment.xml \
    -listenerHost domU-12-31-39-00-C5-C7 \
    -listenerPort 13001 \

    -jvmArgs -cp \
/root/PaymentProcessor/bin/output/PaymentProcessor.jar:/root/downloads/
jboss-4.2.2.GA/server/default/lib/*:/root/downloads/jboss-4.2.2.GA/
lib/*:/root/downloads/ObjectGrid/lib/*;
```

This command line starts an ObjectGrid container process named `server0`. It also tells the container that the catalog services for this deployment run on the host domU-12-31-39-00-C5-C7 on port 2809. The container takes instructions directly from a catalog server. We give the container process an ObjectGrid configuration file so that it knows specifically which ObjectGrid instance it is to become a part of. The container notifies the catalog server of its availability, and to which ObjectGrid instance it belongs to. The ObjectGrid configuration file defines the server-side BackingMaps hosted by the ObjectGrid instance. A catalog server can coordinate the resources of many ObjectGrid instances.

The `-listenerHost` and `-listenerPort` options configure the container to listen on a particular host and port. Setting the host parameter is recommended. The host should not be set to localhost. This is also useful when the box has multiple network interfaces. This prevents an ObjectGrid container from using the incorrect network interface to communicate with other ObjectGrid containers in the deployment.

In the example above, I'm using an Amazon EC2 instance. This instance has two network interfaces, one visible to the outside Internet, and other internal to Amazon's infrastructure. Using `-listenerHost domU-12-31-39-00-C5-C7` as the listener host prevents this container from listening to traffic from the outside Internet. Instead, the ObjectGrid instance uses the internal network.

Specifying a listener port is useful when multiple containers run on the same operating system instance. If we were to start another ObjectGrid container on this box, then we would set the `-listenerPort` option to something different, probably just incrementing the port number by one to 13001. The listener port is used by the container for ORB communication, which is for communicating with ObjectGrid clients. Clients connect to the ObjectGrid container process running on this port to make read and write requests.

Typically, specifying a listener port is unnecessary. When left unspecified, containers will search for an unused port for IIOP communication. When firewalls block ports, it is necessary to specify listener ports for a container based on the firewall rules. Choosing an IIOP port for an ObjectGrid container process, is as simple as finding an unused port on your server. Client processes will use the correct port, thanks to the `ClientClusterContext` object obtained, when connecting to a grid.

A container process should contain something. An ObjectGrid container contains shards.

Shards

A **shard** is the smallest unit of data storage in an ObjectGrid deployment. A shard contains a subset of objects stored in BackingMaps. That set of objects can be the entire set of objects in an unpartitioned BackingMap, which is the case when using a local ObjectGrid instance. There is one container running inside the application process, and that container has one shard. That shard holds the entire set of objects in every BackingMap defined in the instance.

In a distributed deployment, our data is typically partitioned. In this case, a shard contains a subset of the objects in all BackingMaps in a map set. A particular shard may be the only shard with a set of objects, or that set of objects may be duplicated in one or more additional shards.

New to the container startup command line is the -deploymentPolicyFile setting. The deployment policy file is optional, but is a strongly recommended setting. The deployment policy file gives an ObjectGrid deployment a lot of flexibility to scale out and up. The policy file is specific for our deployment, and it tells an ObjectGrid how many shards to use and what role each shard should take:

```xml
<?xml version="1.0" encoding="UTF-8"?>
<deploymentPolicy xmlns:xsi="http://www.w3.org/2001/XMLSchema-instance"
   xsi:schemaLocation="http://ibm.com/ws/objectgrid/deploymentPolicy
   ../deploymentPolicy.xsd"
   xmlns="http://ibm.com/ws/objectgrid/deploymentPolicy">

   <objectgridDeployment
         objectgridName="PaymentProcessorGrid">
      <mapSet name="ppMapSet"
            numberOfPartitions="233"
            minSyncReplicas="1"
            maxSyncReplicas="1"
            maxAsyncReplicas="2">
         <map ref="Payment"/>
         <map ref="Batch"/>
         <map ref="Card"/>
         <map ref="Address"/>
      </mapSet>
   </objectgridDeployment>

</deploymentPolicy>
```

The ObjectGrid deployment policy file tells an ObjectGrid deployment how many shards our deployment uses, but this file does not mention anything about shards. This is because shards may take one of the three different roles: primary, synchronous replica, or asynchronous replica. The number of shards is the total number of primary, synchronous replica, and asynchronous replica shards defined in the ObjectGrid deployment file. The mapSet in the deployment file has numberOfPartitions, minSyncReplicas, MaxSyncReplicas, maxAsyncReplicas as attributes. These mapSet attributes define the total number of shards in an ObjectGrid instance.

Every partition has a primary shard. The mapSet is defined as having one synchronous replica, and two asynchronous replicas per primary shard. This deployment file specifies a mapSet that uses a total of 932 shards.

Map sets

The next building block up from a shard is a **map set**. It is a group of BackingMaps that belong in a shard. Our deployment policy file defines just one map set. A map set simply says that this group of BackingMaps shares a common partition key.

In other words, the BackingMaps in a map set are somehow related. The easiest way to show this is through an object model with classes Batch and Payment. If the data model is defined where a Batch has many Payments, we access the payments through their parent Batch.

This means we need to look up for a Batch in the BackingMap which exists on a particular shard. As the Batch and Payment BackingMaps are in the same map set, the instances of Payment objects that belong to the Batch object live in the same shard. As a result, the related objects are stored close together. This is good for read and write operations because the client application can update just one partition per transaction. Storing related data in the same shard means we don't need to make multiple write calls when we change a Batch/Payment relationship. Storing related data together also gives us a lot of power when we introduce the DataGrid API in the next chapter.

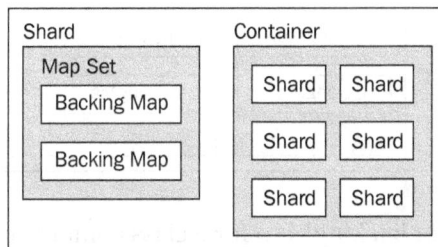

Logically, a shard is a set of objects contained in a group of BackingMaps (as seen above). Replicating this set of objects in different shards provides redundancy and fault tolerance in a deployment. Grouping these replicated shards together gives us a partition.

Partitions

A **partition** is the set of shards that contain the same data. It is always made up of at least one shard, which is the primary shard. A partition can contain up to any number of shards as defined in a map set.

```
<mapSet name="ppMapSet"
        numberOfPartitions="233"
        minSyncReplicas="1"
        maxSyncReplicas="1"
        maxAsyncReplicas="2">
```

The map set in our deployment policy file defines 233 shards to function as primary shards with `numberOfPartitions="233"` (as seen above). We also have 233 replica shards. This comes from `maxSyncReplicas="1"`. This setting tells ObjectGrid to create one synchronous replica shard per primary, bringing the number of shards in this deployment to 466. The `maxAsyncReplicas="2"` instructs ObjectGrid to create up to two asynchronous replica shards per primary, if there are sufficient containers to do so. This brings the total number of shards in the deployment to 932.

In this deployment, we have up to four shards that contain the same objects in the same BackingMaps. Ideally, in a production environment, these shards will exist in a container on a different physical computer.

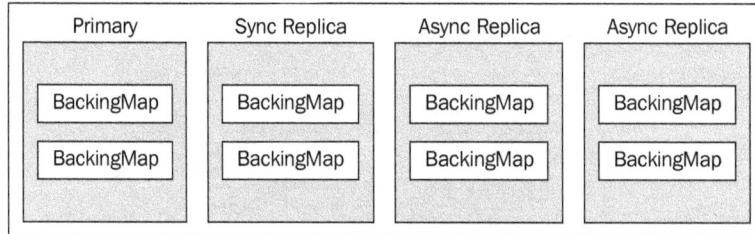

In the diagram above, each BackingMap for a class contains the same objects. The objects placed into the BackingMap depend on the object key. The sum of these four shards makes up the partition. The partition contains a set of BackingMaps that contains a subset of the total number of objects in each logical BackingMap.

Let's look at an example of a partitioned data set that has just one BackingMap:

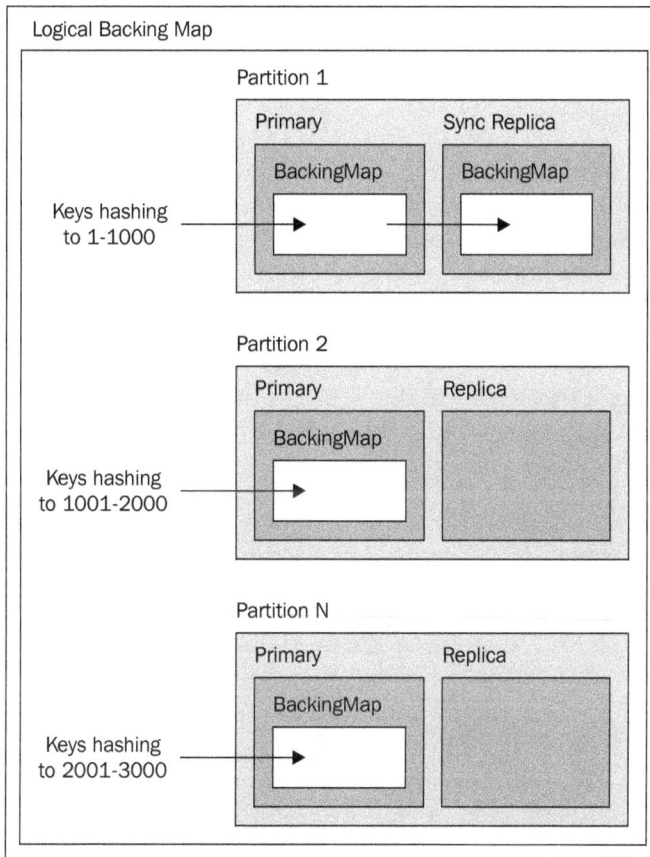

In our applications, we interact with BackingMaps through the ObjectMap and EntityManager APIs. Our applications deal with BackingMaps at the logical level. Our applications (usually) don't care if a BackingMap is partitioned or not. We just want to get and put objects without much hassle. This is the logical view that our application sees through the API.

Behind the scenes, things are a little more interesting. A BackingMap is actually made up of many instances of BackingMap spread across multiple shards and containers. Objects are placed in particular partitions based on the hashCode() of their key, or the key of the parent object if they are in a parent-child relationship.

Replication

Now that we've seen how to enable replication, we should take a step back and ask what does it provide us? Enabling replication provides a degree of fault tolerance. Now, we can lose a container with a primary partition, and still have one or more backups waiting to take over.

Replicating small shards ensures that one partition does not become so big that its failure is catastrophic for the cache and the database it fronts. Ideally, we'll have a large number of small partitions which migrate between containers as they come online and offline. A client does not care which container it gets an object from, only that it gets the object. The physical location of the shard is irrelevant.

By making shards small enough that their failure isn't a big deal, we cushion our availability strategy. ObjectGrid catalog services monitor shard placement and the number of replicas each primary shard should have. If there is a deficiency, the catalog service notifies a container to place a new shard of the missing type.

Replication also lets us scale out read transactions. Read-only transactions can read from synchronous replica if it is enabled in the deployment policy file. This will spread reads out across replicas and puts those nodes to work rather than letting them sit around waiting for a failure. Write transactions are still routed to the primary shard.

Telling ObjectGrid to allow clients to read from replica shards is easy. The `mapSet` node of the deployment policy file has an attribute called `replicaReadEnabled`, which is a Boolean flag. With this attribute set to `true`, ObjectGrid clients will be routed to replica shards for read operations:

```
<mapSet name="ppMapSet"
        numberOfPartitions="233"
        minSyncReplicas="1"
        maxSyncReplicas="1"
        maxAsyncReplicas="2"
        replicaReadEnabled="true">
```

Shard placement

As containers come online and offline, the catalog service places shards on available containers based on the rules in the ObjectGrid deployment configuration file. After starting the catalog service, there are zero containers available for shard placement. Let's use the `xsadmin` tool to find out how shards are placed as we add containers to the deployment. We'll change some of the settings in the `ogdeployment.xml` file we used earlier. We will only change the number of partitions and replicas:

```xml
<?xml version="1.0" encoding="UTF-8"?>
<deploymentPolicy xmlns:xsi="http://www.w3.org/2001/XMLSchema-instance"
  xsi:schemaLocation="http://ibm.com/ws/objectgrid/deploymentPolicy
  ../deploymentPolicy.xsd"
  xmlns="http://ibm.com/ws/objectgrid/deploymentPolicy">
  <objectgridDeployment objectgridName="PaymentProcessorGrid">
    <mapSet name="ppMapSet"
            numberOfPartitions="11"
            minSyncReplicas="1"
            maxSyncReplicas="1"
            maxAsyncReplicas="1">
      <map ref="Payment"/>
      <map ref="Batch"/>
      <map ref="Card"/>
      <map ref="Address"/>
    </mapSet>
  </objectgridDeployment>

</deploymentPolicy>
```

Before we start any containers, let's see what the xsadmin tool can do. Run the following command:

xsadmin

Only one of the following must be specified:

- -containers: Show all containers
- -primaries: Show all primaries
- -unassigned: Show all unassigned shards
- -mapsizes: Show all map sizes
- -hosts: Show all hosts
- -mbeanservers: Show all MBean server end points

xsadmin is a sample application shipped with WebSphere eXtreme Scale. It demonstrates how to interact with the eXtreme Scale JMX interface. We can use it to see how shard placement works as we bring up containers. Though it is a functional and a useful tool, it is not a supported application and shouldn't be expected to behave as such. Also, make sure to use IBM's JVM or make sure the IBM ORB is used by your JVM of choice. This is described under *Getting IBM WebSphere eXtreme Scale* in Chapter 1.

Start up a catalog server and run `xsadmin -ch <catalog server host name> -primaries`:

```
startOgServer catalog0 -catalogServiceEndPoints catalog0:
galvatron:6601:6602


xsadmin -ch galvatron -primaries
Connecting to Catalog service at galvatron:1099
*** Showing all primaries for grid - PaymentProcessorGrid & mapset -
ppMapSet
Primary Partition 0:C[UNASSIGNED], H[UNASSIGNED], S[UNNAMED]
Primary Partition 1:C[UNASSIGNED], H[UNASSIGNED], S[UNNAMED]
Primary Partition 2:C[UNASSIGNED], H[UNASSIGNED], S[UNNAMED]
Primary Partition 3:C[UNASSIGNED], H[UNASSIGNED], S[UNNAMED]
Primary Partition 4:C[UNASSIGNED], H[UNASSIGNED], S[UNNAMED]
Primary Partition 5:C[UNASSIGNED], H[UNASSIGNED], S[UNNAMED]
Primary Partition 6:C[UNASSIGNED], H[UNASSIGNED], S[UNNAMED]
Primary Partition 7:C[UNASSIGNED], H[UNASSIGNED], S[UNNAMED]
Primary Partition 8:C[UNASSIGNED], H[UNASSIGNED], S[UNNAMED]
Primary Partition 9:C[UNASSIGNED], H[UNASSIGNED], S[UNNAMED]
Primary Partition 10:C[UNASSIGNED], H[UNASSIGNED], S[UNNAMED]
```

The output line is in the format of C[container name], H[host name], and S[server name]. None of our primary partition shards are assigned to a container because there are zero containers running at this point. Let's start a container and see what happens:

```
startOgServer server0 -catalogServiceEndpoints galvatron:2809 \
-objectgridFile c:/wxs/workspace/PaymentProcessor/src/jpa-objectgrid.xml
\-deploymentPolicyFile \c:/wxs/workspace/PaymentProcessor/src/
ogdeployment.xml \
-listenerHost galvatron \
-listenerPort 13000 \
-jvmArgs -cp \
c:/wxs/workspace/PaymentProcessor/bin/output/PaymentProcessor.jar:
c:/jboss-4.2.2.GA/server/default/lib/*:c:/jboss-4.2.2.GA/lib/*:c:/wxs/
ObjectGrid/lib/*;
```

Once the container starts, we'll run the `xsadmin` tool again:

```
xsadmin -ch galvatron -primaries
Connecting to Catalog service at galvatron:1099
*** Showing all primaries for grid - PaymentProcessorGrid & mapset -
ppMapSet
Primary Partition 0:C[UNASSIGNED], H[UNASSIGNED], S[UNNAMED]
Primary Partition 1:C[UNASSIGNED], H[UNASSIGNED], S[UNNAMED]
Primary Partition 2:C[UNASSIGNED], H[UNASSIGNED], S[UNNAMED]
Primary Partition 3:C[UNASSIGNED], H[UNASSIGNED], S[UNNAMED]
Primary Partition 4:C[UNASSIGNED], H[UNASSIGNED], S[UNNAMED]
Primary Partition 5:C[UNASSIGNED], H[UNASSIGNED], S[UNNAMED]
Primary Partition 6:C[UNASSIGNED], H[UNASSIGNED], S[UNNAMED]
Primary Partition 7:C[UNASSIGNED], H[UNASSIGNED], S[UNNAMED]
Primary Partition 8:C[UNASSIGNED], H[UNASSIGNED], S[UNNAMED]
Primary Partition 9:C[UNASSIGNED], H[UNASSIGNED], S[UNNAMED]
Primary Partition 10:C[UNASSIGNED], H[UNASSIGNED], S[UNNAMED]
```

Again, our primary shards are not placed. We have a container process, so why didn't the shards get placed? For the answer, we need to look in our `ogdeployment.xml` file:

```
<objectgridDeployment objectgridName="PaymentProcessorGrid">
  <mapSet name="ppMapSet"
          numberOfPartitions="11"
          minSyncReplicas="1"
          maxSyncReplicas="1"
          maxAsyncReplicas="1">
```

Our MapSet definition specifies the minimum number of synchronous replicas required for the deployment. A primary shard cannot live in the same container as one of its replica shards. Having only one container, the minimum deployment requirements of one primary shard and one synchronous replica shard are not met. Starting a second container should allow partition placement:

```
startOgServer server1 -catalogServiceEndpoints galvatron:2809 \
-objectgridFile c:/wxs/workspace/PaymentProcessor/src/jpa-objectgrid.xml
 \-deploymentPolicyFile c:/wxs/workspace/PaymentProcessor/src/
ogdeployment.xml \
-listenerHost galvatron \
-listenerPort 13001 \
-jvmArgs -cp \
c:/wxs/workspace/PaymentProcessor/bin/output/PaymentProcessor.jar:
c:/jboss-4.2.2.GA/server/default/lib/*:c:/jboss-4.2.2.GA/lib/*:c:/wxs/
ObjectGrid/lib/*;

xsadmin -ch galvatron -primaries
```

```
Connecting to Catalog service at galvatron:1099
```

```
*** Showing all primaries for grid - PaymentProcessorGrid & mapset -
ppMapSet
```

```
Primary Partition 0:C[server0_C-0], H[galvatron], S[server0]
```

```
Primary Partition 1:C[server2_C-0], H[galvatron], S[server2]
```

```
Primary Partition 2:C[server0_C-0], H[galvatron], S[server0]
```

```
Primary Partition 3:C[server2_C-0], H[galvatron], S[server2]
```

```
Primary Partition 4:C[server0_C-0], H[galvatron], S[server0]
```

```
Primary Partition 5:C[server2_C-0], H[galvatron], S[server2]
```

```
Primary Partition 6:C[server0_C-0], H[galvatron], S[server0]
```

```
Primary Partition 7:C[server0_C-0], H[galvatron], S[server0]
```

```
Primary Partition 8:C[server2_C-0], H[galvatron], S[server2]
```

```
Primary Partition 9:C[server2_C-0], H[galvatron], S[server2]
```

```
Primary Partition 10:C[server0_C-0], H[galvatron], S[server0]
```

Starting a second container gives the catalog service the resources it needs to place the shards. Notice how the partitions are split between the two containers. We can get a more detailed view of the shards in each container with the xsadmin tool:

```
xsadmin -ch galvatron -containers
```

```
*** Show all online containers for grid - PaymentProcessorGrid & mapset
 - ppMapSet
```

```
Host: galvatron
  Container: server0_C-0, Server:server0, Zone:DefaultZone
    P:0 Primary
    P:10 Primary
    P:2 Primary
    P:4 Primary
    P:6 Primary
    P:7 Primary
    P:1 SynchronousReplica
    P:3 SynchronousReplica
    P:5 SynchronousReplica
    P:8 SynchronousReplica
    P:9 SynchronousReplica
  Container: server2_C-0, Server:server2, Zone:DefaultZone
    P:1 Primary
```

```
P:3 Primary
P:5 Primary
P:8 Primary
P:9 Primary
P:0 SynchronousReplica
P:10 SynchronousReplica
P:2 SynchronousReplica
P:4 SynchronousReplica
P:6 SynchronousReplica
P:7 SynchronousReplica
```

Here, we see that, each container holds a number of primary shards, and the other container holds their synchronous replicas. From this exercise, we see that the minimum number of containers for a deployment to place shard is N+1, where N is the minimum number of synchronous replicas.

What happened to the asynchronous replicas? We have specified one asynchronous replica per partition in the `ogdeployment.xml` file:

```
xsadmin -ch galvatron -unassigned

Connecting to Catalog service at galvatron:1099
*** Showing unassigned containers for grid - PaymentProcessorGrid &
mapset - ppMapSet
0:AsynchronousReplica
1:AsynchronousReplica
2:AsynchronousReplica
3:AsynchronousReplica
4:AsynchronousReplica
5:AsynchronousReplica
6:AsynchronousReplica
7:AsynchronousReplica
8:AsynchronousReplica
9:AsynchronousReplica
10:AsynchronousReplica
```

The asynchronous replica shards are not placed yet. The deployment placed all primary and synchronous replica shards without placing the asynchronous replica shards. There is no setting in the ObjectGrid deployment policy file which specifies the minimum number of asynchronous replicas before shard placement. Asynchronous replicas are added as a deployment has resources for them. They are not on the critical path in shard placement, and have no required minimum before shard placement begins. Asynchronous replica shards are placed only after all primary and synchronous replica shards are placed.

We'll add another container to the deployment to give the catalog server the resources it needs to place the asynchronous replicas:

```
startOgServer server2 -catalogServiceEndpoints galvatron:2809 \
-objectgridFile c:/wxs/workspace/PaymentProcessor/src/jpa-objectgrid.xml
\-deploymentPolicyFile \
c:/wxs/workspace/PaymentProcessor/src/ogdeployment.xml \
-listenerHost galvatron \
-listenerPort 13002 \
-jvmArgs -cp \

c:/wxs/workspace/PaymentProcessor/bin/output/PaymentProcessor.jar:
c:/jboss-4.2.2.GA/server/default/lib/*:c:/jboss-4.2.2.GA/lib/*:c:/wxs/
ObjectGrid/lib/*;


xsadmin -ch galvatron -unassigned

  Container: server2_C-0, Server:server2, Zone:DefaultZone

    P:0 AsynchronousReplica

    P:1 AsynchronousReplica

    P:10 AsynchronousReplica

    P:2 AsynchronousReplica

    P:3 AsynchronousReplica

    P:4 AsynchronousReplica

    P:5 AsynchronousReplica

    P:6 AsynchronousReplica

    P:7 AsynchronousReplica

    P:8 AsynchronousReplica

    P:9 AsynchronousReplica
```

Giving the deployment a third container allows placement of all of the asynchronous replicas in the container server2_C-0. Adding more containers to the deployment now spreads the shards out across the additional containers using the water-fall migration that was described in Chapter 5.

Shard start-up

Each shard type goes through certain events during start-up. Primary shards come to exist in one of two ways, and may come to exist when an ObjectGrid deployment initially places shards onto containers. This happens very soon after the minimum number of containers for the deployment is running.

When a primary shard is placed, it receives a list of replica shards that have also been placed by the ObjectGrid catalog service. These replica shards will function as replicas of that primary shard. After registering the replica shards, the primary shard is ready to accept transactions. The container holding the primary shard notes the events in its log file:

`$ObjectGridHome/bin/logs/server0/SystemOut.log`

```
[3/14/09 15:52:04:250 EDT] 399d399d ReplicatedPar I CWOBJ1511I:
PaymentProcessorGrid:ppMapSet:1 (primary) is open for business.
```

Starting a replica shard is a little more complicated than starting a primary shard. A replica shard must have a copy of all of the objects stored in the primary shard before it enters peer mode. A replica shard enters the peer mode state, when it is included in processing the transactions. The primary shard processes as the primary processes them. It means the replica participates in the transaction lifecycle experienced by a client.

When a replica shard starts, it is empty. Upon registering with the primary shard, the maps in the primary shard enter copy-on-write mode. At replica startup, we must take a snapshot of the objects in all of the maps on the primary, and copy them to the replica. Placing the maps in copy-on-write mode allows us to do this.

Copy-on-write mode is helpful because it keeps a pristine copy of the snapshot data sent to the replica. If a transaction on the primary alters one of the objects in a map, a copy of that object is made. This prevents mangled objects from getting sent to the replica. It also allows us to keep track of any objects that changed during the snapshotting process.

After the objects in the primary are placed in copy-on-write mode, they are copied to the replica shard. After the initial copy is complete, any objects that change during the copy process are merged with the objects on the primary shard and on the replica shard. We know which objects have changed because there is a copy of them, thanks to the copy-on-write on the primary shard.

The copy-on-write/merge process continues until the replica has caught up to the primary. When the replica mirrors the objects in the primary, and can participate in transactions, it enters peer mode. Peer mode means that the objects in the replica mirror the objects on the primary shard. Any transaction processed by the primary shard sends changes from that transaction to the replica shard. Before the transaction on the primary shard commits, the primary must have confirmation that the minimum number of synchronous replicas specified in the deployment policy file have a copy of the changes.

Though the synchronous replicas have a copy of the changes from a transaction, they do not know if the transaction is successfully committed, or not until the next time the primary shard contacts the replica. Once the replica knows the state of the transaction on the primary shard, the replica finalizes the transaction, and the changes become readable to clients. If the primary shard committed the transaction, then the replica applies the changes. If the primary shard rolled back the transaction, then the replica discards the changes.

Lost shards and failover

Running the payment processor application using the ObjectGrid deployment allows inspection of the size of BackingMaps in the grid. As the payment processor application is running, we use the `xsadmin` tool:

```
xsadmin -ch galvatron -mapsizes -fm Payment

************Displaying Results for Grid - PaymentProcessorGrid, MapSet -
ppMapSet**************

*** Listing Maps for server0 ***

Map Name: Payment  Partition #: 1  Map Size: 1750  Shard Type: Primary

Map Name: Payment  Partition #:10  Map Size: 1780  Shard Type:
SynchronousReplica

Map Name: Payment  Partition #: 9  Map Size: 1756  Shard Type:
SynchronousReplica

Map Name: Payment  Partition #: 8  Map Size: 1747  Shard Type:
SynchronousReplica

Map Name: Payment  Partition #: 7  Map Size: 1775  Shard Type:
SynchronousReplica

Server Total: 8808

*** Listing Maps for server1 ***

Map Name: Payment  Partition #: 7  Map Size: 1775  Shard Type: Primary
```

Map Name: Payment   Partition #: 5   Map Size: 1818   Shard Type: Primary

Map Name: Payment   Partition #: 0   Map Size: 1800   Shard Type: Primary

Map Name: Payment   Partition #: 4   Map Size: 1750   Shard Type:
SynchronousReplica

Server Total: 7143

*** Listing Maps for server2 ***

Map Name: Payment   Partition #: 8 Map Size: 1747   Shard Type:
AsynchronousReplica

Map Name: Payment   Partition #: 7 Map Size: 1775   Shard Type:
AsynchronousReplica

Map Name: Payment   Partition #:10 Map Size: 1780   Shard Type:
AsynchronousReplica

Map Name: Payment   Partition #: 3 Map Size: 1850   Shard Type:
AsynchronousReplica

Server Total: 7152

*** Listing Maps for server3 ***

Map Name: Payment   Partition #: 1 Map Size: 1750   Shard Type:
AsynchronousReplica

Map Name: Payment   Partition #: 5 Map Size: 1818   Shard Type:
AsynchronousReplica

Map Name: Payment   Partition #: 4 Map Size: 1750   Shard Type:
AsynchronousReplica

Server Total: 5318

*** Listing Maps for server4 ***

Map Name: Payment   Partition #: 6 Map Size: 1822   Shard Type: Primary

Map Name: Payment   Partition #: 3 Map Size: 1850   Shard Type: Primary

Map Name: Payment   Partition #: 2 Map Size: 1815   Shard Type:
AsynchronousReplica

Map Name: Payment   Partition #: 1 Map Size: 1750   Shard Type:
SynchronousReplica

Server Total: 7237

*** Listing Maps for server5 ***

Map Name: Payment   Partition #: 9 Map Size: 1756   Shard Type:
AsynchronousReplica

Map Name: Payment   Partition #: 6 Map Size: 1822   Shard Type:
SynchronousReplica

Map Name: Payment   Partition #: 0 Map Size: 1800   Shard Type:
SynchronousReplica

```
Server Total: 5378

*** Listing Maps for server6 ***
Map Name: Payment  Partition #:10 Map Size: 1780   Shard Type: Primary
Map Name: Payment  Partition #: 9 Map Size: 1756   Shard Type: Primary
Map Name: Payment  Partition #: 3 Map Size: 1850   Shard Type:
SynchronousReplica
Server Total: 5386

*** Listing Maps for server7 ***
Map Name: Payment  Partition #: 2 Map Size: 1815   Shard Type: Primary
Map Name: Payment  Partition #: 5 Map Size: 1818   Shard Type:
SynchronousReplica
Map Name: Payment  Partition #: 0 Map Size: 1800   Shard Type:
AsynchronousReplica
Map Name: Payment  Partition #: 4 Map Size: 1750   Shard Type: Primary
Server Total: 7183

*** Listing Maps for server8 ***
Map Name: Payment  Partition #: 6 Map Size: 1822   Shard Type:
AsynchronousReplica
Map Name: Payment  Partition #: 2 Map Size: 1815   Shard Type:
SynchronousReplica
Map Name: Payment  Partition #: 8 Map Size: 1747   Shard Type: Primary
Server Total: 5384

Total Domain Count: 58989
```

This is a snapshot of all of the payments in the grid at a point in time. Our deployment is running normally. All nine containers are up and running, and the CPU, memory, and network resources used by each container are not saturated. This is how we want our deployment running.

Unfortunately, we cannot always have all nine containers running. Whether due to JVM crashes, system maintenance, network outage, or some disaster scenario, we'll lose containers from time to time. Let's see what happens when we lose a container in our deployment. Let's just kill the Java process for server0. That container had five shards in it:

```
*** Listing Maps for server0 ***
Map Name: Payment  Partition #: 1  Map Size: 1750   Shard Type: Primary
Map Name: Payment  Partition #:10  Map Size: 1780   Shard Type:
SynchronousReplica
```

```
Map Name: Payment  Partition #: 9  Map Size: 1756  Shard Type:
SynchronousReplica

Map Name: Payment  Partition #: 8  Map Size: 1747  Shard Type:
SynchronousReplica

Map Name: Payment  Partition #: 7  Map Size: 1775  Shard Type:
SynchronousReplica

Server Total: 8808
```

Only one of the five shards was a primary shard. Partition 1 also had shards in `server3` and `server4`. Without the primary shard, let's see what happened to the two replicas:

```
*** Listing Maps for server3 ***

Map Name: Payment  Partition #: 1 Map Size: 1750  Shard Type:
SynchronousReplica

Map Name: Payment  Partition #: 5 Map Size: 1818  Shard Type:
AsynchronousReplica

Map Name: Payment  Partition #: 4 Map Size: 1750  Shard Type:
AsynchronousReplica

Server Total: 5318


*** Listing Maps for server4 ***

Map Name: Payment  Partition #: 6 Map Size: 1822  Shard Type: Primary

Map Name: Payment  Partition #: 3 Map Size: 1850  Shard Type: Primary

Map Name: Payment  Partition #: 1 Map Size: 1750  Shard Type: Primary

Map Name: Payment  Partition #: 2 Map Size: 1815  Shard Type:
AsynchronousReplica

Server Total: 7237
```

This newly-promoted primary shard then receives a list of replicas from the catalog service. As with a new primary shard start-up sequence, the new primary registers the replicas. Unlike the new primary start-up sequence, these replicas already have maps and objects in them. The initial snapshot process is not required if a replica is up-to-date, as will be the case with most synchronous replicas. Any replicas, synchronous or asynchronous, that do not have a current copy of the objects in the new primary are emptied. Once emptied, the snapshot process of copying the current state of objects from the primary to the replica takes place.

We only had one synchronous replica for the partition. By promoting the synchronous replica to primary, we do not have a correct deployment. In the `ogdeployment.xml` file, we specify that a deployment must have a minimum of one synchronous replica shard per primary. To fill this void, the new primary shard promotes the asynchronous replica of the partition to synchronous replica.

As we still have eight containers in the deployment, the primary shard places a new asynchronous replica shard in container server7_C-0:

```
*** Listing Maps for server7 ***

Map Name: Payment  Partition #: 2 Map Size: 1815  Shard Type: Primary

Map Name: Payment  Partition #: 5 Map Size: 1818  Shard Type:
SynchronousReplica

Map Name: Payment  Partition #: 1 Map Size: 1750  Shard Type:
AsynchronousReplica

Map Name: Payment  Partition #: 0 Map Size: 1800  Shard Type:
AsynchronousReplica

Map Name: Payment  Partition #: 4 Map Size: 1750  Shard Type: Primary

Server Total: 8933
```

Placing the asynchronous replica is done automatically by ObjectGrid. If replacing lost shards is not a recommended behavior, then it can be turned off with the `autoReplaceLostShards` attribute on mapSet:

```
<objectgridDeploymentobjectgridName="PaymentProcessorGrid">
  <mapSet name="ppMapSet"
          numberOfPartitions="11"
          minSyncReplicas="1"
          maxSyncReplicas="1"
          maxAsyncReplicas="1"
          autoReplaceLostShards="false"
          replicaReadEnabled="true">
```

This attribute only affects the last shard in the promotion chain. If we had set it to `false` in our `ogdeployment.xml` file, then the asynchronous replica shard for partition would not occur. Losing either the primary, or synchronous replica, would now leave the partition running with only one primary shard and zero replicas.

The next attribute of interest on mapSet is `replicaReadEnabled`. Using replicas for disaster recovery is fine, but client applications can read from them too. This attribute defaults to `false`, meaning all read requests (get, find, and so on) from a client go to the primary shard. Setting `replicaReadEnabled="true"` spreads the load among a primary shard and its replicas. Client read requests now go to any one of the primary or replica shards. All write requests (put, delete, update, and insert) only go to the primary shard. From there, it is the primary's responsibility to copy the changes to its replicas.

We use `replicaReadEnabled="true"` when the client-side near cache has frequent object evictions or invalidations, or the near cache does not exist (when using the pessimistic lock strategy).

Physical location

Another mapSet attribute affecting shard placement is the `developmentMode` attribute. By default, this value is set to `true`, meaning the deployment is in development mode. Development mode allows primary and replica shards to be placed on the same host. It also allows us to start all of our containers on the same host, be it our laptop, desktop, test system, or wherever. We cannot run these examples without the development mode as well as without at least two different host operating systems, whether they may be physical boxes or virtual.

When a deployment is not in development mode, two shards from the same partition cannot live on the same host, even if they are in different containers. With `developmentMode="false"`, multiple containers on the same host will not contain any duplicate objects. The entire set of objects is unique because only one shard from each partition may live in a container on that host.

This is significant because a production environment should never have data loss due to the failure of one host. If a physical box goes down, or network traffic is congested rendering it unreachable, then the ObjectGrid deployment still exists without data loss. If a primary and synchronous replica for the same partition were on the box that went down, then the data in that partition is lost. If we were using a loader with maps in that partition, then the database would be in an inconsistent state with no way to report if something went wrong to the client application.

With the shards on different hosts, we have a shot at recovery through the promotion chain. When using a loader, the synchronous replica is usually at least one commit behind the primary. Losing the host with a primary partition triggers the synchronous replica's promotion to primary.

Immediately after promotion, the new primary tries to commit any active transactions for which the old primary didn't send a final transaction status. If both the primary and replica shards were lost, then these transactions don't reach the database. The client application functions after the primary loss by communicating with the new primary.

Controlled data separation

ObjectGrid separates shards that make up a partition by placing those shards on different hosts. We control the hosts on which a shard is placed by defining zones.

An ObjectGrid deployment exists in a data center. In the data center are racks of blade servers. These servers run the container processes which make up the ObjectGrid deployment. In the event of a rack failure, or if there is a loss of power to the room, then we want to ensure that our shards are physically placed significantly far enough that we can avoid disaster and allow the ObjectGrid to recover.

A **zone** is a collection of hosts that run containers containing a certain shard type or types. The ObjectGrid deployment policy file defines a set of zone rules for a particular map set. Using these zone rules, we can split shards across two racks instead of letting ObjectGrid decide which of the 14 blades can hold a shard. Letting ObjectGrid decide only ensures that shards for the same partition don't go on the same host. With zones, we can ensure that shards for the same partition don't go on the same rack if that was our goal.

Zone rules are defined in the mapSet in a deployment policy file. Let's say we want to separate primary shards from replica shards. We want all primary shards running on one rack, and all replica shards running on a different rack.

```
<mapSet name="ppMapSet"
        numberOfPartitions="11"
        minSyncReplicas="1"
        maxSyncReplicas="1"
        maxAsyncReplicas="1">
    <map ref="Payment" />
    <map ref="Batch" />
    <map ref="Card" />
    <map ref="Address" />

    <zoneMetadata>
        <shardMapping shard="P"
                zoneRuleRef="rack1Rule" />

        <shardMapping shard="S"
                zoneRuleRef="rack2Rule" />

        <zoneRule name="rack1Rule"
              exclusivePlacement="true">
            <zone name="rack1" />
        </zoneRule>

        <zoneRule name="rack2Rule"
                exclusivePlacement="true">
            <zone name="rack2" />
        </zoneRule>
    </zoneMetadata>
</mapSet>
```

We add zone metadata to the mapSet in the ogdeployment.xml file (seen above). Shard placement is done by shard type, shown in the shardMapping element. "P" defines a rule for primary shards, "S" for synchronous replicas, and "A" for asynchronous replicas.

A shard mapping refers to a zone rule. A zone rule has a name, an exclusive placement flag, and a list of zones that fall under this rule. The zone name is only used to map a shard type to a rule. Having the exclusivePlacement flag set to false allows shards of one partition to occupy the same zone. If we set exclusivePlacement to true, it means two shards from one partition cannot be placed in the same zone. With the above zone metadata, we see that network I/O to rack one will be significantly higher than that of rack two. All of the primary partitions are on rack one, and all write operations go to rack one. Rather than heavily loading rack one, we can spread the load of primaries and replicas across those two racks.

```
<zoneMetadata>
    <shardMapping shard="P"
                    zoneRuleRef="evenLoadRule" />
    <shardMapping shard="S"
                    zoneRuleRef="evenLoadRule" />
    <zoneRule name="evenLoadRule"
                    exclusivePlacement="true">
      <zone name="rack1" />
      <zone name="rack2" />
    </zoneRule>
</zoneMetadata>
```

In the code above, we consolidate down to one rule shared by both primary and synchronous replica shard types. The exclusive placement flag is set to true. If a primary shard for partition one is placed on rack one, a replica shard for partition one cannot be placed on rack one. It must go in the zone named rack2. If we have more server racks available for our deployment, then they can be added to the zones in a zone rule:

```
<zoneMetadata>
    <shardMapping shard="P"
                    zoneRuleRef="evenLoadRule" />
    <shardMapping shard="S"
                    zoneRuleRef="evenLoadRule" />
    <zoneRule name="evenLoadRule"
                    exclusivePlacement="true">
      <zone name="rack1" />
      <zone name="rack2" />
      <zone name="rack3" />
      <zone name="rack4" />
    </zoneRule>
</zoneMetadata>
```

Sharing the zone rule between partition types, and keeping exclusive placement, allows the deployment to more effectively use physical resources. Rather than loading a set of boxes with a vast majority of read/write operations, we have ObjectGrid spread them across predefined sets of boxes.

We can specify a zone for asynchronous replicas too. Perhaps we want to keep asynchronous replica shards in a different room in the data center, or across town, or across the country. Due to the fire-and-forget nature of sending transactions to asynchronous replicas, they can be located further away from the primary than a synchronous replica.

```
<zoneMetadata>
    <shardMapping shard="P"
                    zoneRuleRef="evenLoadRule" />
    <shardMapping shard="S"
                    zoneRuleRef="evenLoadRule" />
     <shardMapping shard="A"
                    zoneRuleRef="asyncRule" />

    <zoneRule name="evenLoadRule"
             exclusivePlacement="true">
        <zone name="rack1" />
        <zone name="rack2" />
        <zone name="rack3" />
        <zone name="rack4" />
    </zoneRule>

    <zoneRule name="asyncRule"
             exclusivePlacement="true">
        <zone name="rack1A" />
        <zone name="rack2A" />
    </zoneRule>
</zoneMetadata>
```

We define a new zone rule with two zones in it (as seen above). These two new zones could be racks in any of the locations just mentioned. As long as the containers on those hosts are reachable by the primary shards, the replication works as usual. Along with the new zone rule, we have added a shard mapping. Asynchronous shards use the `asyncRule` for shard placement. Asynchronous shards can only be placed in `rack1A` and `rack2A`.

For zone rules to take effect, we must specify a zone when starting an ObjectGrid container process. This is easy to do by adding the `-zone` argument to the `startOgServer` script:

```
startOgServer server0 -catalogServiceEndpoints galvatron:2809 \
-objectgridFile c:/wxs/workspace/PaymentProcessor/src/jpa-objectgrid.xml
\
-deploymentPolicyFile \
c:/wxs/workspace/PaymentProcessor/src/ogdeployment.xml \
-listenerHost galvatron \
-listenerPort 13000 \
-zone rack1 \
-jvmArgs -cp \
c:/wxs/workspace/PaymentProcessor/bin/output/PaymentProcessor.jar:
c:/jboss-4.2.2.GA/server/default/lib/*:c:/jboss-4.2.2.GA/lib/*:c:/wxs/
ObjectGrid/lib/*;
```

At container startup, the zone that each container belongs to must be specified. Containers running on each server in rack one will use the `-zone rack1` argument. Containers running on each server in rack two will use the `-zone rack2` argument. With these rules, we have everything we need for an ObjectGrid instance to span data centers. Starting containers in zones rack1, rack2, and rack3, rack4 should be done in the same data center. These zones contain our primary and replica shards. These shard types should be physically close enough so that the latency of synchronous replica transactions does not noticeably reduce the transaction throughput.

Zones for `rack1a` and `rack1b` (and any other zones we want this rule applied to) can be physically located anywhere. As asynchronous replicas populate these zones, they are not in the main code path when committing a transaction. We don't care about latency with asynchronous replicas. We understand that committed transactions won't immediately be readable on an asynchronous replica. With this relaxed stance on latency, ObjectGrid is free to replicate transactions in environments that may be in different geographic regions.

Preferred zones

Locating ObjectGrid containers in different cities is a common use. Consider our ObjectGrid deployment policy file with zones named rack1, rack2, rack3, and rack4 running in New York City (NYC), and zones named rack1a and rack2a running in Boston. Working with the grid a client in NYC will read from primary and synchronous replicas with very low latency. A client will only read from an asynchronous replica in Boston if no shard in NYC is available to fulfill the request.

However, a grid client in Boston, will also prefer to read from primary and synchronous replicas in NYC. Each read and write request will make an RPC, not to the asynchronous replicas in Boston, but to the shards in NYC. Making this RPC for every grid request kills throughput because of the latency involved in going to a shard located in NYC. The Boston-based asynchronous replicas are essentially backups, in case all shards in NYC become unavailable.

We stress that locality of reference is very important in achieving high scalability and performance. Obviously, the asynchronous replicas should be worked harder than being just an object cache backup. One of the great features of WebSphere eXtreme Scale is that we can tell our clients which zones they should prefer when performing read and write operations.

At runtime, ObjectGrid uses an instance of the `ClientProperties` interface to set client preferences on the `ClientClusterContext` obtained from the `ObjectGridManager#connect(...)` methods. We can interact with the instance of `ClientProperties`, which we get by calling the `ClientClusterContext#getClientProperties("gridName")` method. Replace `gridName` with the actual name of the ObjectGrid instance you want to set preferences for. We call setter methods on this instance of `ClientProperties` returned by `getClientProperties(gridName)`. Once we call the setter methods for our preferences, we don't need to set the `ClientProperties` on the `ClientClusterContext` object. The `ClientProperties` we modify is a reference to the instance used by `ClientClusterContext`. If we set `ClientProperties`, then we must do so before calling an `ObjectGridManager#get(...)` method. Otherwise, our preferences will not be applied to the `ClientClusterContext` sent to the `get(...)` method.

Though we can set preferences programmatically, it's easier and more portable to set them in a configuration file. This way, the `ClientProperties` are set when the client obtains a `ClientClusterContext`, without polluting the client code with client preferences.

An easy way to use `ClientProperties` is by making a file called `objectGridClient.properties`. This file can be on the client `classpath` root, or in the file system directory, where the client start command is executed. The format of this file is `setting=value`. The value is a comma-separated list of values.

Configuring a client in Boston to use the Boston-based asynchronous replicas gives us this `objectGridClient.properties` file:

```
preferZones=rack1a,rack2a,rack4
```

With this file on the client `classpath` root, or in the executable directory, the `ClientProperties` are applied to any `ClientClusterContext` obtained by an `ObjectGridManager.connect(...)` method. From an application point of view, we can set some clients to read from `rack1a` and some to read from `rack2a`. Here, we have clients preferring `rack1a` if it's available, then `rack2a`, then `rack4` in NYC, if both asynchronous replica racks are unavailable. We avoid going to the rack1, rack2, rack3, and rack4 zones if rack1a and rack2a are available, keeping read requests local to Boston. Write operations still go to NYC because all primary shards are located there.

Additional client preferences and methods of setting ClientProperties are documented in the `com.ibm.websphere.objectgrid.client` Javadoc package.

Summary

We covered a lot of ground in this chapter. By now, we should have a clear idea of what happens when an ObjectGrid deployment starts. We have introduced the ObjectGrid deployment policy file and what its uses are. Shard types and placement are influenced by elements and attributes in the deployment policy file. Though it's not required, the deployment policy file unlocks a lot of eXtreme Scale's power. The deployment policy file also gives us control over a few things.

First, we have the power to partition our data sets. This lets us spread the load over many servers. We gain the power of all of the servers used to host the ObjectGrid instance. The deployment policy file also gives us control over replication and shard placement. It lets us define how many copies of shards should be kept and where they are located. We can place shards in specific racks (and even finer-grained placement than that if we want), in local or far-away data centers, based on the zone rules defined in the deployment policy.

You should now be comfortable defining partitions and setting up shard replication. You should know how to use zones to your advantage. Zone rules help define shard placement and are valuable for disaster scenarios.

We also used the `xsadmin` tool to find out where shards are placed as well as the current size of a BackingMap in a container. You should feel comfortable enough using `xsadmin` on your own to continue exploring your WebSphere eXtreme Scale deployment topologies.

Finally, we covered client apps using zones in different regions. Through ClientProperties, we tell client apps to rely on ObjectGrid shards that are closer to where the client app runs. Remember, keeping code and data close together produces applications with high scalability and performance.

7
The DataGrid API

The previous chapters dealt with local and client-server ObjectGrid interaction. Local ObjectGrid instances run in the same memory process as the business application. Access to objects stored in the grid is extremely fast, and there are no network hops or routing done on ObjectGrid operations. The disadvantage with a local ObjectGrid instance is that all objects stored in the grid must fit into the heap space of one JVM.

The client-server distributed ObjectGrid instances we studied in the previous chapters overcame that single heap space disadvantage by combining the resources of multiple JVMs on multiple servers. These combined resources hide behind the façade of an ObjectGrid instance. The ObjectGrid instance has far more CPU, memory, and network I/O available to it than the resources available to any single client.

In this chapter, we'll learn how to use those resources held by the ObjectGrid instance to co-locate data and business logic on a single JVM. The client-server model relies on a client pulling objects across a network from an ObjectGrid shard. The client performs some operations on those objects. Any object whose state has changed must be sent back across the network to the appropriate shard. The client-server programming model co-locates data and code by moving data to the code. The data grid programming model does the opposite by moving code to the data. Rather than dragging megabytes of objects from an ObjectGrid shard to a client, only to send it right back to the ObjectGrid, we instead send our much smaller application code to an ObjectGrid shard to operate on the data in place. The end result is the same: code and data are co-located. We now have the resources of an entire data grid available to run that code instead of one client process.

Co-locating data and logic on the same JVM requires a different model of programming. This chapter deals with the DataGrid API which makes co-location possible. In this chapter, we'll explore:

- Concepts implemented by the DataGrid API
- The programming model for sending logic to ObjectGrid partitions
- Where we would use the DataGrid classes

What does DataGrid do for me?

The DataGrid API provides encapsulation to send application-specific methods into the grid and operate directly on the objects in shards. The API consists of only five public classes. These five classes provide us with several patterns to make an ObjectGrid instance do the heavy lifting for a client application. In the previous chapters, the client application did a lot of work by operating on the objects in the grid. The client requires a network hop to get an object from the grid and performs an operation on it, persisting that the object requires another network hop to the grid.

In a single client environment, the probable bottlenecks in dealing with ObjectGrid are all on the client side. A single client will not stress the resources in the ObjectGrid deployment. The client application is most likely the bottleneck. With all computers in a deployment being equal, one client application on one computer will not stress the combined resources of the grid.

In a naïve application that performs single object `get` and `put` operations, our application will first notice a bottleneck due to data starvation. This is where a client cannot get the data it needs fast enough, caused by network latency. Single object `get` and `put` operations (and the corresponding Entity API calls) won't saturate a gigabit ethernet connection by any means, but the latency in making the RPC is higher than what the CPU can handle. The application works, but it's slow.

A smarter application would use the `ObjectMap#getAll` method. This would go out to the grid and get an object for every key in the list. Instead of waiting for each individual object, the client application waits for the entire list to come over the network. While the cost of network RPC is amortized over the size of the list, the client still incurs that cost.

In addition to these network latency concerns, we may not want a near-cache that eats up client-side memory. Turning off the near-cache means that every `get` operation is an RPC. Turning it on means that some of our JVM heap space is used to store objects, which we may not need after the first use.

The fundamental problem is that our objects and client application are architecturally separated. For our application to do anything, it needs to operate on objects that exist in the grid. In the client-server model, we copy data from the server to the client. At this point, our data and code are co-located, and the application can perform some business logic with that data. This model breaks down when there are huge data sets copied between boxes.

Databases co-locate data and code with stored procedures. The processing power of the stored procedure is a product of the CPU and memory resources of the computer running the database. The stored procedure is code compiled into a module and executed by the database. Within that process, the stored procedure accesses data available in the same process.

ObjectGrid gives us the ability to run code in the same process that gives an object access via the DataGrid API. Unlike the database example, where the throughput and latency of getting the store procedure result is limited to the power of the server it's on, ObjectGrid's power is limited by the number of CPUs in the deployment, and it can scale out at any time.

ObjectGrid co-locates our code and objects by sending serialized classes with our application code methods to primary partitions in the grid. There are two ways to do this. The first way sends the code to every primary partition in the grid. The code executes and returns a result to the client. In the second way, we supply a collection of keys to the DataGrid API. With a list of keys, ObjectGrid only sends the application code to the partitions that contain at least one object with a key in the list. This reduces the amount of container processes doing the work for our client application, and is preferred instead of making the entire grid service on one client request.

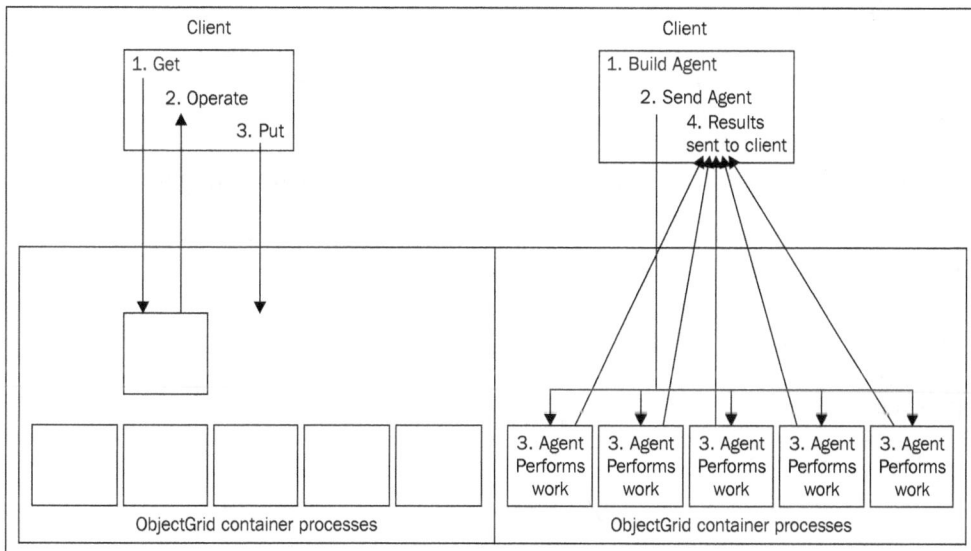

Let's look at finding an object by key in the client-server distributed model. The client has a key for an object. Calling the ObjectMap#get(key) method creates some work for the client. It first needs to determine to which partition the key belongs. The partition is important because the ClientClusterContext, already obtained by the client, knows how to get to the container that holds the primary shard in one hop. We find out the partition ID (pID) for a key with the PartitionManager class:

```
BackingMap bMap = grid.getMap("Payment");
PartitionManager pm = bMap.getPartitionManager();
int pId = pm.getPartition(key);
```

After obtaining the partition ID and the host running the container process, the client performs a network hop to request the object. The object is serialized and sent back to the client, where the client performs some operation with the object. Persisting an updated object requires one more network hop to put it back in the primary shard.

We can now repeat that process for every object in our multi-million object collection.

On second thought, that may not be such a great idea. Instead, we'll create an agent that we send to the grid. The agent encapsulates the logic we want to perform. An AgentManager serializes the agent and sends it to each primary shard in the deployment. Once on a primary shard, the agent executes and produces a result which is sent back to the client.

Borrowing from functional programming

The DataGrid API borrows the "map" and "reduce" concepts from the world of functional programming. Just so we're all on the same page, let's go over the concepts behind these two functions. Functional programming focuses more on what a program does, instead of how it does it. This is in contrast to the most imperative programming we do in the **C** family of languages. That's not to say we can't follow a functional programming model, it's just that we don't. Other languages, like **Lisp** and its descendants, make functional programming the natural thing to do.

Map and reduce are commonly found in functional programming. They are known as higher-order functions because they take functions as arguments. This is similar to how we would use a function pointer in C, or an anonymous inner class in Java, to implement callbacks. Though the focus is on *what* to do, at some point, we need to tell our program *how* to do it. We do this with the function passed as an argument to map or reduce.

Let's look at a simple example in Ruby, which has both functional and imperative programming influences:

```
>> numbers = [0,1,2,3,4,5,6,7,8,9]
>> numbers.map { |number| number * 2 }
=> [0, 2, 4, 6, 8, 10, 12, 14, 16, 18]
```

We assign an array of numbers 0-9 to the variable numbers. The array has a method called map that we call in the second line. Map is a higher-order function and accepts a function as its argument. The Array#map method calls the passed-in function for each element in the array. It passes the element in the variable numbers. In this way, we return a new array that contains the results of each call to our function which performs number * 2.

Let's look at the reduce method. In Ruby, reduce is called inject but the concept is the same:

```
>> numbers = [0,1,2,3,4,5,6,7,8,9]
>> numbers.inject(0) { |sum, number| sum = sum + number }
=> 45
```

The inject (read as reduce) method takes a function that performs a running total on the numbers in the array. Instead of an array as our return type, we only get one number. The reduce operation returns a single result for an entire data set. The map operation returns a new set based on running the original set through a given function.

These concepts are relevant in the data grid environment because we work with large data sets where we frequently need to work with large segments of data. Pulling raw data across the network, and operating over the data set on one client, are both too slow. Map and reduce helps us by using the remote CPU resources of the grid to cut down on the data sent across the network and the CPU power required on the client. This help comes from writing methods that work like map and reduce and sending them to our objects in the grid.

java.util.Map, BackingMaps, ObjectMaps, HashMaps, like we need one more use for the word "map". We just saw the functional origin of the map concept. Let's take a look at a Java implementation. Map implements an algorithm that performs an operation on each element in a collection and returns a new collection of results:

```
public Collection doubleOddInts(Collection c) {
    Collection results = new HashSet();
    Iterator iter = c.iterator();
    while (iter.hasNext()) {
        int i = (Integer)iter.next();
        if (i % 2 == 0) {
```

```
            results.add(i);
        } else {
            results.add(i*2);
        }
    }
    return results;
}
```

Our needs go beyond performing a map function over an array. In order to be useful in a DataGrid environment, the map function must operate on a distributed collection of objects in an ObjectGrid instance. The DataGrid API supports this by giving us the MapGridAgent interface. A business logic class implements the two methods in MapGridAgent to encapsulate the code we intend to run in the grid. Classes that implement MapGridAgent must implement two methods, namely, MapGridAgent#process(Session session, ObjectMap map, Object key) and MapGridAgent#processAllEntries(Session session, ObjectMap map).

Let's implement the doubleOddInts algorithm with MapGridAgent. We first create a class that implements the MapGridAgent interface. We give this class a meaningful name that describes the map operation implemented in the process methods:

```
public class DoubleOddIntsMapAgent implements Serializable,
    MapGridAgent {

    public Object process(Session session, ObjectMap map, Object key)
    {
        int i = (Integer)map.get(key);
        if (i % 2 == 0) {
            return i;
        } else {
            return i*2;
        }
    }

    public Map processAllEntries(Session session, ObjectMap map) {
        // nothing to do here for now!
    }
}
```

The map function itself is called by our client code. The process (session, map, key) method performs the *how* in the map function. Because ObjectGrid gives us the *what* for free (the map function), we only need to implement the *how* part. Like the Ruby example, this process (session, map, key) method is performed for each element in a collection. The Session and ObjectMap arguments are supplied by the AgentManager based on the current session and ObjectMap that starts the map function. The key is the crucial object for a given value in the collection, and that collection is supplied by us when we run the DoubleOddIntsMapAgent.

After implementing the MapGridAgent#process(session, map, key) method, the DoubleOddIntsMapAgent is ready to run. We want it to run on each shard in an ObjectGrid instance that has a key in the collection we pass to it. We do this with an instance of the AgentManager class. The AgentManager class has two methods to send a MapGridAgent to the grid: AgentManager#callMapAgent(MapGridAgent agent, Collection keys) and AgentManager#callMapAgent(MapGridAgent agent).

The first method provides a set of keys for our agent to use when run on each partition. Using this method is preferable to the non-keyed version because the non-keyed version runs the code on every primary shard in the grid. The Agent Manager#callMapAgent(agent, keys) method only runs the code on primary partitions that contain at least one key in the key collection. Whenever we have the choice to use part of the grid instead of the entire grid, we should take the choice that uses only part of the grid. Whenever we use the entire grid for one operation, we limit scalability and throughput. The AgentManager serializes the DoubleOddIntsMapAgent agent and sends it to each partition that has a key in the keys collection. Once on the primary partition, the process(session, map, key) method is called for each key in the keys collection supplied to AgentManager#c allMapAgent(agent, keys). This set of keys is a subset of all of the keys in the BackingMap, and likely a subset of keys in each partition.

Let's create an instance of this agent and submit it to the grid:

```
Collection numbers = new ArrayList();
for(int i = 0; i < 10000; i++) {
    numbers.add(i);
}

MapGridAgent agent = new DoubleOddIntsAgent();
AgentManager am = session.getMap("Integer").getAgentManager();
am.callMapAgent(agent, numbers);
```

This example assumes that we have a BackingMap of Integer for both the key and value objects. The numbers collection is a list of keys to use. Once we create the agent, we submit it to the grid with the 10,000 keys to operate on. Before running the agent, the AgentManager sorts the keys by partition. The agent only runs on partitions that have a list of keys that hash to that partition. The agent runs on each partition that has a list of keys that hash to it. In each primary partition, the DoubleOddIntsMapAgent#process(session, map, key) method is called only for the keys that map to that partition.

GridAgent and Entity

GridAgent works with Entity classes as well. We don't directly use key objects when working with Entity objects. The Entity API hides the key/value implementation from us to make working with Entity objects easier than working with the ObjectMap API.

The method definition for `MapGridAgent#process(session, map, key)` normally expects an object to be used as a key for an ObjectMap. We can still find the value object by converting key and value objects to their Tuple representations, but the DataGrid API makes it much easier for us. Instead of passing a key to the process method, we can convince the primary shard to pass us the Entity object itself, rather than a key using the EntityAgentMixin interface. EntityAgentMixin has one method, namely, `EntityAgentMixin#getClassForEntity()`. The implementation of this method should return the class object of the Entity. DataGrid needs this method defined in the grid agent implementation so it can provide the Entity object itself, rather than its key to the `MapGridAgent#process(session, map, key)` method.

Let's assume that we have an Entity `MyInteger` that acts as a wrapper for Integer:

```
public class DoubleOddIntsMapAgent implements Serializable,
    MapGridAgent, EntityAgentMixin {

    public Object process(Session session, ObjectMap map, Object key)
    {
        MyInteger myInt = (MyInteger)key;
        if (myInt.mod(2) == 0) {
            return myInt;
        } else {
            return myInt.multiplyBy(2);
        }
    }

    public Map processAllEntries(Session session, ObjectMap map) {
        // nothing to do here for now!
    }

    public Class getClassForEntity() {
        return MyInteger.class;
    }
}
```

Our agent now implements the EntityAgentMixin interface and the `getClassForEntity()` method. The key is converted to the correct class before the `MapGridAgent#process(session, map, key)` method is called. Instead of the Tuple key for an Entity, the process method is passed a reference to the Entity itself. Because it is passed as an object, we must cast the Entity to its defined class. There is no need to look up for the Entity in its BackingMap because it's already the Entity we want to work with. This means the collection of keys passed to `AgentManager#callMapAgent(agent, keys)` is a collection with all elements of the class returned by `getClassForEntity()`.

GridAgent with an unknown key set

We may not always know the keys for each object we want to submit to an agent. In this situation, we send an agent into the grid without a key set. The grid agent cannot call the process (`session`, `map`, `key`) method because we don't know which keys to use. Instead, our grid agent method relies on the Query API to narrow the number of objects in each partition we work with. The MapGridAgent interface gives us the `MapGridAgent#processAllEntries(Session session, ObjectMap map)` method for this situation.

The `MapGridAgent#processAllEntries(session, map)` method lets us specify what to do when we potentially need to work with all objects in a partition. Particularly, it lets us narrow the field with a query. In the past, we used a query to find card and address objects in a local ObjectGrid instance. This was fine for local instances with only one partition. The real power of the Query API is revealed when used with the DataGrid API.

Query does not work across partitions when called from an ObjectGrid client in a distributed environment. It works with just one partition. In a distributed deployment, where we use the DataGrid API, a grid agent instance runs on one partition. Each partition has an instance of the grid agent running in it and each agent can see the objects in its partition. If we have 20 partitions, then we have 20 grid agents running, one in each partition. Because we're working with a single partition in each grid agent, we use the Query API to determine which objects are of interest to the business logic.

Now that we know how to run code in the grid, the Query API is suddenly much more useful. Now, we want a query to run against just one partition. Using a query in a GridAgent is a natural fit. Each agent runs on one partition, and each query runs on that partition in the primary shard container process:

```
public class DoubleOddIntsMapAgent implements Serializable,
    MapGridAgent, EntityAgentMixin {
    public Object process(Session session, ObjectMap map, Object key)
    {
```

```
        MyInteger myInt = (MyInteger)key;
        if (myInt.mod(2) == 0) {
            return myInt;
        } else {
            return myInt.multiplyBy(2);
        }
    }

    public Map processAllEntries(Session session, ObjectMap map) {
        EntityManager em = session.getEntityManager();
        Query q = em.createQuery("select m from MyInteger m " +
                                "where m.integer > 0 " +
                                "and m.integer < 10000");
        Iterator iter = q.getResultIterator();

        Map<MyInteger, Integer> results =
            new HashMap<MyInteger, Integer)();

        while (iter.hasNext()) {
            MyInteger mi = (MyInteger)iter.next();
            results.put(mi, (Integer)process(session, map, mi));
        }
        return results;
    }

    public Class getClassForEntity() {
        return MyInteger.class;
    }
}
```

The `MapGridAgent#processAllEntries(session, map)` method generally follows the same pattern when implemented:

1. Narrow the scope of objects in the partition. This is important in the MapGridAgent because it returns a result for *every object it processes*. This can result in hundreds of megabytes of objects sent back to a client from every partition for an indiscriminate query.

2. Create a map to hold the results of each process operation. This map is keyed with the key object, or the value object, when using ObjectMap. The client application can perform its own `gets` if the keys are returned. Otherwise, it works directly with the value objects. We can also return a map of key/value objects. The map is keyed with the Entity class itself when using Entity.

3. Iterate over the query results calling `MapGridAgent#process(session, map, key)` for each result. Calling the process method is required here since we didn't pass a collection of keys to the `AgentManager#callMapAgent(agent)` method. The key set is unknown before the agent runs. The agent finds all objects in a partition that meet our criteria for processing, and then we call process to get each result.

4. Return the results. This map contains an entry for each object that meets our processing criteria in this partition. This map is merged, client-side, with the maps from every other partition where the agent ran. The merged map is the final result, and it is the return value to the `AgentManager#callMapAgent (agent)` method.

Following the call to `AgentManager#callMapAgent (agent)`, we have a Map that contains the combined agent results from every partition. We also split the workload between N partitions rather than performing all of the processing on the client. The ObjectGrid deployment performed our business logic because we passed the business logic to the grid rather than pulling objects out of the grid.

One of the great things about this pattern is that our task on many partitions completes in about $1/N^{th}$ the amount of time it would take for one huge partition containing the same objects running on one computer. Of course, there is the overhead of the merge operation and network connections, but this is amortized over the number of primary partitions used by the agent. This is distinctly different than scaling up a database server when it needs more CPU speed for stored procedures. Instead of incurred downtime for database server migration, we simply add more containers on additional computers. The power of our grid increases as easily as starting a few more JVMs.

Aggregate results

One thing to be aware of with the MapGridAgent interface is its potential for a partition to send huge result maps to a client. This is the nature of the map function. Its output size can be proportional to its input size if we don't use a query to select specific objects to work with or specify a key set. In this case, we need a specific result for every key, with the key set as narrow as we can make it. We then just need to deal with large maps once in a while.

What if we need an aggregate result for a key set? Instead of an operation and result for each element, we need an operation over all elements with just one result. Simple examples include the highest or lowest number in a set, and the earliest or total payroll expenses in a management hierarchy. In these examples, we need data from a set of elements in a partition, but we don't need a result for each. We only want one result for the entire set of objects.

Going back to our functional programming reference, this is where the reduce function shines. Like the map function, reduce has a corresponding grid agent interface. The reduce function takes a collection of input keys and only produces one result for the entire collection. The result is typically an aggregate result: a sum, product, max, min, average, or any other aggregate function.

Classes that implement ReduceGridAgent are used as parameters to the `AgentManager#callReduceAgent (ReduceGridAgent agent, Collection keys)` and `AgentManager#callReduceAgent (agent)` methods. The implementation itself is similar to the MapGridAgent pattern. The reduce grid agent we write operates on a collection of known keys or an unknown key set. If we have a known key set, then we will run the agent with `AgentManager#callReduceAgent (agent, keys)`. If the key set is not known, and if we need a query to find the interesting objects, then we will call the `AgentManager#callReduceAgent (agent)`.

Let's write a ReduceGridAgent that finds the largest integer in a set. We'll start with a naïve implementation for finding the largest integer in an array:

```
public int findLargestInteger(Integer[] ints) {
    int largestInt = ints[0];
    for (int i = 0; i < ints.length; i++) {
        if (ints[i] > largestInt) {
            largestInt = ints[i];
        }
    }
    return largestInt;
}
```

Implementing ReduceGridAgent requires three methods. Two of those methods look like the process methods in MapGridAgent. We have `ReduceGridAgent#reduce(session, map, keys)` and `ReduceGridAgent#reduce(session, map)`. Like its MapGridAgent counterparts, the reduce method that accepts keys in the signature works with keys or Entity objects. The reduce method without keys in the signature should use a Query to find the objects most interesting to our business logic.

```
public class LargestIntReduceAgent implements ReduceGridAgent,
    EntityAgentMixin {

    public Object reduce(Session session, ObjectMap map,
      Collection keys) {

        MyInteger largestInt = null;
        Iterator iter = keys.iterator();
        while (iter.hasNext()) {
            (MyInteger)myInt = (MyInteger)iter.next();
            if (myInt.greaterThan(largestInt)) {
```

```
                largestInt = myInt;
            }
        }
        return largestInt;
    }

    public Object reduce(Session session,ObjectMap map) {
        // Nothing to do for now!
    }

    public Object reduceResults(Collection results) {
        // Nothing to do for now!
    }

    public Class getClassForEntity() {
        return MyInteger.class;
    }
}
```

The first reduce method is similar in signature to the `MapGridAgent#process` `(session, map, key)` method. The difference here is that the third argument in `Red uceGridAgent#reduce(session, map, keys)` is a collection of keys rather than one key. This immediately illustrates the difference between the two. A Map operation takes place on only one element. Reduce operates on the entire collection.

With a known key set, the `ReduceGridAgent#reduce(session, map, keys)` method is called. Without a key set passed to the `AgentManager#callReduceAgent(agent)` method, the `GridReduceAgent#reduce(session, map)` method is called. This method should use a Query to find the objects we want to use in our business logic. The keys or entity objects can then be passed to the `ReduceGridAgent#reduce` `(session, map, keys)` method for the actual business logic.

We submit this agent to the grid in almost the same way as we submit a MapGridAgent to the grid. AgentManager has two `callReduceAgent` methods. The first takes a collection of keys as an argument, while the second does not.

Submitting this agent to the grid looks like this:

```
Collection numbers = new ArrayList();
for(int i = 0; i < 10000; i++) {
    numbers.add(i);
}

ReduceGridAgent agent = new LargestIntReduceAgent();
AgentManager am = session.getMap("MyInteger").getAgentManager();
am.callReduceAgent(agent, numbers);
```

This looks so similar to submitting a MapGridAgent to the grid and you may miss the method change to am.callReduceAgent(agent, keys). The programming models are so similar you may ask why there isn't just one generic callAgent method. Take a look at the ReduceGridAgent, particularly the ReduceGridAgent#reduceResults(results) method. This method is called *on the client side* after all instances of the agent return their results. At this point, we have a collection of results for each partition. It is acceptable for the AgentManager#callMapAgent(agent, keys) to return the merged results here. AgentManager#callReduceAgent(agent, keys) must return one result for the entire operation. The ReduceGridAgent#reduceResults(results) method aggregates each partition's aggregate results:

```
public class LargestIntReduceAgent implements ReduceGridAgent,
    EntityAgentMixin {

    public Object reduce(Session session, ObjectMap map,
        Collection keys) {
        return findLargestInt(keys);
    }

    public Object reduce(Session session,ObjectMap map) {
        // Nothing to do for now!
    }

    public Object reduceResults(Collection results) {
        findLargestInt(results);
    }

    public Class getClassForEntity() {
        return MyInteger.class;
    }

    private MyInteger findLargestInt(Collection keys) {
        MyInteger largestInt = null;
        Iterator iter = keys.iterator();
        while (iter.hasNext()) {
            (MyInteger)myInt = (MyInteger)iter.next();
            if (myInt.greaterThan(largestInt)) {
                largestInt = myInt;
            }
        }
        return largestInt;
    }
}
```

`ReduceGridAgent#reduceResults(keys)` is responsible for producing the final result passed back to the `AgentManager#callReduceAgent(agent, keys)` caller. Sometimes, the reduce operation performed in this final aggregation is the same as the operation performed in the `ReduceGridAgent#reduce(session, map, keys)` method. Sometimes, the operation is different. In our case, it is the same, and we refactor the reduce operation into a private method.

Finishing off the ReduceGridAgent, we come to `ReduceGridAgent#reduce (session, map)`. The method signature is similar to `MapGridAgent#processAllE ntries(session, map)` and should be a hint that they have a similar purpose. The `ReduceGridAgent#reduce(session, map)` is called when a key list is not provided to `AgentManager#callReduceAgent(agent)`.

`ReduceGridAgent#reduce(session, map)` should limit the number of objects used in the reduce operation. Like `MapGridAgent#processAllEntries(session, map)`, we typically use a Query. While the reduce agent does not send large results back to the client, we still care about finding objects that meet our criteria to use in the reduce operation:

```
public Object reduce(Session session,ObjectMap map) {
    EntityManager em = session.getEntityManager();
    Query q = em.createQuery("select m from MyInteger m " +
                             "where m.integer > 0 " +
                             "and m.integer < 10000");
    Iterator iter = q.getResultIterator();

    Collection<MyInteger> keys = new ArrayList<MyInteger)();

    while (iter.hasNext()) {
        MyInteger mi = (MyInteger)iter.next();
        keys.add(mi);
    }
    return reduce(session, map, keys);
}
```

Though these are not strict rules, this method usually follows a pattern like `MapGridAgent#processAllEntries(session, map)`.

1. Run a query to limit the number of objects used in the reduce operation.

2. Create a collection of keys used by the reduce operation. We're using entities here. Rather than duplicating the reduce operation in this method, we use put entities from the Query in the key collection. `ReduceGridAgent#reduce (session, map, keys)`, when using Entities, expects a collection of MyInteger objects.

3. Call `ReduceGridAgent#reduce(session, map, keys)` using the key collection we just created. There is no rule against re-implementing the reduce operation in each method but we'll be good software engineers and keep it DRY. If we can massage the query results into arguments, the reduce method accepts, and then we have enough reason to reuse it.

At this point, we can submit this agent to the grid with or without a set of known keys and get the largest MyInteger back. In both, the MapGridAgent and ReduceGridAgent, we used a Query to limit the number of objects used in each operation:

```
Query q = em.createQuery("select m from MyInteger m " +
                         "where m.integer > 0 " +
                         "and m.integer < 10000");
Iterator iter = q.getResultIterator();
```

Obviously, this query is limited in what it can do. The criteria is hardcoded into the query. This query can only find MyIntegers with values between 0 and 10,000. Initially, we hardcoded these values because the agent runs on a partition in a container. Fortunately, we can pass additional data along with our agent.

Using ephemeral objects in agents

In the previous examples, we hardcoded the query criteria in the process and reduce methods. We should let the client-side program set those parameters instead of dictating what range of numbers the queries operate on. Right now, our queries are limited to exactly what is coded. A grid agent is just a POJO. It can have fields, getter and setter methods, and any other methods outside of the implemented grid agent interface. It's probably best to limit functionality to grid agent functionality but that doesn't mean that we can't have fields or other objects on the implementing class.

Classes that implement the agent interfaces are POJOs. We'll send additional data to the grid by adding fields to the implementing class:

```
public class LargestIntReduceAgent implements ReduceGridAgent,
    EntityAgentMixin {

    private Integer minValue;
    private Integer maxValue;

    // Reduce methods omitted for brevity

    public void setMinValue(Integer min) {
        this.minValue = min;
    }
}
```

```
public void setMaxValue(Integer max) {
    this.maxValue = max;
}
}
```

The only requirement for sending these additional fields to the grid is that they must each be serializable. Sending these objects to the grid is probably a one-way trip. Unless they're passed back as part of a map result, we cannot use them to communicate the state between client and grid. The grid agent instance used on the client side does not get a copy of the state of grid agent variables when the agents finish execution in the grid. Including grid state objects in the result set is bad practice and unnecessary. Before we pass the agent to AgentManager#callReduceAg ent(agent), we set the fields used in the partition-side query:

```
ReduceGridAgent agent = new LargestIntReduceAgent();
agent.setMinValue(500);
agent.setMaxValue(5000);
AgentManager am = session.getMap("MyInteger").getAgentManager();
am.callReduceAgent(agent);
```

· The ReduceGridAgent#reduce(session, map) method requires a small change to use our new query parameters:

```
public Object reduce(Session session,ObjectMap map) {
    EntityManager em = session.getEntityManager();
    Query q = em.createQuery("select m from MyInteger m " +
                            "where m.integer > ?1 " +
                            "and m.integer < ?2");
    query.setParameter(1, minValue);
    query.setParameter(2, maxValue);
    Iterator iter = q.getResultIterator();

    Collection<MyInteger> keys = new ArrayList<MyInteger)();

    while (iter.hasNext()) {
        MyInteger mi = (MyInteger)iter.next();
        keys.add(mi);
    }
    return reduce(session, map, keys);
}
```

It's almost the same as before. We've just parameterized the query. It now uses the two values we sent into the grid with the agent.

We can send more than query parameters along with an agent. We can send additional, complex business logic. If we obey the principles of object-oriented design, then we favor composition over inheritance. This allows the composition of agents with complex map or reduce operations, without cluttering the agent implementation class with business logic. To demonstrate, we'll refactor the `findLargestInt(collection)` method out of the `LargestIntReduceAgent` class:

```java
public interface MyHelper {
    public MyInteger call(Collection keys);
}

public class AgentHelper implements MyHelper, Serializeable {
    public MyInteger call(Collection keys) {
        MyInteger largestInt = null;
        Iterator iter = keys.iterator();
        while (iter.hasNext()) {
          (MyInteger)myInt = (MyInteger)iter.next();
           if (myInt.greaterThan(largestInt)) {
              largestInt = myInt;
           }
        }
        return largestInt;
    }
}
```

This is just a class that encapsulates the method formerly known as `findLargestInt (collection)`. The name changed to conform to an imaginary calling convention is used by our agents. The ReduceGridAgent changes a bit to accommodate this calling convention:

```java
public class LargestIntReduceAgent implements ReduceGridAgent,
    EntityAgentMixin {

    private Integer minValue;
    private Integer maxValue;
    private MyHelper helper;

    public Object reduce(Session session, ObjectMap map,
        Collection keys) {
        return helper.call(keys);
    }

    public Object reduce(Session session,ObjectMap map) {
        EntityManager em = session.getEntityManager();
        Query q = em.createQuery("select m from MyInteger m " +
                                 "where m.integer > ?1 " +
                                 "and m.integer < ?2");
        query.setParameter(1, minValue);
```

```
        query.setParameter(2, maxValue);
        Iterator iter = q.getResultIterator();

        Collection<MyInteger> keys = new ArrayList<MyInteger)();

        while (iter.hasNext()) {
            MyInteger mi = (MyInteger)iter.next();
            keys.add(mi);
        }
        return reduce(session, map, keys);
    }

    public Object reduceResults(Collection results) {
        helper.call(results);
    }

    public getClassForEntity() {
        return MyInteger.class;
    }

    public void setMinValue(Integer min) {
        this.minValue = min;
    }

    public void setMaxValue(Integer max) {
        this.maxValue = max;
    }

    public void setHelper(MyHelper helper) {
        this.helper = helper;
    }
}
```

LargestIntReduceAgent's concern is interacting with the grid. Refactoring the
findLargestInt method into different classes keeps our code clean and more easily
testable. It also allows algorithm replacement. If we come up with a better map or a
reduce method, then the GridAgent implementation doesn't change.

LargestIntReduceAgent calls the helper.call(collection) method. The
AgentHelper class is serialized with the agent and sent to each partition the agent is
sent to. Once on the grid, the AgentHelper#call(collection) method is available
to the agent. The normal Java serialization process handles agent serialization.
Anything serializable in that processes is sent to the grid. Serializing these objects,
and sending them to the grid requires that the appropriate class files be on the
classpath of each ObjectGrid container process before the agent is sent to the grid.

Updates with agents

The agents we've seen so far are idempotent. They do not change any objects in the grid. They create new objects as a result of their operation but the objects queried by the agents remained unchanged.

There is no rule against updating objects in an agent. Any operation valid inside an ObjectGrid transaction can also be performed in an agent, including inserts, updates, and deletes. In this way, an agent doesn't necessarily need to perform a map or reduce operation. It acts as a code transport between the client and server. We should be cautious with this relaxed approach to agents because there is a lot of potential for abuse. Used with caution, running agents on the grid for inserts, updates, and deletes creates a powerful application controlled by submitting agents to the grid. Building an application around agents reduces the need for running large numbers of client processes.

Let's go back to our payment processor example to look at updates using a GridAgent. Specifically, we'll update a batch of deposit payments with a status of `BatchStatus.SENT_TO_NETWORK` after we receive the payments from the merchant and check for duplicates.

We need to make a choice between using a MapGridAgent and a ReduceGridAgent. The choice depends on the behavior our application needs with the result of the operation. If we want to do more work with each payment after it is sent to the network, then we choose a MapGridAgent. Because we only care that the payments are updated, we'll choose the ReduceGridAgent. ReduceGridAgent gives one result for the entire operation, which in this case is the status of the operation, either success or failure.

We don't have a particular known key set for all of the payments in a batch. A large batch has payments spread across nearly all partitions. We call our PaymentStatusReduceAgent with the `AgentManager#callReduceAgent(agent)` method:

```
PaymentStatusReduceAgent agent = new PaymentStatusReduceAgent();
agent.setBatch(batch);
agent.setFromStatus(PaymentStatus.WAITING);
agent.setToStatus(PaymentStatus.SENT_TO_NETWORK);

AgentManager am = session.getMap("Payment").getAgentManager();
am.callReduceAgent(agent);
```

We use the `AgentManager#callReduceAgent(agent)` method because we want all partitions in the grid to participate in the reduce operation. The reduce operation begins by finding all payments that match a certain criteria. We want all payments for a batch that have a status of `WAITING`. We set these properties on the agent so that the AgentManager serializes them and sends them to the grid along with the agent. They are used as query parameters in the `ReduceGridAgent#reduce(session, map)` method:

```
public Object reduce(Session session,ObjectMap map) {
    EntityManager em = session.getEntityManager();
    Query q = em.createQuery("select p from Payment p " +
                        "where p.batch = ?1 " +
                        "and p.status = ?2");
    query.setParameter(1, batch);
    query.setParameter(2, fromStatus);
    Iterator iter = q.getResultIterator();

    Collection<MyInteger> keys = new ArrayList<MyInteger)();

    while (iter.hasNext()) {
        Payment payment = (Payment)iter.next();
        keys.add(payment);
    }
    return reduce(session, map, keys);
}
```

We create a collection of payments to pass to the `ReduceGridAgent#reduce(session, map, keys)` method. In there, we perform the update payment status operations. Instead of an aggregate result based on calculations of objects in the grid, it is based on the success or failure of the update operations to each object. The `ReduceGridAgent#reduce(session, map, keys)` method returns a Boolean value if the update succeeds, and throws an exception if it does not:

```
public Object reduce(Session session, ObjectMap map,
  Collection keys) {
    try{
        Session s = session.getObjectGrid().getSession();
        EntityManager em = s.getEntityManager();

        Iterator iter = keys.iterator();
        while (iter.hasNext()) {
            Payment payment = (Payment)iter.next();
            payment.setStatus(toStatus);
            em.merge(payment);
        }
```

```
        return Boolean.TRUE;
    } catch(ObjectGridException e) {
        throw new ObjectGridRuntimeException(e);
    }
}
```

Throwing an exception doesn't exactly follow the spirit of the reduce operation. If the update operation fails, then the exception is thrown up the call stack and across the network to `AgentManager#callReduceAgent(agent)`. If the update operation fails, then we have bigger problems to worry about than the exception uncovered by the update operation. We throw the exception here because the situation is unrecoverable by the reduce operation. A call to `ReduceGridAgent#reduceResults (results)` is meaningless when there is an exception.

Absent from this code are explicit transaction demarcations. When the MapGridAgent and ReduceGridAgent methods are called, they are under an already-active transaction on the session passed in to them. Should the grid agent methods throw an exception, the transaction is rolled back. This transaction is independent of the client transaction and any other active agent transactions. If one of the agent transactions rolls back, then the client transaction rolls back too.

We see a few interesting things from the payment update implemented as a reduce operation. In the happy-path case, each agent will return `Boolean.TRUE`. We only return `Boolean.TRUE` to conform to the method signature. A collection of values of `Boolean.TRUE` is passed to the `ReduceGridAgent#reduceResults(Collection results)` method. There is nothing more to do in the reduce operation. The values in the results collection do not play any part in the update operation. The update was successful. We know this because an exception wasn't thrown in any of the reduce methods.

These two things let us implement a very simple `ReduceGridAgent#reduceResults (Collection results)` method:

```
public Object reduceResults(Collection results) {
    return null;
}
```

Either the update succeeds and we don't need to do any more, or we know the update failed by getting an exception thrown out of the `AgentManager#callReduceAgent(agent)` method. It may seem strange that we don't confirm the update is successful. Do we always explicitly check that JDBC updates were successful? No. We assume that because there was no thrown exception, the update happened. The same goes for our update in the ReduceGridAgent.

For clarity, let's look at the PaymentStatusReduceAgent in its entirety:

```
public class PaymentStatusReduceAgent implements ReduceGridAgent,
    EntityAgentMixin {

    private Batch batch;
    private PaymentStatus fromStatus;
    private PaymentStatus toStatus;

    public Object reduce(Session session, ObjectMap map,
      Collection keys) {
        try{
            Session s = session.getObjectGrid().getSession();
            EntityManager em = s.getEntityManager();

            Iterator iter = keys.iterator();

            em.getTransaction().begin();
            while (iter.hasNext()) {
                Payment payment = (Payment)iter.next();
                payment.setStatus(toStatus);
                em.merge(payment);
            }
            em.getTransaction().commit();
            return Boolean.TRUE;
        } catch(ObjectGridException e) {
            throw new ObjectGridRuntimeException(e);
        }

    }

    public Object reduce(Session session,ObjectMap map) {
        EntityManager em = session.getEntityManager();
        Query q = em.createQuery("select p from Payment p " +
                                 "where p.batch = ?1 " +
                                 "and p.status = ?2");
        query.setParameter(1, batch);
        query.setParameter(2, fromStatus);
        Iterator iter = q.getResultIterator();

        Collection<MyInteger> keys = new ArrayList<MyInteger)();

        while (iter.hasNext()) {
            Payment payment = (Payment)iter.next();
            keys.add(payment);
        }
        return reduce(session, map, keys);
    }
    public Object reduceResults(Collection results) {
```

```
        return null;
    }

    public getClassForEntity() {
        return Payment.class;
    }

    public void setBatch(Batch b) {
        this.batch = b;
    }

    public void setFromStatus(PaymentStatus status) {
        this.fromStatus = status;
    }

    public void setToStatus(PaymentStatus status) {
        this.toStatus = status;
    }
}
```

Scheduling agents

The AgentManager methods are blocking methods. A method call on any method in AgentManager remains at that point in execution, while the data grid runs the agent instances against its primary partitions. The thread that calls the AgentManager method must wait for a return from the call before it proceeds. In case blocking is unacceptable, we should schedule the call to the AgentManager methods using the `java.util.concurrent` API.

There are two cases to consider when thinking about scheduling agents. The first is with the `AgentManager#callReduceAgent(agent)` and `AgentManager#callMap Agent(agent)` methods. These methods do not pass any keys to the agents. In this case, the agent is executed on all primary partitions. It may be okay for a client application to block here while it waits for the result from the grid. Obviously, scheduling insert, update, and delete operations provides some performance improvement, if we work at the client-side in the future, that does not depend on those objects being in the grid (or not, as the case may be). A read operation where the client depends on the result before proceeding probably shouldn't schedule the agent.

One case where scheduling read operations is important is when we have multiple sets of keys passed to agents of the same type. Given a large object set, where the objects partition many different primaries, we don't want to pass the entire key set to an agent. For a sufficiently large key set, an agent will spend most of its time processing (ignoring) keys that do not belong to its partition. Instead, we can pre-sort the keys into collections of objects where all belong to the same partition. We then send the smaller, pre-sorted collections to the grid.

We determine an object's partition with a PartitionManager. Each BackingMap has a PartitionManager associated with it, which is obtained with the `BackingMap#get PartitionManager()` method. `PartitionManager#getPartition(Object key)` returns the 0-based partition number, which is the partition the PartitionManager puts the object in. This is easy when working with the ObjectMap API. Let's assume:

```
MyInteger mi = (MyInteger)myIntMap.get(35);
BackingMap map = session.getObjectGrid().getMap("MyInteger");

int partitionId = map.getPartitionManager().getPartition(35);
```

We don't need the first line. It only shows that we have a MyInteger with a key of 35. We obtain the ObjectGrid reference, and then the BackingMap for the MyInteger map from the session. We then call the `getPartition(key)` method for that same key. The result of this call is the ID of the partition that holds the MyInteger object with the key 35.

Now, we can use object and entity keys to sort objects based on partitions. After sorting the objects into smaller collections, we pass them to `AgentManager#callMap Agent(agent, keys)` and `AgentManager#callReduceAgent(agent, keys)`. These calls should now be scheduled in different threads, rather than making each call in a loop. If we then make these method calls in a loop, we then effectively turn the data grid into an expensive client program. The client program blocks during each call to the AgentManager methods. If we have 20 key collections that map to 20 different partitions, we will send only one request at a time to the grid if we send the agents in a loop. Instead, we want them to execute in parallel. We can do this by sending each instance of grid agent to the grid using a `java.util.concurrent.ExecutorService`.

Summary

We covered a lot of ground again in this chapter. Working with objects where they live produces much higher throughput than dragging objects to a client and pushing them back to the grid when we're done. Co-locating logic and data is easy to do with the DataGrid API.

DataGrid gives us a few patterns to follow when writing agents. It also makes us think in terms of map operations and reduce operations. Though these two methods seem limiting at first, they are useful when operating on very large data sets. The map operation gives us a way to perform an algorithm on each object in a set. The reduce operation lets us create aggregate results from a set.

We aren't limited to only sending logic to the grid with an agent. Thanks to Java serialization, we send any serializable object referenced by our agent to the grid along with it. This gives us flexibility in running queries in an agent, and in passing helper logic.

We also looked at pre-sorting objects into maps based on their partition ID. This reduces the size of the bytes sent from the client to a partition, and lets the agent run only for keys known to be in the partition the agent runs on.

With a little imagination, we can put more work on the grid. This gives us much higher throughput and scales horizontally with the resources given to our grid. Appropriately partitioned, a grid can scale out and return results at a predictable rate, no matter how many objects it stores.

8
Data Grid Patterns

Now that we have covered the major ObjectGrid APIs, we can look at how we apply them in our software projects. The concept of a design pattern has been around for long enough that experienced developers should know of a few. Patterns become part of the software nomenclature as they evolve and help us solve different problems. A pattern is not an API or library that we call directly, but a general outline for designing software. A pattern is a concept that is implementable in any programming language, and on any platform.

With the focus on reusable patterns, keep in mind the topics that we discuss in this chapter apply to any IMDG, not just WebSphere eXtreme Scale. We'll cover the eXtreme Scale implementation of these patterns.

IMDGs allow massive scale-out, horizontal deployment growth. In these situations, we solve a problem by throwing *more* hardware at it, not necessarily *more powerful* hardware like in a scale-up deployment. In this chapter, we'll cover how to classify problems as suitable for scale-out or scale-up deployments.

The data model used in an application is an important factor in building scalable software. We looked at locality of reference in previous chapters. In this chapter, we'll look at storing our objects as they are used, and breaking patterns that relational databases taught us.

In detail, this chapter covers:

- **XTP, extreme transaction processing**: Though not a new concept, we have new tools and patterns to build XTP systems.
- **Data modeling and usage patterns**: Effective data modeling for use with an IMDG looks a little different than a data model used in traditional ORM. Most notably, we use simpler data models here.
- **Getting the most out of object placement**: We revisit shard placement and the near-cache and how they work together to bring about ultra-high performance and scalability.

XTP: Extreme Transaction Processing

Recent industry focus may lead one to believe extreme transaction processing is a new concept. The concept isn't new, but we have new tools that make building XTP-classified systems easier. XTP is a fuzzy classification of software architecture and performance. XTP systems have three main responsibilities. They must offer high performance, scalability, and manageability. Other definitions exist, but these three things are consistent across all XTP definitions.

We have covered enough IMDG features, and the WebSphere eXtreme Scale APIs, to compare in-memory data grids with in-memory databases. In-memory databases were popular in the late-90s and early-00s as a way to build XTP-style applications. As we have seen, storing data in memory has a much lower latency than storing data on disk. An in-memory database allows SQL access to data since it's stored in rows and columns just like any other SQL-based database. In-memory databases are popular for smaller datasets thanks to the low-latency access to that data.

The in-memory databases use traditional database deployment topologies. Master-master, master-slave, and more complex topologies based on combinations of those two are possible. All writes must take place on a master instance, and each replica is used for read-only or backup purposes. Each database instance must be installed and configured to replicate the data in the master instance.

Performance using an IMDB is much higher, as compared to a disk-based approach. Using a hybrid approach and keeping a fraction of the data in memory while the rest is on disk is also possible. However, the scalability of such a system suffers. With only one box available for writes, the deployment can scale up and out until the master database instance reaches its limits.

The in-memory database is vulnerable to two kinds of limitations. First, the size of data stored in memory can exceed the size of each server memory. Fixing this involves scaling up, and therefore, we need a box with more memory. Scale-up typically involves extended downtime and presents a high-risk to data availability and integrity while we migrate the database instance to its new physical server. CPU and network bandwidth may be saturated too. Each replica instance presents additional workload to the master database instance. Each one requires CPU and network bandwidth to get a copy of the data from the master. Again, we can scale-up the master to service more replicas in addition to its transactional load. The master instance is a bottleneck that we just can't overcome by adding more hardware. When high performance is a requirement, without the need to grow web-scale application size, in-memory databases work very well. Though in-memory databases offer high performance required from XTP systems, they suffer from poor scalability and manageability. Like their disk-based cousins, IMDBs have their place in XTP systems.

As compared with in-memory databases, in-memory data grids offer much more for scalability and manageability. These two factors are closely related. Who wants to scale up to hundreds or thousands of nodes without good management? WebSphere eXtreme Scale provides scalability for reads, writes, and total data size through partitioning and shard placement. eXtreme Scale's scale-out requires no additional configuration. The `objectgrid.xml` and `ogdeployment.xml` files are the only files needed by eXtreme Scale to start additional nodes. The catalog service manages shard placement. Scale-out is a matter of starting a new container on a new box. eXtreme Scale takes care of the management. The catalog services handle shard placement, heart-monitoring, shard organization, and more. As these things are under the control of the catalog servers, we only need to provide container processes for the catalog services to use.

An IMDG also improves the performance offered by in-memory databases. IMDGs store data as POJOs, not rows and columns. There is no ORM required after getting an object from an IMDG. It is immediately usable by our application. A result set from an in-memory database requires an object/relational mapping framework to make the result set useful in our software. An IMDG provides inherently faster performance because it serves POJOs, instead of SQL result sets.

The data model

XTP is achieved by either scaling up or scaling out. Certain problem domains require scale-up, and others lend themselves well to scale-out. Scale-up deployments generally have a few computers that are very powerful. Scale-out deployments generally have many computers that are not the most powerful computers in the market.

The biggest factor in deciding scale-up versus scale-out is the data model. A non-partitionable data model lends itself better to a scale-up solution. Data is non-partitionable when a single step in an algorithm requires a large fraction (most or all) of the data available to the application. Partitioning the data causes significant performance reduction due to fetching of data from different locations, either in memory or on disk. Without high performance, we don't have an XTP system.

Before we go on, we should note that XTP is a subjective term. We've been doing XTP for years, though we may laugh at the throughput and performance of some XTP systems from 25 years ago. XTP is more about implementing the concepts, rather than comparing performance statistics. High performance is generally considered for a particular problem domain, not on an absolute scale. Airline reservation systems and financial trading systems are two examples of XTP-style apps that aren't close in terms of transactions-per-second. Airline reservation systems work with a limited number of flights, planes, and users making reservations doing thousands of transactions per second. Banks' electronic trading systems need to do hundreds of thousands to millions of transactions per second. Both applications are classified as XTP.

Remember that locality of reference is important for performance. It's the reason we send grid agents to an ObjectGrid to do work there, rather than drag objects back to the client. With a non-partitionable data model, our work and our data must be located on a massive SMP box within a single 64-bit address space. If we are unable to create logical data partitions, we cannot scale out. Scale-up is the only choice we can make. As the data set in a non-partitionable data model grows, we need to make more storage available to the box. An in-memory database running on this box would require more memory. The CPU may be pegged continuously at 99 percent. The only way to scale-up is by migrating to a new, more powerful computer. Scale-up is the brute-force solution to achieving XTP with non-partitionable data models. The WebSphere eXtreme Scale team classifies this style of XTP system as type 1.

A partitionable data model is one where a single step in an algorithm requires a small fraction of the total data available in the system. An algorithm which operates on one customer, one user, one payment, one trade, one frame, or one picture out of millions is an algorithm that works with a partitionable data model. All of the data required by the transaction must exist in the same address space as the root entity. We constrain the accessible data model to one address space because the entirety of the data model does not fit in one address space.

Schema root

Putting this in eXtreme Scale terms, a partitionable data model is one where one transaction works with one *root entity* and its children. Of course, the root entity is Entity API-specific. We can build XTP systems using the ObjectMap API as well. Each object in an ObjectMap is analogous to the root entity when using the Entity API.

What exactly do we mean by *root entity*? The Entity annotation gives us a `schemaRoot` property. We set it to `true` or `false` to denote a class being a schema root:

```
@Entity(schemaRoot=true)
@javax.persistence.Entity
public class LineItem implements Serializable {
    @javax.persistence.Id
    @Id int id;
    int accountId;
    int amount;
// getters and setters omitted
}
```

Large data models look like graphs. The relationships between different classes may not give unique paths to a node object. The first step in using eXtreme Scale with an application, and enabling XTP, is distilling all or part of a data model to a constrained tree. Billy Newport calls this a constrained tree schema.

Constrained trees are trees with a limited depth. In a tree, each object is reachable from the root node. This may not be true for a graph-like data model. A constrained tree does not need to encompass the entirety of the graph-like data model. In fact, it is probably only a subset of the total data model when starting to use eXtreme Scale with an existing application.

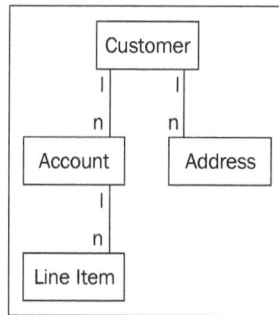

A new application is not burdened with translating a graph data model to a constrained tree data model. A new application can build the data model with each class reachable from the root right from the start. An existing data model should be studied to see where the largest gains from using the XTP concepts are.

Let's work with the example of a customer having many accounts. Each account has many line items. This fits the definition of our constrained tree schema. It has a limited depth, and all nodes are reachable from the entity root. In this case, our entity root is the customer. Customer became the entity root almost by default here. We picked the class that sits at the top of the object hierarchy and made it the entity root.

eXtreme Scale partitions objects based on the entity root. With Customer as the schema root, its child entities (and their children) are all placed on the same partition as the root entity. It is placed in the grid that would look something like as shown below:

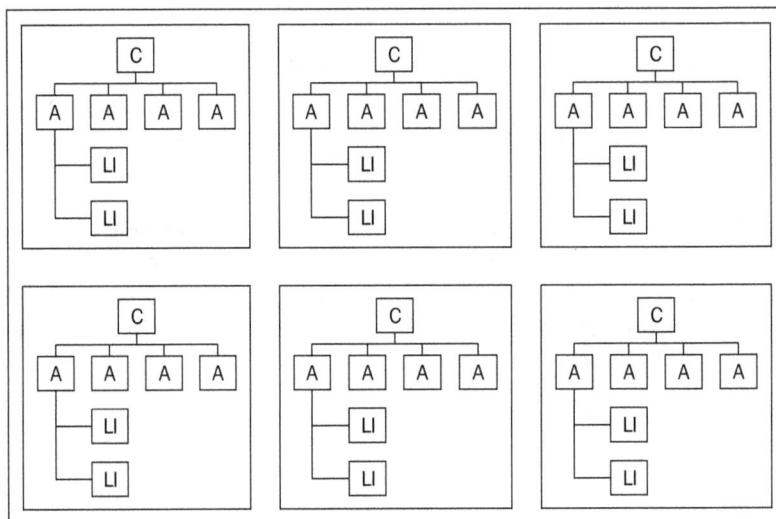

Each large square represents a partition.

When each customer has roughly the same number of accounts, and each account has roughly the same number of line items, then each eXtreme Scale container experiences roughly the same load as the other containers in the deployment.

When certain customers accumulate more accounts, and certain accounts accumulate significantly more line items than others, we start to run into a load balancing problem. If enough big customers or big accounts are placed in shards on the same container, then that container will experience higher load than the other containers in the deployment. When an entity's descendants have wildly varying sizes, we may want to reconsider using that as our schema root.

Rather than making customer the schema root, we can make account the schema root. We already established that there are many more accounts than customers. Our schema now looks similar to the following image:

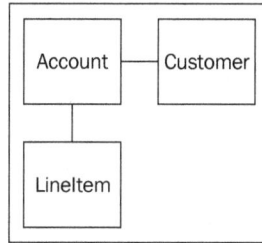

With account as the schema root, we only care that the number of line items per account are roughly equal. In this case, "roughly equal" may mean the same order of magnitude. What happens to the customer? It becomes *reference data* in the grid. Reference data is the data which we don't mind duplicating (duplicating is not replicating) in multiple partitions. This is duplication at the application level, not at the ObjectGrid replica shard level. This means we get something as shown in the following diagram:

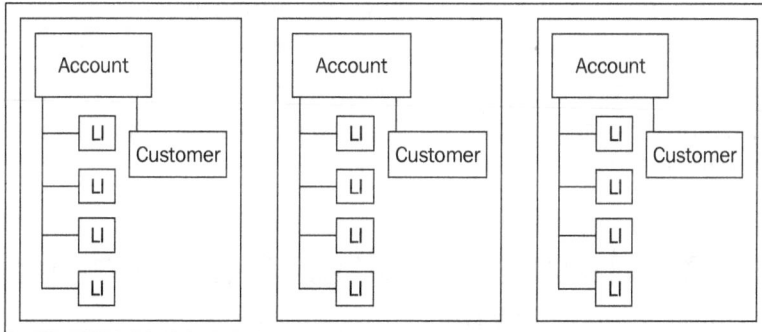

Each large rectangle represents a partition.

Now, let's look at the situation where accounts have a wildly different number of line items. Obviously, this means looking at line item as the schema root:

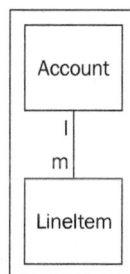

LineItem has a many-to-one relationship with Account.

Partitioning now takes place based on line items. We know we have many more line items than accounts and customers. The account each line item belongs to is now reference data along with the customer:

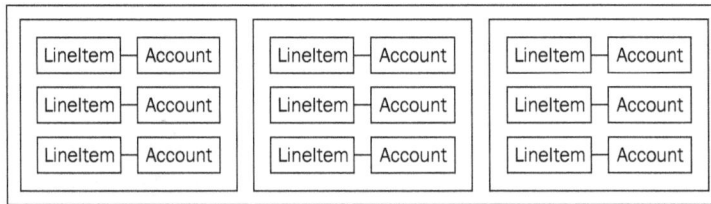

Each large rectangle represents a partition.

Even simple constrained trees give us different ways to partition our data model. Choosing the right schema root is important in giving us predictable scalability. The guidelines we should follow when choosing a schema root are:

- Choose a class that has a high number of runtime instances
- Consider the size and number of descendants of the root entity
- Don't be afraid to look at non-obvious choices for schema root
- Transactions should work on constrained tree schemas that are about the same size at runtime.

Reference data and object duplication

Previously in this chapter, we briefly touched on reference data as part of CTS. Reference data consists of objects that are not the object we partition on. In the case where we use line item as the tree root, we have account and customer as reference data. This reference data doesn't typically change often. It's there to give the root entity context.

If we have orders of magnitude more line items than accounts and customers, then we would create a line item, and set its account to the right parent account. We would then use the entity manager to insert the new line item into the grid. The insert operation places the line item in the correct partition. With a Loader configured, the line item is saved to the database:

```
for (int i = 0; i < 1000; i++) {
    LineItem item = new LineItem();
    item.setId(i);
    Account account = (Account)accounts.get(
                        (int)(Math.random() * 100));
    item.setAccountId(account.getId());
    item.setAmount(250 + i);
```

```
            try {
                em.getTransaction().begin();
                em.persist(item);
                em.getTransaction().commit();
            } catch (Exception e) {
                e.printStackTrace();
            }
        }
    }
```

We define the Account as an ObjectMap, not an Entity, with a JPALoader as the Loader plug-in. Account is not defined as an Entity due to the difficulty persisting many-to-one relationships where the non-owning side (Account) is not defined as the schema root:

```xml
<objectGridConfig>
    <objectGrids>
        <objectGrid name="AccountGrid"
                    entityMetadataXMLFile="ppEntities.xml">

            <bean id="TransactionCallback"
                className=
                "com.ibm.websphere.objectgrid.jpa.JPATxCallback">
                <property name="persistenceUnitName"
                        type="java.lang.String"
                        value="Account" />
            </bean>

            <backingMap name="Account"
                    ttlEvictorType="CREATION_TIME"
                    timeToLive="43200"
                    evictionTriggers="MEMORY_USAGE_THRESHOLD"
                    pluginCollectionRef="Account" />

            <backingMap name="LineItem"
                    pluginCollectionRef="LineItem" />
        </objectGrid>
    </objectGrids>

    <backingMapPluginCollections>
        <backingMapPluginCollection id="Account">
            <bean id="Loader"
                className=
                    "com.ibm.websphere.objectgrid.jpa.JPALoader">
                <property name="entityClassName"
                        type="java.lang.String"
                        value="wxs.sample.models.Account"/>
            </bean>
        </backingMapPluginCollection>

        <backingMapPluginCollection id="LineItem">
```

```
<bean id="Loader"
    className=
    "com.ibm.websphere.objectgrid.jpa.JPAEntityLoader">
    <property name="entityClassName"
              type="java.lang.String"
              value="wxs.sample.models.LineItem"/>
</bean>
</backingMapPluginCollection>

</backingMapPluginCollections>
</objectGridConfig>
```

Applications are built on transactional data. We've been conditioned to normalize transactional data as much as possible. Normalization reduces data duplication so that a datastore has only factual data, and any derivable data is not included in the datastore. This is acceptable when the entirety of the datastore is located on one box.

When data is distributed, we've already seen that locality of reference is important for performance and scalability. Rather than saturating an authoritative source for derivable data, we should calculate and duplicate that data if it is mostly static.

In ObjectGrid terms, that means we should duplicate the contents of the Account BackingMap in each partition that needs access to Accounts.

Duplicating data makes sense when the data is small enough to fit into a single JVM and does not change often. The entire map doesn't need to fit in a single JVM. Maybe we're only interested in Accounts that have been touched in the last 24 hours.

Duplicating data is acceptable with an IMDG because reference data is cheap to store compared to transactional data. Reference data should be orders of magnitude smaller than transactional data, the class on which we base partitioning. We throw enough hardware at storing our transactional data with plenty of room to grow the deployment, so duplicating reference data should not be a capacity planning concern.

How do we duplicate objects?

Duplicating objects takes place on the ObjectGrid partition level. We're saying, we have LineItems partitioned across the grid, and we want to look up to a parent account.

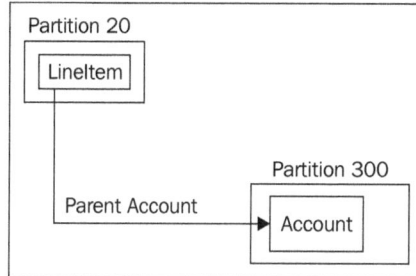

Our Account BackingMap is partitioned just like the LineItem BackingMap (as seen above). So far, this is no different from what we've been doing. Here, a LineItem references an Account that lives in a different container process. We want to avoid a network hop to other container process when working with that LineItem in the grid.

In the previous chapter, we worked with the DataGrid API. We'll work with it again here, so we can work directly on the partitions. Recall how the `ReduceGrid Agent#reduce(session, map, collection)` and `ReduceGridAgent#reduce(se ssion, map)` work with an AgentManager. When called with a collection of keys, the AgentManager has some work to do. If we pass a collection of keys that spans multiple partitions, then the AgentManager separates those keys based on the partition to which they belong to, before passing each subset of properly sorted keys to each grid agent. In this way, the grid agent gets only the keys that map to the partition where the grid agent runs:

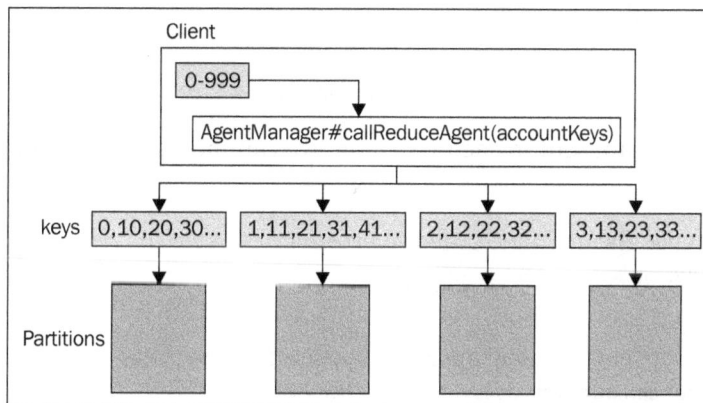

Let's see an example of that behavior in the ReduceGridAgent#reduce (session, map, collection) method. Let's build a grid agent that just displays the keys that it works with:

```
public class AccountReduceAgent implements ReduceGridAgent {

    @Override
    public Object reduce(Session session, ObjectMap map) {
        return null;
    }

    @Override
    public Object reduce(Session arg0,
                         ObjectMap arg1,
                         Collection arg2) {
        for (Object o : arg2) {
            int i = (Integer)o;
            System.out.println("Working with key: " + i);
        }
        return null;
    }

    @Override
    public Object reduceResults(Collection arg0) {
        System.out.println("DONE!");
        return null;
    }

}
```

Now, we'll call that grid agent from the LineItemProcessor:

```
Collection<Integer> c = new ArrayList<Integer>();
for (int i = 0; i < 1000; i++) {
    c.add(i);
}
am.callReduceAgent(new AccountReduceAgent(), c);
```

As all 1000 keys are not sent to each partition, we cannot rely on this reduce method to duplicate objects.

Instead, we can use the ReduceGridAgent#reduce(session, map) method to duplicate objects:

```
    @Override
    public Object reduce(Session session, ObjectMap map) {
        System.out.println("STARTING AGENT");
        try {
```

```
        Session s = session.getObjectGrid().getSession();
        ObjectMap m = s.getMap(map.getName());

        Account account = (Account)m.getAll(keys);

    } catch (Exception e) {
        throw new ObjectGridRuntimeException(e);
    }
    return true;
}
```

Calling the `ObjectMap#getAll(list of keys)` method on the Account map is our goal. We call the `getAll(list of keys)` method with the expectation that it returns our Account value objects. This agent runs on every partition in the grid. In every partition, the agent calls `ObjectMap#getAll(list of keys)` for all 1000 keys in the collection.

Our Account BackingMap does not have a value for all 1000 objects in the key collection though. In order for this to work, we need to configure the Account BackingMap with a JPALoader.

For completeness, let's look at the entire `objectgrid.xml` file:

```xml
<?xml version="1.0" encoding="UTF-8"?>
<objectGridConfig xmlns:xsi="http://www.w3.org/2001/XMLSchema-
instance"
    xsi:schemaLocation="http://ibm.com/ws/objectgrid/config ../
objectGrid.xsd"
    xmlns="http://ibm.com/ws/objectgrid/config">
    <objectGrids>
        <objectGrid name="AccountGrid"
                    entityMetadataXMLFile="ppEntities.xml">

         <bean id="TransactionCallback"
           className="com.ibm.websphere.objectgrid.jpa.JPATxCallback">
                <property name="persistenceUnitName"
                          type="java.lang.String"
                          value="Account" />
         </bean>

            <backingMap name="Account"
                        pluginCollectionRef="Account" />
            <backingMap name="LineItem"
                        pluginCollectionRef="LineItem" />
            <backingMap name="IBM_SYSTEM_MAP_defaultMapSet" />
        </objectGrid>
    </objectGrids>
```

```
<backingMapPluginCollections>
    <backingMapPluginCollection id="Account">
        <bean id="Loader"
          className="com.ibm.websphere.objectgrid.jpa.JPALoader">
            <property name="entityClassName"
                      type="java.lang.String"
                      value="wxs.sample.models.Account"/>
        </bean>
    </backingMapPluginCollection>

    <backingMapPluginCollection id="LineItem">
        <bean id="Loader"
className="com.ibm.websphere.objectgrid.jpa.JPAEntityLoader">
            <property name="entityClassName"
                      type="java.lang.String"
                      value="wxs.sample.models.LineItem"/>
        </bean>
    </backingMapPluginCollection>

</backingMapPluginCollections>
</objectGridConfig>
```

With a JPALoader, the Account BackingMap performs a read-through to the database when the Account with key *key* is not found in the BackingMap. Using the `ObjectMap#get(key)` method loads the Account object into the BackingMap on the partition where the agent runs. This is repeatable across all partitions:

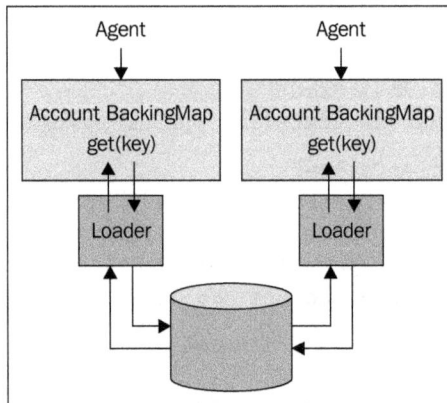

Now this agent loads Accounts with keys 0-999 in all partitions in the grid. The two important points to remember are:

- `ObjectMap#get(key)` still functions as described way back when we first discovered Loaders. If an object is not found in a BackingMap with a Loader, the GET method acts as a read-through to the database. If the object is present in the database, it is loaded into the BackingMap in the requesting partition.

- Once in the grid agent, a call to `ObjectMap#get(key)` loads an object that keys to any partition. We can load objects from maps that don't correspond to the map from which we obtained the AgentManager.

Coding the keys into the agent method obviously isn't the best thing to do for production systems. More realistically, we would duplicate accounts based on an operation to LineItems. We'll use `LineItemReduceAgent` for that:

```
public class LineItemReduceAgent implements ReduceGridAgent {

    @Override
    public Object reduce(Session session, ObjectMap map) {
        System.out.println("STARTING LineItemReduceAgent");
        try {
            Session s = session.getObjectGrid().getSession();
            ObjectMap m = s.getMap(map.getName());
            ObjectMap accounts = s.getMap("Account");
            Query q = s.getEntityManager().createQuery("select item
                    from LineItem item");

            s.getEntityManager().getTransaction().begin();
            Iterator iter = q.getResultIterator();

            while (iter.hasNext()) {
                LineItem item = (LineItem)iter.next();
                Account account =
                    (Account)accounts.get(item.getAccount().getId());
                String line = "\nWorking with line item: " +
                            item.getId() +
                                "\n--- Account ID: " +
                            account.getId();
                System.out.println(line);
            }

            s.getEntityManager().getTransaction().rollback();
        } catch (Exception e) {
            throw new ObjectGridRuntimeException(e);
        }
        return null;
```

```
    }

    @Override
    public Object reduce(Session arg0, ObjectMap arg1, Collection
        arg2) {
        // TODO Auto-generated method stub
        return null;
    }

    @Override
    public Object reduceResults(Collection arg0) {
        System.out.println("DONE!");
        return null;
    }


}
```

Our reduce agent performs a Query to find all LineItems in this partition. A Query does not perform an `ObjectMap#get(key)` operation. It operates on the BackingMap, without reading-through to the database. The Query is for data in the grid only.

Iterating over each LineItem, we look up the Account associated with it. This Account is not the Account managed by a BackingMap. Instead, this Account object is from the JPA relationship between LineItem and Account.

```
<entity class="wxs.sample.models.Account" access="FIELD">
    <attributes>
        <id name="id"/>
    </attributes>
</entity>

<entity class="wxs.sample.models.LineItem" access="FIELD">
    <attributes>
        <id name="id"/>
        <many-to-one name="account"
                     target-entity="wxs.sample.models.Account"
                     fetch="LAZY"/>
    </attributes>
</entity>
```

The example above shows that it is possible to maintain JPA relationships between JPA entities and not use ObjectGrid Entities. We use this relationship to get the Account ID which is the key for the Account BackingMap.

After obtaining the Account ID, we perform an `ObjectMap#get(key)` operation with that ID. For every line item in this partition, we look up the Account in the BackingMap. If the Account is not in the BackingMap in this partition, the BackingMap performs a read-through to the database and loads it in this partition. The result is an Account BackingMap populated with every unique Account for each LineItem in this partition. It could be a subset of all Account objects, or it could be the complete set.

Rather than storing the JPA relationship Account object along with each LineItem, we should store a soft-reference to the Account. Storing the Account object with every line item is wasteful and *does* impact grid capacity. Storing an Account once per partition is okay, but storing an Account with each of a million LineItems is not.

We briefly touched on soft-references when we first discussed Loaders. A **soft-reference** is a reference to an object by some key, managed manually. It is not a managed relationship, as provided by JPA or ObjectGrid Entities. Instead of setting a reference to the parent Account, a LineItem stores the Account ID as an integer value:

```
@Entity(schemaRoot=true)
@javax.persistence.Entity
public class LineItem implements Serializable {
    @javax.persistence.Id
    @Id int id;
    int accountId;
    int amount;
// getters and setters omitted
}
```

The JPA `orm.xml` file looks like this:

```
<entity class="wxs.sample.models.Account" access="FIELD">
    <attributes>
        <id name="id"/>
    </attributes>
</entity>

<entity class="wxs.sample.models.LineItem" access="FIELD">
    <attributes>
        <id name="id"/>
    </attributes>
</entity>
```

We just removed the many-to-one mapping between LineItem and Account. JPA automatically handles the Account ID field because it is a non-transient primitive type.

Setting the Account ID on a LineItem now looks like this:

```
for (int i = 0; i < 10000; i++) {
    LineItem item = new LineItem();
    item.setId(i);
    Account account = (Account)
                        accounts.get((int)(Math.random() * 100));
    item.setAccountId(account.getId());
    item.setAmount(250 + i);

    try {
        em.getTransaction().begin();
        em.persist(item);
        em.getTransaction().commit();
    } catch (Exception e) {
        e.printStackTrace();
    }
}
```

And the `LineItemReduceAgent` looks like:

```
public Object reduce(Session session, ObjectMap map) {
    System.out.println("STARTING LineItemReduceAgent");
    try {
        Session s = session.getObjectGrid().getSession();
        ObjectMap m = s.getMap(map.getName());
        ObjectMap accounts = s.getMap("Account");

        Query q = s.getEntityManager()
                    .createQuery("select item from LineItem item");

        s.getEntityManager().getTransaction().begin();
        Iterator iter = q.getResultIterator();

        while (iter.hasNext()) {
            LineItem item = (LineItem)iter.next();
            Account account =
                (Account)accounts.get(item.getAccountId());
            String line = "\nWorking with line item: " +
                            item.getId() +
                            "\n--- Account ID: " +
                            account.getId();
            System.out.println(line);

        }
        s.getEntityManager().getTransaction().rollback();
```

```
    } catch (Exception e) {
        throw new ObjectGridRuntimeException(e);
    }
    return null;
}
```

Removing the Account from each LineItem reduces the amount of data grid storage required for each LineItem. The right way to duplicate the Account data is on a per-partition basis, not a per-object basis. Calling the `ObjectMap#get(key)` method from within an agent method will load the object into the Account BackingMap because the Account BackingMap is configured with a JPALoader. Once in the BackingMap on each partition where it is needed, the Account object is available without a read-through to the database. It is stored in the BackingMap. In this way, we can lazy-load duplicate objects across the grid. This eliminates the network hops to other grid nodes for data lookup.

Time-to-live keeps us out of trouble

Duplicating objects across partitions is great for locality of reference. Duplicating enough objects leads to OutOfMemoryExceptions. We need to keep enough data in the memory to be useful, but not so much that our grid crashes after loading too many objects. The time-to-live property on BackingMap helps us avoid this problem.

The time-to-live property tells a BackingMap how long to keep an object in the memory. After that time has elapsed, the object is eligible for eviction from the BackingMap. Eviction takes place with an Evictor plug-in. Most commonly, we use the (default) time-to-live evictor, LRUEvictor, and LFUEvictor.

The LRU and LFU evictors are based on the usual suspects of least-recently used, and least-frequently used objects. We can avoid trouble with our duplicated Account objects by setting an LRUEvictor as its BackingMap evictor. We give it a time-to-live of 12 hours:

```
<backingMap name="Account"
            ttlEvictorType="CREATION_TIME"
            timeToLive="43200"
            pluginCollectionRef="Account" />
```

That Account may be removed 12 hours after inserting an Account into a BackingMap. A call to `ObjectMap#get(key)` after eviction triggers another read-through operation, if the BackingMap has a Loader.

Storing objects for 12 hours may be acceptable on a frequently accessed server. A client process with a near-cache probably doesn't want to store objects for that long. This is a great time to create an `objectgrid.xml` file for client use only. The setting in this file is merged with the container processes settings when a client obtains a reference to a grid. These merged settings only affect the client-side near-cache. Settings on container processes are not changed.

```
<backingMap name="Account"
            ttlEvictorType="CREATION_TIME"
            timeToLive="600"
            pluginCollectionRef="Account" />

<backingMap name="LineItem" pluginCollectionRef="LineItem" />
```

The client-side near-cache stores Account objects in its local BackingMap for just 10 minutes (as seen above). This should be enough time to process all line items that refer to an account, and not so long that keeping it around for 10 minutes is detrimental to client performance and memory allocation.

Early eviction

The best planning is still subject to unexpected load. BackingMap evictors and TTL are no different. We've set the container-side TTL to 12 hours, and the client-side near-cache TTL to 10 minutes, but the BackingMaps may fill up under load. If BackingMap fills up before the evictor removes stale objects, then we run in to the OutOfMemoryException that we tried to avoid by setting a reasonable TTL.

ObjectGrid containers can trigger early eviction based on the used heap percentage. We do this in a container server properties file. An example of this file is found in your `$ObjectGridHome/properties` directory. Look for the line that has the `memoryThresholdPercentage` setting:

```
memoryThresholdPercentage=-1
```

By default, the memory threshold that triggers eviction is not set to any meaningful value. If we want eviction to start when we use 70 percent of heap space, we put:

```
memoryThresholdPercentage=70
```

We tell our Account BackingMap to use memory-based eviction by adding an additional eviction trigger property to the container-side `objectgrid.xml` configuration file:

```
<backingMap name="Account"
            ttlEvictorType="CREATION_TIME"
            timeToLive="600"
            evictionTriggers="MEMORY_USAGE_THRESHOLD"
            pluginCollectionRef="Account" />
```

Specifying the evictionTriggers property triggers the evictor when the JVM heap is 70 percent full. Under unexpected load, there may not be any objects that meet the normal eviction criteria. When this happens, and until the heap usage is used below 70 percent, the evictor removes objects that are most qualified for removal. When `CREATION_TIME` is the `ttlEvictorType`, the "most qualified" objects are the oldest objects. If there are 100 objects, and the 10 oldest were created only 11 hours ago, then those 10 objects will be removed. The number of objects removed from a BackingMap in this way grows until heap usage is back under the threshold usage amount.

Memory heap-based eviction is not a cure-all. It is still possible for heap usage to grow to 100 percent and crash a container process if the load is too intense. Also, memory heap-based eviction does not work with generational garbage collectors. A non-generational garbage collector must be used with memory-based eviction. Memory heap-based eviction is just another tool in keeping our grid available longer while the load subsides naturally or administratively. Even the best capacity and load planning is subject to unexpected spikes. Gracefully handling these spikes is a market place expectation. It is still possible to get into trouble using the TTL, LRU, and LFU eviction methods. Keep this in mind when building grid applications. Remember that an additional evictionTrigger based on heap usage can save off that trouble while you come up with a way to handle the unexpected spike in demand. This is a great problem to have, if your application suddenly becomes very popular.

Rely on partitions, not the entire grid

Working with a data grid is different than working with a database because our objects are distributed. The centralized nature of data in a database has bred some bad habits that work against us when building scalable software.

When we query a database table, we query a complete set of data. That query runs in the database query engine and returns matching rows. One query runs against one database instance. An IMDG presents many partitions on many boxes.

Our goal in running a distributed system is workload isolation. Based on object key, we know which partition holds a particular object. We get that object directly with an `ObjectMap#get(key)` or `EntityManager#find(class, id)` call. This is analogous to querying a single database table by primary key only.

Obviously, all database queries are not confined to a single table using its primary key. A user login, for example, doesn't require the user to enter the primary key of the row that corresponds to their user data. A user logs in with their username.

By using a database, we would query the Users table after the user authenticates and loads their user data into the app server. With a normalized data model, a user BackingMap is keyed by a User ID. Querying for that same data in an IMDG requires a grid agent. We could make a class that implements ReduceGridAgent and send it to the grid to find a user matching the user that just authenticated.

Though this implementation is easy, it is a waste of grid resources. Every user login requires every partition in the grid to search for that user. Only one partition at most can return the user object. The other N-partitions just wasted CPU time that could have been used for other queries.

This anti-pattern is easily avoided by keeping in mind the following two guidelines:

- Don't use every grid node for every operation. Objects are distributed, so we can work with a subset when we do meaningful work.
- Store data in the way that it will be used. Duplicating data is encouraged when it enables horizontal scalability.

Let's look at both of these in a little more detail.

One transaction, one node

We partition data so that the grid supports more clients than a master-multi-slave database topology. Clients that rely on the entire grid reduce the scalability and throughput for all other applications using that grid. When clients submit agents like the user query agent, it's as if we're querying the monolithic database. We're treating the grid as one big box instead of hundreds of containers, across hundreds of boxes. Building clients that utilize the entire grid for most operations is not horizontally scalable. Getting higher throughput from the grid topology requires faster servers, instead of more commodity hardware. This defeats the purpose of using a data grid.

Each container in the grid services multiple clients. As long as each container in the grid isn't servicing the *same* clients, we achieve near-linear scalability. Clients need to use keys when searching for individual objects. In the case of user login, we need to lookup the user object by its key. The user hasn't provided their key, though they provided a name.

Object schema denormalization

Rather than struggling with finding the user by their ID, we create a new BackingMap of user objects keyed by username. After authentication, we use the username to lookup the user object in the BackingMap. As we have the key to the BackingMap, the client is routed to the one partition that contains the user object. The login process now touches just one partition, in one container, instead of all partitions.

Denormalizing data so that it is stored in a way it is used is a key component in building horizontally scalable software. Each node must increase the total number of simultaneously supported clients. If each node processes the same requests from every client, then the grid would support a static number of clients.

No matter how much hardware was thrown at it, the number of clients would remain the same. Squeezing more power out of this requires faster computers. If each node independently supports 20 clients when the clients know they need data on that node, we can add a node and support 20 clients out of the box. Each node added increases the total grid capacity by 20 new clients.

We may find that we have many maps that store data on how it is used. Each map may key a value object, or a soft-reference to another map. The user map may return a User ID when `ObjectMap#get(key)` is called. The User ID is then the key for all other maps where we store user-related data.

When we use an IMDG, we assume that storage is cheap for concerns other than the problem we are trying to solve. As long as we don't duplicate the objects that we partition, we can denormalize a duplicate data until we have something fast and predictably scalable. The predictable piece is the most important.

Going a little bit further into predictable scaling, we assume that we have a website where users can send and receive messages and comments. In this case, we'll partition on users, and each user has many comments and many messages.

Let's say we want a page where each user can see their comment and message history. Using a database query, we would query the comments and messages table for all rows with a User ID of **X**. This database supports a static number of clients.

Using a normalized object schema, we would use a ReduceGridAgent to query all partitions that hold the Comment map and Message map for all objects that have the matching User ID. Again, we don't want the entire grid performing one operation. Instead, we'll denormalize the comments and messages.

As all of the comments and messages displayed on the page belong to one user, we create a BackingMap called UserMessages. The UserMessages map is keyed by User ID. Its value is a hash of array lists that contain the comments and messages associated with this user. The hash has an array list for user sent messages, user received messages, user posted comments, and replies to user comments.

Whenever a user makes a comment, that comment is stored in the Comment BackingMap, and in the UserMessages map in the user posted comments bucket. When another user replies to that comment, it is stored in the Comment map, also in their UserMessages bucket, and the original comment poster's bucket.

Getting all comments and messages that belong to a user is much easier now. Let's look at how it's done:

1. Log in with a username. Look up user object in username-keyed BackingMap.

2. User ID is stored in the user object.

3. User goes to their messages and comments page.

4. UserMessages is keyed by User ID, which we already have. Look up all user messages and comments in the map by using this key.

This creates a predictably scalable application. I don't get all of my user comments in one network hop like I would with a database, but my grid supports a lot more simultaneous clients. This lookup also has the added benefit of a finite number of network hops to find the data in O(1) time. This lookup is done in two network hops every time. No matter how many users, comments, or messages are added to the BackingMaps, this operation is completed in two hops. One hop to look up the User ID, and another to get all comments and messages. The lookup is based on one key and one value object. It does not depend on the size of the BackingMap, or the size of a database table. Two network hops and an O(1) lookup every time, regardless of data size, is predictable and fast.

A more resource-conservative approach would store comments keyed by an ID in a Comments BackingMap. The Comment ID is stored in a CommentList on a User object. This approach still uses two hops and does not duplicate the comment text.

Summary

As usual, we covered a lot of ground in this chapter. Although we dealt mostly with concepts and patterns that apply to any IMDG, we saw plenty of WebSphere eXtreme Scale example code.

We started the chapter with XTP. XTP systems require high-performance, high-scalability, and strong manageability. In the past years, we've had middleware that supply all three to varying degrees of success. IMDGs are new tools used to build XTP-class software due to their leaps forward in scalability and manageability. Co-locating data and application logic in the same JVM offers huge performance increase over previous generations of tools.

A common requirement when using IMDGs is a reduction of network hops. Accessing data stored exclusively in different partitions is a scalability limitation when using a grid. We duplicate data where it is used, instead of fetching it every time. We saw in depth how to duplicate objects in each partition when needed.

Staying on the data duplication theme, we discussed the advantages of denormalizing and duplicating data based on usage, not strict normalization rules. Duplicating data eliminates the need for queries because we look up data by key instead. If we didn't duplicate the data and message it into the key/value form, we would be limited in throughput because each container would need to perform a query for a client.

Relying on just one partition for an operation increases the horizontal scalability of our grid, along with the number of simultaneous clients it supports. When we duplicate data and put it in key/value form, we can get our data workflow down to a predictable number of network hops and O(1) lookups. We duplicate data because storage is cheap and predictable. Manageable scalability is more valuable than data storage.

Spring Integration

9

If you've been working with Java professionally for a while, then you must have at least heard of the Spring framework. Spring does a lot of things, but its most important function is that of an inversion of control container. Rather than looking up for dependencies in our class, we inject the dependencies. This opens up the possibility of injecting WebSphere eXtreme Scale beans into our Spring-wired software. Now that we have seen the different WebSphere eXtreme Scale APIs and configuration files, we can integrate it with applications built using the Spring framework.

Injecting WebSphere eXtreme Scale beans into our software implies that we can configure the WebSphere eXtreme Scale components as beans in the first place. This chapter walks through the process of creating reusable WebSphere eXtreme Scale configuration beans that can be used in any application which requires an ObjectGrid instance. The eXtreme Scale/Spring integration goes the other way too. We can use Spring-defined beans in our WebSphere eXtreme Scale configuration files. Making a consistent, reusable WebSphere eXtreme Scale client or server configuration available to different project teams is much easier with Spring-defined beans.

One more thing that we will pay close attention to is Spring's transaction management. Throughout the book, we've manually managed our ObjectGrid transactions. Spring gladly handles transaction management for us as long as we provide both Spring and ObjectGrid with the correct configuration.

When we're done with this chapter, we'll be able to:

- Define reusable ObjectGrid beans in a Spring bean definitions file, and use those beans in a project
- Configure ObjectGrid instances using Spring-defined beans
- Let Spring manage our ObjectGrid transactions
- Use the ObjectMap and Entity APIs from within a Spring-managed transaction
- Configure an ObjectGrid client application using Spring

Injecting ObjectGrid instances

One of the most important things you'll do when using WebSphere eXtreme Scale with Spring is wiring the instances of ObjectGrid, Session, or EntityManager into data access layers. A common application activity is finding and saving users to some data store. Let's see how we would do it with a data grid. If we have an existing DAO interface like this:

```
public interface UserDAO {
    public User find(int id);
    User find(String username);
    public void addUser(User user);
}
```

We expect to use any implementation of this in our application. Chances are that we have an implementation that uses an ORM framework with a database backing it. Calling methods on implementations of this DAO are probably already established, and we should conform to the expected usage when we try to work WebSphere eXtreme Scale into the development environment. This means that our implementation should not require any setup or initialization beyond what can be accomplished via dependency injection. Dependency lookup from within a WebSphere eXtreme Scale implementation is a bad form, and isn't reusable.

```
<bean id="hibernateUserDAO"
    class="net.anthonychaves.bookmarks.dao.HibernateUserDAO">
        <property name="txnManager" ref="transactionManager"/>
        <property name="sessionFactory" ref="hibernateSessionFactory"/>
</bean>
```

An existing implementation is seen above. The `HibernateUserDAO` bean provides the two find methods, and the add user method without revealing any of its implementation details to the developer. It also doesn't perform any resource lookup because any additional beans it needs, such as a transaction manager and session factory, are provided to it by wiring those pre-defined beans into the `HibernateUserDAO` definition. We need to provide something like this for the WebSphere eXtreme Scale implementation.

It may be easier to show one of the find methods in our implementation before we move on to wiring the Spring beans. It will help us wire what's most useful to us by seeing our dependencies in one of the method implementations:

```
public class ObjectGridUserDAO implements UserDAO {

    private SpringLocalTxManager txnManager;
    private ObjectGrid grid;

    @Override
    public User find(int id) {
        txnManager.setObjectGridForThread(grid);
        EntityManager em = txnManager.getSession().getEntityManager();
        em.getTransaction().begin();
        User user = (User)em.find(User.class, id);
        em.getTransaction().commit();
        return user;
    }
    // additional methods omitted for now...
}
```

The `ObjectGridUserDAO` class expects an instance of ObjectGrid to work correctly. We'll cover the `SpringLocalTxManager` dependency later in this chapter. For now, we'll just provide it when wiring the bean.

The `ObjectGridUserDAO` bean should be wired just like any other Spring bean, which means something like this:

```
<bean id="ogUserDAO"
    class="net.anthonychaves.bookmarks.dao.ObjectGridUserDAO">
    <property name="txnManager" ref="transactionManager"/>
    <property name="grid" ref="myGrid"/>
</bean>
```

The bean property `grid` is set to reference to another bean, `myGrid`. This reference is an instance of ObjectGrid which is somehow defined using Spring. Let's look back at how we programmatically obtain an ObjectGrid instance that connects to a distributed eXtreme Scale deployment:

```
ObjectGridManager ogm = ObjectGridManagerFactory
                                        .getObjectGridManager();
ClientClusterContext context = gm.connect("accoungGrid", null,
                            new URL("c://wxo/objectgrid.xml"));
ObjectGrid grid = ogm.getObjectGrid(context, "MyGrid");
```

We go through three steps to get a reference to an ObjectGrid. We start with an ObjectGridManagerFactory which provides a factory method to get a reference to an ObjectGridManager. The factory method should give us a hint about how to use the ObjectGridManagerFactory with Spring. Spring allows us to configure beans as the product of factory methods. We can create an ObjectGridManager bean using the Spring factory method configuration.

```
<bean id="ogManager"
    class="com.ibm.websphere.objectgrid.ObjectGridManagerFactory"
    factory-method="getObjectGridManager">
</bean>
```

Above, we create a bean named ogManager, and when the Spring container initializes, it calls the ObjectGridManagerFactory.getObjectGridManager() method. Writing the bean definition this way gives us an ObjectGridManager instance available to our other Spring beans. This is equivalent to this line of code:

```
ObjectGridManager ogm = ObjectGridManagerFactory
                                    .getObjectGridManager();
```

With our ObjectGridManager in hand, we're one step closer to getting an ObjectGrid reference. The next step on our way is getting a ClientClusterContext. We'll use our ogManager bean to get one. We need to do something analogous to this line of code:

```
ClientClusterContext context = ogm.connect("accoungGrid", null,
                            new URL("c://wxs/objectgrid.xml"));
```

The ObjectGridManager#connect(String gridName, ClusterSecurity cSecurity, URL configFileName) method gives us the ClientClusterContext associated with our distributed eXtreme Scale deployment. Configuring the ClientClusterContext as a Spring bean is interesting because we obtain a reference to it from a non-getter method on an ObjectGridManager bean. This means that we don't configure it as a template bean. Instead, we configure it as the product of a factory bean like we did with the ObjectGridManager bean.

```
<bean id="clientConfigFile"
    class="java.net.URL">
  <constructor-arg type="java.lang.String"
                        value="file://c:/wxs/objectgrid.xml"/>
</bean>
<bean id="clientClusterContext" factory-bean="ogManager"
    factory-method="connect">
  <constructor-arg index="0" type="java.lang.String"
                value="galvatron:2809"/>
  <constructor-arg index="1"><null/></constructor-arg>
  <constructor-arg index="2" ref="clientConfigFile"/>
</bean>
```

Our `ClientClusterContext` instance is defined as a bean named `clientClusterContext`. All instances of this bean come from the factory bean `ogManager`. We use the `ogManager` bean defined in the previous step because it's our instance of ObjectGridManager. The `ogManager` bean has the connect method which we need to call to get a ClientClusterContext. The `clientClusterContext` bean instances come from the Spring container calling the `ogManager.connect(String gridname, SecurityPolicy policy, URL configFile)` method. Spring calls that method by configuring `ogManager` as a factory bean, and the connect method as the factory method. Because factory methods look like constructors to Spring, we pass in the grid name and configuration file name as constructor-args. Spring calls the correct connect method based on the number of constructor-arg arguments passed in the bean definition.

Now that we have an `ObjectGridManager` bean and a `ClientClusterContext` bean, we can perform the third step to create an ObjectGrid bean. This is equivalent to calling the `ObjectGrigManager#getObjectGrid(ClientClusterContext ccc, String gridName)` method:

```
ObjectGrid grid = ogm.getObjectGrid(context, "MyGrid");
```

Again, we rely on the factory bean style of bean configuration when wiring the ObjectGrid bean. We will use the `ogManager` bean as the factory bean once again:

```
<bean id="myGrid" factory-bean="ogManager"
      factory-method="getObjectGrid">
  <constructor-arg index="0" ref="clientClusterContext"/>
  <constructor-arg index="1" type="java.lang.String"
                    value="MyGrid"/>
</bean>
```

Using `ogManager` as the factory bean, we use the `ObjectGridManager#get ObjectGrid` method as the factory method. This method requires a reference to a `clientClusterContext` bean we defined in the previous step. It also requires the String name of the distributed ObjectGrid instance we want to connect to. This ObjectGrid instance is defined in the file referenced by the `java.net.URL` `clientConfigFile` bean.

Here, we have a reference to an ObjectGrid which uses a distributed eXtreme Scale deployment. The `myGrid` bean can be wired into any other Spring bean, such as our `ObjectGridUserDAO` bean:

```
<bean id="ogUserDAO"
      class="net.anthonychaves.bookmarks.dao.ObjectGridUserDAO">
  <property name="txnManager" ref="transactionManager"/>
  <property name="grid" ref="myGrid"/>
</bean>
```

One of the nicest things about defining our classes and dependencies via Spring is that we can easily distribute the bean definition files to other projects that use the same eXtreme Scale deployment. Or, with a small change to the `clientConfigFile` bean, we can point it to a completely different grid, but preserve the hard work of setting up the dependencies to obtain a grid reference. We can pull out all of the eXtreme Scale-specific beans into a standalone bean definition file. Let's call it `objectgridbeans.xml` and import it into our other bean definition files:

```xml
<?xml version="1.0" encoding="UTF-8"?>
<beans xmlns="http://www.springframework.org/schema/beans"
       xmlns:xsi=http://www.w3.org/2001/XMLSchema-instance
      xsi:schemaLocation="http://www.springframework.org/schema/beans
     http://www.springframework.org/schema/beans/spring-beans-2.0.xsd
     http://www.springframework.org/schema/aop
     http://www.springframework.org/schema/aop/spring-aop-2.0.xsd
     http://www.springframework.org/schema/tx
     http://www.springframework.org/schema/tx/spring-tx.xsd">

    <import resource="objectgridbeans.xml"/>

    <bean id="ogUserDAO"
     class="net.anthonychaves.bookmarks.dao.ObjectGridUserDAO">
        <property name="txnManager" ref="transactionManager"/>
        <property name="grid" ref="myGrid"/>
    </bean>
</beans>
```

Here is the `objectgridbeans.xml` file:

```xml
<?xml version="1.0" encoding="UTF-8"?>
<beans xmlns="http://www.springframework.org/schema/beans"
       xmlns:xsi="http://www.w3.org/2001/XMLSchema-instance"
       xsi:schemaLocation="http://www.springframework.org/schema/beans
     http://www.springframework.org/schema/beans/spring-beans-2.0.xsd
     http://www.springframework.org/schema/aop
     http://www.springframework.org/schema/aop/spring-aop-2.0.xsd
     http://www.springframework.org/schema/tx
     http://www.springframework.org/schema/tx/spring-tx.xsd">

    <bean id="transactionManager"
    class="com.ibm.websphere.objectgrid.spring.ObjectGridSpringFactory"
         factory-method="getLocalPlatformTransactionManager">
    </bean>

    <bean id="ogManager"
       class="com.ibm.websphere.objectgrid.ObjectGridManagerFactory"
         factory-method="getObjectGridManager">
    </bean>

    <bean id="clientConfigFile" class="java.net.URL">
```

```xml
        <constructor-arg type="java.lang.String"
                         value="file://c:/wxs/objectgrid.xml"/>
    </bean>

    <bean id="clientClusterContext"
          factory-bean="ogManager"
          factory-method="connect">
        <constructor-arg index="0" type="java.lang.String"
                         value="galvatron:2809"/>
        <constructor-arg index="1"><null/></constructor-arg>
        <constructor-arg index="2" ref="clientConfigFile"/>
    </bean>

    <bean id="myGrid"
          factory-bean="ogManager"
          factory-method="getObjectGrid">
        <constructor-arg index="0" ref="clientClusterContext"/>
        <constructor-arg index="1" type="java.lang.String"
                         value="MyGrid"/>
    </bean>
</beans>
```

And for the sake of completeness, here is the `objectgrid.xml` file used in the `clientClusterContext` bean:

```xml
<?xml version="1.0" encoding="UTF-8"?>
<objectGridConfig xmlns:xsi="http://www.w3.org/2001/
  XMLSchema-instance"
  xsi:schemaLocation="http://ibm.com/ws/objectgrid/config ../
objectGrid.xsd"
  xmlns="http://ibm.com/ws/objectgrid/config">

  <objectGrids>
    <objectGrid name="MyGrid"
                entityMetadataXMLFile="MyGridEntities.xml">

      <bean id="TransactionCallback"
            className="{spring}sampleJpaTxCallback"/>

      <backingMap name="User" pluginCollectionRef="User" />
    </objectGrid>
  </objectGrids>

  <backingMapPluginCollections>
    <backingMapPluginCollection id="User">
      <bean id="Loader" className="{spring}userEntityLoader"/>
    </backingMapPluginCollection>
  </backingMapPluginCollections>

</objectGridConfig>
```

Hmm. What are those {spring} things doing in here? We haven't seen those before.

Spring-managed eXtreme Scale configuration

Before we go any further, we need to make sure that the $OG_HOME/lib/ogspring.jar file is on the classpath.

WebSphere eXtreme Scale allows us to wire Spring-defined beans into our plugin collections. We do this by defining the Spring bean elsewhere and pre-pending {spring} to the bean name when wiring it in to the plugin collection. An eXtreme Scale configuration file may contain any number of {spring} referenced beans.

There isn't a Spring bean factory defined in our objectgrid.xml configuration file, so we must be using some default file. By default, eXtreme Scale looks for a file named GridName_spring.xml in the classpath root. The grid defined in the objectgrid.xml file is "MyGrid", so eXtreme Scale looks for a file named MyGrid_spring.xml in the classpath root.

```xml
<?xml version="1.0" encoding="UTF-8"?>
<beans xmlns="http://www.springframework.org/schema/beans"
    xmlns:xsi="http://www.w3.org/2001/XMLSchema-instance"
    xmlns:objectgrid="http://www.ibm.com/schema/objectgrid"
    xsi:schemaLocation="http://www.ibm.com/schema/objectgrid
    http://www.ibm.com/schema/objectgrid/objectgrid.xsd
    http://www.springframework.org/schema/beans
    http://www.springframework.org/schema/beans/spring-beans-2.0.xsd">

    <objectgrid:JPATxCallback id="sampleJpaTxCallback"
                              persistenceUnitName="PersistenceUnit0"/>

    <objectgrid:JPAEntityLoader id="userEntityLoader"
        entityClassName="net.anthonychaves.bookmarks.dataobject.User"/>
</beans>
```

Notice the inclusion of the objectgrid namespace in the sample above. eXtreme Scale includes the objectgrid namespace in which it makes available a shorthand way to configure our Spring-managed beans. The objectgrid namespace contains 10 namespace elements for configuring the most common types of bean plugins.

Our sample file configures a `JPATxCallbackManager` and a `JPAEntityLoader`. The shorthand objectgrid namespace configuration is the short way of wiring the beans as:

```
<bean id="sampleJpaTxCallback"
      class="com.ibm.websphere.objectgrid.jpa.JPATxCallback">
   <property name="persistenceUnitName" value="PersistenceUnit0"/>
</bean>

<bean id="userEntityLoader"
      class="com.ibm.websphere.objectgrid.jpa.JPAEntityLoader">
   <property name="entityClassName"
             value="net.anthonychaves.bookmarks.dataobject.User"/>
</bean>
```

The 10 objectgrid namespace elements can be found in the `ogspring.jar` file under `com/ibm/ws/objectgrid/spring/namespace/objectgrid.xsd`. Take a look at that file for the remaining namespace elements and their parameters. They work like the two we've seen in this sample.

Transaction management

Before we get to the configuration files, we should first review the Spring transaction management concepts. The two main reasons we want to use Spring's transaction support are first for consistent programming model for different transactional APIs and secondly, the availability of declarative transaction management.

The consistent transactional API is most evident when an application uses different data sources. Out of the box Spring lets our applications use the transactional capabilities of Hibernate, JPA, JTA, JDBC, and more using the same programming model. All of these transactional APIs are hidden behind one Spring abstraction, the transaction strategy.

The transaction strategy is an example of a strategy pattern. The strategy pattern is a way of abstracting some algorithm behind a common interface. This creates a pluggable software system where the appropriate algorithm is plugged in at the appropriate time. In this case, the "appropriate algorithm" is transactional advice for an ObjectGrid session.

Applications already using a data access layer with the Spring framework benefit the most when plugging ObjectGrid into the software stack. A data access layer that abstracts away all transactional operations is a prime candidate for ObjectGrid integration. Application logic does not change, only the configuration does.

Using ObjectGrid in an application that obeys these principles requires a new DAL class that implements the `IDataAccessLayer` interface. Once we have an implementation, we wire it in the Spring configuration, and the application works the same as before, now with ObjectGrid as the data store.

Spring's consistent programming model for transactions also means that there is a consistent configuration for different transaction managers. Later in this chapter, we'll migrate an existing Hibernate data access layer to an ObjectGrid data access layer, and then compare the two different configurations.

Because we configure our transaction managers using Spring, we can use declarative transaction management. Declarative transaction management means Spring handles transaction `begin()`, `commit()`, and `rollback()` calls. This removes transaction management from our application logic and DAL. Instead, Spring wraps our service-level classes with a proxy class using aspect-oriented programming. The proxy class is invisible to our application logic. The proxy begins and ends transactions using the transactional advice we provide in our Spring configuration file.

The Spring framework supports the philosophy that transaction management is invasive to the application programming. Programmatic transaction management looks like what we did in previous chapters:

```
public void persist(Account account) {
    try {
        em.getTransaction().begin();
        em.persist(account);
        em.getTransaction().commit();
    } catch (Exception e) {
            em.getTransaction().rollback();
            e.printStackTrace();
    // somehow handle the exception based on business rules
    }

}
```

Here, we're using declarative transaction management for the same function:

```
public void persist(Account account) {
    em.persist(account);
}
```

Transaction management code disappears from our method. The AOP proxy now begins the transaction before calling the persist method. The proxy also commits the transaction when the method returns. Exception handling code disappears from this method as well. Typically, when an exception is thrown at the data access layer level, it is fatal. Our software cannot repair a database connection, free disk space, or somehow recover from a system exception *at this point*. Catching an exception means rolling back the transaction, which is now handled by the Spring framework, based on the transaction advice we give our transaction manager.

Basic configuration

We're going to use the same ObjectGrid XML configuration file we used in the previous chapter:

```xml
<?xml version="1.0" encoding="UTF-8"?>
<objectGridConfig xmlns:xsi="http://www.w3.org/2001/
  XMLSchema-instance"
  xsi:schemaLocation="http://ibm.com/ws/objectgrid/config ../
objectGrid.xsd"
   xmlns="http://ibm.com/ws/objectgrid/config">
   <objectGrids>
      <objectGrid name="AccountGrid"
                  entityMetadataXMLFile="ppEntities.xml">
         <bean id="TransactionCallback"
          className="com.ibm.websphere.objectgrid.jpa.JPATxCallback">
            <property name="persistenceUnitName"
                      type="java.lang.String" value="Account" />
         </bean>
         <backingMap name="Account" ttlEvictorType="CREATION_TIME"
                     timeToLive="43200"
                     evictionTriggers="MEMORY_USAGE_THRESHOLD"
                     pluginCollectionRef="Account" />
         <backingMap name="LineItem" pluginCollectionRef="LineItem" />
         <backingMap name="IBM_SYSTEM_MAP_defaultMapSet" />
      </objectGrid>
   </objectGrids>

   <backingMapPluginCollections>

      <backingMapPluginCollection id="Account">
            <bean id="Loader"
className="com.ibm.websphere.objectgrid.jpa.JPALoader">
               <property name="entityClassName"
                         type="java.lang.String"
                         value="wxs.sample.models.Account"/>
```

```
            </bean>
        </backingMapPluginCollection>

        <backingMapPluginCollection id="LineItem">
            <bean id="Loader"
   className="com.ibm.websphere.objectgrid.jpa.JPAEntityLoader">
                <property name="entityClassName"
                          type="java.lang.String"
                          value="wxs.sample.models.LineItem"/>
            </bean>
        </backingMapPluginCollection>

    </backingMapPluginCollections>
</objectGridConfig>
```

Two BackingMaps and a plugin for each! This configuration remains untouched
for now. Instead, we'll create a Spring configuration file and configure our
transaction manager. The Spring configuration file is named application.xml
in the META-INF directory:

```
<?xml version="1.0" encoding="UTF-8"?>
<beans xmlns="http://www.springframework.org/schema/beans"
    xmlns:xsi="http://www.w3.org/2001/XMLSchema-instance"
    xsi:schemaLocation="http://www.springframework.org/schema/beans
    http://www.springframework.org/schema/beans/spring-beans-2.5.xsd">

    <aop:aspectj-autoproxy />
    <tx:annotation-driven />

    <bean id="transactionManager"
   class="com.ibm.websphere.objectgrid.spring.ObjectGridSpringFactory"
        factory-method="getLocalPlatformTransactionManager">
    </bean>
</beans>
```

The abstraction behind the Spring transaction management is the
PlatformTransactionManager interface:

```
public interface PlatformTransactionManager {
    TransactionStatus getTransaction(TransactionDefinition definition)
        throws TransactionException;

    void commit(TransactionStatus status)
        throws TransactionException;

    void rollback(TransactionStatus status)
        throws TransactionException;

}
```

We must provide an ObjectGrid class that implements this interface. We do that by defining the `transactionManager` bean as creating classes from a factory method. The `ObjectGridSpringFactory` class method `getLocalPlatformTransactionManager()` returns an instance of `SpringLocalTxManager`. The `SpringLocalTxManager` provides these methods to the calling proxies.

Let's look back at our ideal DAL persist method:

```
public void persist(Account account) {
    em.persist(account);
}
```

We use an instance of EntityManager. Instances of ObjectMap and EntityManager must come from an ObjectGrid Session. To interact with BackingMaps via these APIs, we need a session in our DAL. We get it from the `SpringLocalTxManager` interface. It has a `getSession()` method that gives us a session just like the `ObjectGrid#getSession()` method. Instead of creating a new transaction using the session API, the `SpringLocalTxManager` already has an open transaction, and returns the session associated with it. `SpringLocalTxManager` has an open transaction because it was started before the persist(account) method was called. Our persist method should now look like this:

```
public void persist(Account account) {
    EntityManager em = txnManager.getSession().getEntityManager();
    em.persist(account);
}
```

Something is missing though. Our session must correspond to exactly one ObjectGrid instance. That is not set through Spring, though. We need to set it programmatically on the `SpringLocalTxManager` before calling any transactional methods.

Applications running as clients to a remote grid will just set this once per thread and then leave it. Agents or server-side plugins will need to set it to the shard ObjectGrid instance before entering code using Spring managed beans.

```
@Transactional(propagation=Propagation.REQUIRED)
public class ObjectGridLineItemDAO implements LineItemDAO {

    private SpringLocalTxManager txnManager;
    public void initialize(ObjectGrid grid) {
        txnManager.setObjectGridForThread(grid);
    }
    public void persist(LineItem item) {
        EntityManager em = txnManager.getSession().getEntityManager();
```

```
        em.persist(item);
    }
    public SpringLocalTxManager getTxnManager() {
        return txnManager;
    }
    public void setTxnManager(SpringLocalTxManager txnManager) {
        this.txnManager = txnManager;
    }
}
```

We'll use the class above to persist the LineItem objects. In order to use it, we first inject the SpringLocalTxManager using Spring.

```
<beans>
    <aop:aspectj-autoproxy />
    <tx:annotation-driven />
    <bean id="transactionManager"
            class="com.ibm.websphere.objectgrid.spring.
ObjectGridSpringFactory"
            factory-method="getLocalPlatformTransactionManager">
    </bean>
    <bean id="lineItemDAO"
            class="wxs.sample.models.ObjectGridLineItemDAO">
        <property name="txnManager"
                    ref="transactionManager"/>
    </bean>
    <bean id="lineItemProcessor"
            class="wxs.sample.app.LineItemProcessor">
        <property name="lineItemDAO"
                    ref="lineItemDAO"/>
    </bean>
</beans>
```

Upon creation, the lineItemDAO bean has a SpringLocalTxManager injected by Spring (as seen above). For now, let's get a reference to an ObjectGrid programmatically. We'll configure it with Spring soon:

```
public class LineItemProcessor {
    private String ogHost = "galvatron";
    private int ogPort = 2809;
    private URL clientConfig;

    private ObjectGridManager ogm;
    private ObjectGrid grid;
```

```
private ClientClusterContext context;

private EntityManager em;
private SpringLocalTxManager txnManager;
private LineItemDAO lineItemDAO;
private AccountDAO accountDAO;

public static void main(String args[]) throws Exception {
    ApplicationContext applicationContext =
        new ClassPathXmlApplicationContext("application.xml");

    LineItemProcessor lp = (LineItemProcessor)
            applicationContext.getBean("lineItemProcessor");

    lp.setClientConfig(args[0]);
    lp.connectToObjectGrid();
    lp.initializeSession(applicationContext);

    Map accounts = lp.populateAccounts();
    lp.populateLineItems(accounts);

    System.out.println("Finished.");
}

private void populateLineItems(Map accounts) {
    for (int i = 0; i < 1000; i++) {
        LineItem item = new LineItem();
        item.setId(i);
        Account account = (Account)accounts.get((int)(Math.random()
                                                        * 100));

        item.setAccountId(account.getId());
        item.setAmount(250 + i);

        lineItemDAO.persist(item);
    }
}

private Map populateAccounts() {
    Map accounts = new HashMap();

    for (int i = 0; i < 1000; i++) {
        Account account = new Account();
        account.setId(i);
        account.setBalance("100");
        account.setName("Anthony's account " + i);
        account.setType("Savings");

        accounts.put(account.getId(), account);
        accountDAO.persist(account);
    }
    return accounts;
}
```

```
        private void connectToObjectGrid() {
            ogm = ObjectGridManagerFactory.getObjectGridManager();
            String clusterHost = ogHost + ":" + ogPort;
            try {
            context = ogm.connect(clusterHost, null, clientConfig);
            } catch (ConnectException e) {
                throw new RuntimeException(e);
            }
            grid = ogm.getObjectGrid(context, "AccountGrid");
        }
        private void initializeSession(
                ApplicationContext applicationContext) {
            SpringLocalTxManager txnManager = (SpringLocalTxManager)
                    applicationContext.getBean("transactionManager");
            txnManager.setObjectGridForThread(grid);
        }
        public ObjectGrid getGrid() {
            return grid;
        }
        public void setClientConfig(String clientConfigFile)
            throws MalformedURLException {
            this.clientConfig = new URL("file://" + clientConfigFile);
        }
        public LineItemDAO getLineItemDAO() {
            return lineItemDAO;
        }
        public void setLineItemDAO(LineItemDAO lineItemDAO) {
            this.lineItemDAO = lineItemDAO;
        }
        public AccountDAO getAccountDAO() {
            return accountDAO;
        }
        public void setAccountDAO(AccountDAO accountDAO) {
            this.accountDAO = accountDAO;
        }
    }
```

The main method starts by obtaining a reference to the `lineItemProcessor` bean we created in our `application.xml` Spring configuration file. That bean already has its DAO dependencies injected by Spring. After creating a connection to the ObjectGrid named AccountGrid using the `LineItemProcessor` methods, we have the ObjectGrid reference needed to initialize the `SpringLocalTxManager`. The `lp.initializeSession()` method passes the ObjectGrid reference to the `SpringLocalTxManager`. From that point on, each transaction and session in this thread is bound to AccountGrid.

Moving on to the `populateAccounts` and `populateLineItems` methods, they have changed very little since the last chapter. Instead of using the ObjectMap and EntityManager APIs directly, the DAO classes handle the persistence. Because they implement the `AccountDAO` and `LineItemDAO` interfaces, we could have plugged in a JPA or JDBC DAO just as easily. It's this pluggable configuration that makes integrating ObjectGrid with your application very easy.

In fact, this may be your first step to using ObjectGrid in an existing application. Configuring the ObjectGrid reference programmatically is easy enough at this point. If your data access layer has a well-defined interface, then using ObjectGrid instead of your existing persistence is as easy as changing the Spring wiring to your service layer.

ObjectGrid client configuration

If you're using Spring, then you may want to move your entire ObjectGrid client configuration into your Spring application context, instead of obtaining a reference to an ObjectGrid instance programmatically. Moving ObjectGrid client configuration details into the application context XML file makes it easy to use different grids in different situations. We could have three different grids with the same BackingMaps, each with a different purpose, development, testing, and production. Depending on the build type, the appropriate grid reference is injected into the application at runtime. Overriding client-side BackingMap settings is easier as well. We specify the client-side configuration file in the Spring configuration file.

In the `LineItemProcessor` class, we used this method to connect to an ObjectGrid instance named AccountGrid:

```
private void connectToObjectGrid() {
    ogm = ObjectGridManagerFactory.getObjectGridManager();
    String clusterHost = ogHost + ":" + ogPort;
    try {
        context = ogm.connect(clusterHost, null, clientConfig);
    } catch (ConnectException e) {
        throw new ObjectGridRuntimeException(e);
    }
    grid = ogm.getObjectGrid(context, "AccountGrid");
}
```

We end up with a reference to an ObjectGrid with the private instance variable grid. This method starts with nothing, and the LineItemProcessor instance has a grid reference by the end. Using Spring, we need to inject an ObjectGrid reference into the LineItemProcessor instance using setter-based injection. That means LineItemProcessor must have a setter which takes a reference to an ObjectGrid as an argument:

```
public class LineItemProcessor {
// other methods omitted
    public void setGrid(ObjectGrid grid) {
        this.grid = grid;
    }
}
```

In order to get to this point, we must have an ObjectGridManager. ObjectGridManager provides methods to get a reference to a ClientClusterContext and connect to an ObjectGrid instance. In connectToObjectGrid(), we get an ObjectGridManager from the static method ObjectGridManagerFactory.getObjectGridManager(). This is a factory method which means that we need to configure this Spring bean as if it were coming from a factory method. The following goes in application.xml:

```
<bean id="ogManager"
class="com.ibm.websphere.objectgrid.ObjectGridManagerFactory"
factory-method="getObjectGridManager">
</bean>
```

This snippet creates a Spring bean named ogManager. The bean is created by the factory method getObjectGridManager() in the ObjectGridManagerFactory class. Later in our configuration, we refer to this bean by its ID ogManager. The code in the connectToObjectGrid() method that does this is:

```
ogm = ObjectGridManagerFactory.getObjectGridManager();
```

Next, we need an instance of ClientClusterContext. The connectToObjectGrid() method requires two pieces of information to get a ClientClusterContext. It needs the host and port of the catalog service, and the client-side ObjectGrid configuration file. We create the ClientClusterContext bean using a factory method again. We obtain a reference to a ClientClusterContext from one of the ObjectGridManager#connect(...) methods. Though we've chosen the ObjectGridManager#connect(catalogServerAddress, securityPropsFile, clientConfigurationFile) method here, we can use any #connect(...) method, provided we pass the appropriate parameters when setting it up with the factory method configuration.

```xml
<bean id="clientConfigFile"
      class="java.net.URL">
    <constructor-arg type="java.lang.String"
       value="file://c:/wxs/workspace/AccountLineItem/src/
              jpa-objectgrid.xml" />
</bean>

<bean id="clientClusterContext"
      factory-bean="ogManager"
      factory-method="connect">
    <constructor-arg index="0" type="java.lang.String"
                     value="galvatron:2809"/>
    <constructor-arg index="1"><null/></constructor-arg>
    <constructor-arg index="2" ref="clientConfigFile"/>
</bean>
```

As the connect method above requires a `java.net.URL` of the configuration file, we create a bean named `clientConfigFile`. We pass the location of the client-side configuration file we'd like to use as the `constructor-arg`. With a bean for the configuration file, we call the `ObjectGridManager#connect( catalogServerAddress, securityPropsFile, clientConfigurationFile)` method. Again, we use the factory bean and factory method configuration. This is because the ClientClusterContext is obtained from a connect method, not a ClientClusterContext constructor. This snippet does the same as the code in `connectToObjectGrid()`:

```java
String clusterHost = ogHost + ":" + ogPort;
try {
    context = ogm.connect(clusterHost, null, clientConfig);
} catch (ConnectException e) {
    throw new RuntimeException(e);
}
```

The factory bean used references the `ogManager` bean we created in the previous step. This is because the connect methods are instance methods, not class methods. The `ogManager` bean is an instance of ObjectGridManager. The factory method specified is the name of the method. Because there is more than one `connect(...)` method on an ObjectGridManager instance, we rely on the constructor-args to determine which connect method is called. To avoid ambiguity, we specify the index of the constructor argument as part of the configuration. The constructor-args with indices of 0 and 2 are the two we are most interested in. We are not passing a security properties file right now so we give null to the `constructor-arg` with index 1.

The constructor-arg with index 0 is the catalog server address. This value is no longer in the source code, or passed as a command-line argument. This makes application startup easier now that we configure our settings at build-time, rather than on startup. This is just the `java.lang.String` of the catalog server in the `host:port` format. The constructor-arg with index 2 is the `java.net.URL` of the client-side ObjectGrid configuration file.

Now that we have a reference to an ObjectGridManager and a ClientClusterContext, we obtain a reference to the ObjectGrid named AccountGrid:

```
<bean id="accountGrid"
      factory-bean="ogManager"
      factory-method="getObjectGrid">
  <constructor-arg index="0" ref="clientClusterContext"/>
  <constructor-arg index="1" type="java.lang.String"
                   value="AccountGrid"/>
</bean>
```

This snippet creates an ObjectGrid bean with the ID `accountGrid`. We need this ID to inject the AccountGrid reference into the `LineItemProcessor` bean. As with the `ClientClusterContext` bean, we obtain a reference to the grid using a factory method on the `ogManager` bean we created. This time, the factory method is `getObjectGrid` with two arguments. The first is the reference to the `clientClusterContext` bean we just created. The second is the `java.lang.String` name of the ObjectGrid we want to connect to. This snippet does the same thing as the method call in `connectToObjectGrid()`:

```
ogm.getObjectGrid(context, "AccountGrid");
```

Notice how the `grid` = part of that line did not make it into that snippet. That happened because we only have a reference to the AccountGrid ObjectGrid. We still need to set the reference on the `LineItemProcessor` bean:

```
<bean id="lineItemProcessor"
      class="wxs.sample.app.LineItemProcessor">
  <property name="accountDAO" ref="accountDAO"/>
  <property name="lineItemDAO" ref="lineItemDAO"/>
  <property name="grid" ref="accountGrid"/>
</bean>
```

Now, our ObjectGrid client is configured with Spring. Back in our `LineItemProcessor` main method, we obtain a reference to the grid:

```
LineItemProcessor lp = (LineItemProcessor)
                  applicationContext.getBean("lineItemProcessor");
```

The reference to the ObjectGrid instance named AccountGrid is already injected into the `LineItemProcessor` instance when we call `getBean("lineItemProcessor")`. There is no reason to call `connectToObjectGrid()` anymore, and it should be removed from the LineItemProcessor class. The entire main method looks like this:

```
public static void main(String args[]) throws Exception {
    ApplicationContext applicationContext =
                        new ClassPathXmlApplicationContext(
                            "/META-INF/application.xml");

    LineItemProcessor lp = (LineItemProcessor)
                applicationContext.getBean("lineItemProcessor");

    lp.initializeSession(applicationContext);

    Map accounts = lp.populateAccounts();
    lp.populateLineItems(accounts);

    System.out.println("Finished.");
}
```

Though we have an ObjectGrid reference, we still need to associate the grid with the transaction manager. This is the only piece we do in code now. It's easy to call the `initializeSession(applicationContext)` method once we have the `LineItemProcessor` bean. Remember, the `txnManager.setObjectGridForThread(grid)` method must be called before starting any transactions on each thread the client will use. There is just one thread in this example:

```
public void initializeSession(
                        ApplicationContext applicationContext) {
    SpringLocalTxManager txnManager = (SpringLocalTxManager)
    applicationContext.getBean("transactionManager");
    txnManager.setObjectGridForThread(grid);
}
```

After configuring our application with Spring, there are no ObjectGrid dependencies in the data access layer. Additionally, the client configuration is reduced to three lines of code. For completeness, we can remove all ObjectGrid and Spring dependencies from our business logic class, `LineItemProcessor`. The remaining ObjectGrid dependency is in the `initializeSession()` method. The Spring dependencies are the `applicationContext` creation and `getBean` methods. Instead of keeping these in the business logic class, we can put them in a driver class:

```
public class LineItemDriver {
    private ObjectGrid grid;
    private LineItemProcessor lineItemProcessor;

    public static void main(String args[]) throws Exception {
```

```
        ApplicationContext applicationContext = new
            ClassPathXmlApplicationContext("/META-INF/application.xml");
        LineItemDriver driver = (LineItemDriver)
                applicationContext.getBean("lineItemDriver");

        driver.initializeSession(applicationContext);
        driver.getLineItemProcessor().run();

        System.out.println("Finished.");
    }

    private void initializeSession(ApplicationContext
                                    applicationContext) {
        SpringLocalTxManager txnManager = (SpringLocalTxManager)
                    applicationContext.getBean("transactionManager");
        txnManager.setObjectGridForThread(grid);
    }

    public ObjectGrid getGrid() {
        return grid;
    }

    public void setGrid(ObjectGrid grid) {
        this.grid = grid;
    }

    public LineItemProcessor getLineItemProcessor() {
        return lineItemProcessor;
    }

    public void setLineItemProcessor(LineItemProcessor
                                        lineItemProcessor) {
        this.lineItemProcessor = lineItemProcessor;
    }

}
```

The main method and `initializeSession` methods have been pulled out of
`LineItemProcessor` and put in `LineItemDriver`. The `LineItemDriver` needs a
reference to an ObjectGrid and a `LineItemProcessor` to work:

```
<bean id="lineItemDriver"
      class="wxs.sample.app.LineItemDriver">
    <property name="lineItemProcessor"
                ref="lineItemProcessor"/>
    <property name="grid"
                ref="accountGrid"/>
</bean>
```

This changes the `lineItemProcessor` bean definition to:

```xml
<bean id="lineItemProcessor"
      class="wxs.sample.app.LineItemProcessor">
    <property name="accountDAO"
              ref="accountDAO"/>
    <property name="lineItemDAO"
              ref="lineItemDAO"/>
</bean>
```

`LineItemProcessor`, where our business logic is, only has dependencies on some class that persists accounts, and some class that persists line items. We're still using our `ObjectGrid*DAO` classes, but the point is we don't need to.

Without a main method, the `LineItemProcessor` class needs a method to invoke its workflow. Let's call that method run:

```java
public void run() {
    populateLineItems();
    populateAccounts();
}
```

This is what any client application calls to invoke the `LineItemProcessor` workflow. It's called in the `LineItemDriver` main method:

```java
public static void main(String args[]) throws Exception {
    ApplicationContext applicationContext = new
        ClassPathXmlApplicationContext("/META-INF/application.xml");
    LineItemDriver driver = (LineItemDriver)
        applicationContext.getBean("lineItemDriver");

    driver.initializeSession(applicationContext);
    driver.getLineItemProcessor().run();

    System.out.println("Finished.");
}
```

Why is this important? Take a look at the `LineItemProcessor` class and the two DAO interfaces:

```java
public interface AccountDAO {

    public void persist(Account account);
}
public interface LineItemDAO {

    public void persist(LineItem item);
}
public class LineItemProcessor {
```

```
        private LineItemDAO lineItemDAO;
        private AccountDAO accountDAO;

        private Queue lineItems = new LinkedList();
        private Collection accounts = new ArrayList();

        public void run() {
            populateLineItems();
            populateAccounts();
        }

        private void populateLineItems() {
        //...
        }

        private void populateAccounts() {
        //...
        }

        public LineItemDAO getLineItemDAO() {
            return lineItemDAO;
        }

        public void setLineItemDAO(LineItemDAO lineItemDAO) {
            this.lineItemDAO = lineItemDAO;
        }

        public AccountDAO getAccountDAO() {
            return accountDAO;
        }

        public void setAccountDAO(AccountDAO accountDAO) {
            this.accountDAO = accountDAO;
        }
    }
}
```

There are no traces of ObjectGrid or Spring dependencies in the business logic. This makes it much easier to port an application from one persistence stack to another. Plugging in an ObjectGrid in front of an existing persistence layer only requires changing the DAO bean references in the Spring configuration file.

Remembering our patterns

In our somewhat generic example, we have Accounts and LineItems. Initially, we partition on LineItems. We expect there will be many more LineItems than Accounts. We partition on LineItems because we expect our application to have more random LineItem operations than Account operations.

As we're dealing with a pluggable persistence layer, we need to think about what happens when we have an interface that looks like this:

```
public interface LineItemDAO {
    public void persist(LineItem item);
    public void persist(Collection items);
}
```

Using a database-based persistence layer, this interface presents no problems to the programming model. The database operations to save tens or hundreds of LineItems are batched up and committed as one transaction using one remote procedure call. An unpartitioned data grid also doesn't prove to be much of a problem. Again, the objects are batched up and sent to the grid in one transaction and one RPC.

Implementing the persist(Collection items) method with a partitioned data grid requires a little more thought. Remember, with ObjectGrid, we can write to just one partition per transaction. If the collection has 10 objects that each map to a different partition, we will then need 10 transactions and 10 RPCs to persist these objects.

One way to handle this is by using the partition-sorting code we used in Chapter 7 to sort the objects into sub-collections per partition. This should happen inside the persist(Collection items) method. Object sorting inside the method preserves the lack of ObjectGrid dependencies inside application logic:

```
public void persist(Collection items) {
    Map<Integer,Collection<LineItem>> partitions = new
            HashMap();<Integer,Collection<LineItem>>

    Session session = txnManager.getSession();
    EntityManager em = session.getEntityManager();

    ObjectMap map = null;
    try {

        for (Object o : items) {
            LineItem item = (LineItem)o;

        BackingMap bmap = session.getObjectGrid().getMap("LineItem");
         int partId = bmap.getPartitionManager().getPartition(key);item

            Collection<LineItem> c = (Collection)partitions.get(key);new
              Integer(partId)
            if (c == null) {
            c = new ArrayList();
        }        partitions.put(new Integer(partId), c);
        c.add(item);
        }
```

```
    } catch (UndefinedMapException e) {
        e.printStackTrace();
    }
    Set keys = partitions.keySet();
    for (Integer o : keys) {
        Collection<LineItem> c = partitions.get(o);
        persist(c, true);
    }
}
@Transactional(propagation=Propagation.REQUIRES_NEW)
private void persist(Collection<LineItem> partition, boolean b) {
    EntityManager em = txnManager.getSession().getEntityManager();
    for (iLineItem tem : partition) {
        em.persist(item);
    }
}
```

The `persist(collection)` method takes care of sorting the LineItems by partition into new collections. These new collections are passed on to the `persist(collection, true)` method, one collection at a time, where the `EntityManager#persist(item)` method is called. This works because we start a new transaction for every call to `persist(collection, true)` due to the `@Transactional(propagation=Propagation.REQUIRES_NEW)` annotation. This annotation instructs Spring to suspend the currently running transaction (if any) and start a new one. This new transaction then writes to just one partition, persisting all of the objects in the collection. Once the partition-keyed objects are saved, the transaction commits. This process repeats for each partition-keyed collection. The worst we could do for 10 objects is sorting them into 10 different collections, each requiring a transaction and RPC.

Another approach to this problem is to partition on Account instead of LineItem. This is helpful when the LineItem operations are clustered around Accounts. If more than one LineItem is inserted or updated per Account, then it would be helpful to partition on Account because persisting the Account can cascade that operation to any LineItems associated with it. This requires the business logic to be set up like this already, or it requires changing the business logic. This approach may not work if changing the business logic is a political challenge.

```
@Entity(schemaRoot=true)
@javax.persistence.Entity
public class Account implements Serializable {
    @javax.persistence.Id
    @Id int id;
    String name;
    String type;
    String balance;
    @OneToMany(cascade=CascadeType.ALL)
```

```
    Collection<LineItem> lineItems = new ArrayList<LineItem>();
// ... methods omitted...
}
```

Now we define Account as the root entity with a one-to-many relationship to LineItem. This relationship is also reflected in the orm.xml file:

```
<entity class="wxs.sample.models.Account" access="FIELD">
    <attributes>
        <id name="id"/>
        <one-to-many name="lineItems">
            <cascade>
                <cascade-all/>
            </cascade>
        </one-to-many>
    </attributes>
</entity>
```

The application logic in LineItemProcessor changes a bit too:

```
public void run() {
    populateLineItems();
    populateAccounts();
}
private void populateLineItems() {
    for (int i = 0; i < 5000; i++) {
        LineItem item = new LineItem();
        item.setId(i);
        item.setAmount(250 + i);
        lineItems.add(item);
    }
}
private void populateAccounts() {
    accounts = new ArrayList();
    for (int i = 0; i < 1000; i++) {
        Account account = new Account();
        account.setId(i);
        account.setBalance("100");
        account.setName("Anthony's account " + i);
        account.setType("Savings");
        for (int j = 0; i < 5; i++) {
            LineItem item = (LineItem)lineItems.poll();
            account.getLineItems().add(item);
        }
        accounts.add(account);
        accountDAO.persist(account);
    }
}
```

The `populateAccounts()` method now picks five LineItems from a queue and associates them with an Account. Calling `accountDAO.persist(account)` saves the account, and all of the associated LineItems, in one transaction, and one RPC. Partitioning on Account means that the associated LineItems live in the same partition as their parent Account. This reduces the number of transactions and RPCs to the number of modified Accounts, rather than the number of LineItems. This is most helpful if your application usage clusters LineItem updates around Accounts. It is less helpful if there is mostly random LineItem access.

Summary

In this chapter, we covered how to integrate our ObjectGrid code with the Spring framework. For those familiar with Spring, this should be a good introduction to what you can do with ObjectGrid and Spring. It should now be easy to create Spring-managed, ObjectGrid-backed persistence layers, and plug them into existing applications with little modification to your existing beans.

We saw how to write interfaces using Spring-managed, declarative transactions. This removes a lot of invasive transaction-handling code and exception-checking from our business logic. The business logic is the business logic, and the persistence logic exists safely in a data-access layer. Any Spring transaction advice can be given to the transaction manager associated with an ObjectGrid instance.

We wrote an example `application.xml` file that showed how to build a small application using the Spring framework. This configuration created all of the ObjectGrid classes and instances that we needed to use an ObjectGrid instance in a client application. Finally, we covered what happens when existing interfaces make new, distributed architectures a little more interesting to build. Sometimes, we encounter a problem that makes it seem like using a database will be faster than a data grid. If we look at the problem from a few different points of views, then we can come up with a few different solutions to use, depending on our application usage. Application usage patterns are a very important consideration when building software with a data grid. Awareness of this consideration in the data layer gives us options. Some may not be as fast as a database-backed architecture, but they should be more easily scalable.

10
Putting It All Together

We rarely get to write software from scratch. Most software projects continue development of an existing code base. Data grids are relatively new middleware, and our projects probably don't have an immediate migration path to using one. If we are to introduce a data grid into these existing projects, then we need somehow to work WebSphere eXtreme Scale into the existing architecture. In this chapter, we'll go over a sample project which was initially written without thought of a data grid. Think of the previous chapters as reference, where you can find a quick recipe for performing a task with WebSphere eXtreme Scale. This chapter shows how we might apply those recipes.

Through this chapter we'll see:

- Data access considerations—what made sense without a data grid may not make sense with a data grid acting as an in-line cache. How do we deal with models and methods in a mixed-access environment?

- Migration toward data grid methods—a messy service layer means a messy data access layer. How do we refactor the service layer using WebSphere eXtreme Scale?

- Up and running—which patterns should we apply and where? How do we get the most functionality out of the grid?

- Digging deeper—what is the structure of our cache? Where does the user see the most benefit?

The bookmarks app

I wrote the first version of the bookmarks app sometime in early 2003. How many computers do you use each day? How many web browsers on each computer? If you're like me, you use different computers at work and a few more at home. Between all of those computers, there wasn't a good way to sync web bookmarks (2003 remember). Have you ever found yourself at an unfamiliar computer without the web references you need handy? Email is not a good way to manage bookmarks, and therefore the bookmarks app was born.

But it's from 2003! Well we need an existing project that would benefit from using a data grid. This is an existing project that uses the classic Java stack: database (MySQL), Hibernate, service layer and Spring Web MVC, all deployed to JBoss. This sounds like a typical example of what we face in the wild. It's as good a choice as any to work with, and honestly, the code base is a mess. Let's see what we can do about it.

The data model

The data model is simple. Users have bookmarks, and bookmarks have tags. Let's take a look at the relationships between these classes. Most of the interesting relationships are defined in the `Bookmark.hbm.xml` file. This is an excerpt from that file, including only relationships to other classes:

```xml
<hibernate-mapping package="net.anthonychaves.bookmarks.dataobject">
    <class name="Bookmark"
            table="bookmarks">

        <many-to-one name="url" column="url_id" class="Url"
                        unique="false" lazy="false" fetch="select"
                        cascade="all"/>

        <set name="tags" table="bookmarks_to_tags" cascade="none"
            lazy="false">
          <key column="bookmark_id"/>
          <many-to-many column="tag_id" class="Tag"/>
        </set>

        <many-to-one name="user" column="user_id" class="User"
                        fetch="select" lazy="false" cascade="refresh"/>
    </class>
</hibernate-mapping>
```

There are two things to note here. At first, we define a many-to-one relationship from bookmark to user, but **not** the inverse relationship from user to bookmark. This has a profound effect on our data access pattern. Defining the relationship as many bookmarks to one user, without the inverse, makes a user reference data for a bookmark. Accessing a bookmark is done by Bookmark ID. Thinking in ObjectGrid terms, Bookmark is our schema root.

Considering our data access patterns, does this approach make sense? Look at the service-level call made to show a user all of their bookmarks:

```
private List<Bookmark> getUserBookmarks(String sessionId,
                                        int offset,
                                        int numberOfBookmarks,
                                        boolean force) {
    String userBookmarksKey = sessionId +
                                BookmarksConstants.USER_NAME;
    List<Bookmark> bookmarks = (List<Bookmark>)
                            cacheService.get(userBookmarksKey);
    if (bookmarks == null ||
        bookmarks.size() == 0 ||
        force) {
        String userName = getUserNameFromSession(sessionId);
        DetachedCriteria dc = DetachedCriteria.forClass(
                            Bookmark.class, "bookmarks");
        dc.add(Restrictions.sqlRestriction(
                        "{alias}.user_id = (select bu.user_id " +
                        "from bookmark_users bu where " +
                        "bu.user_name = ?)", userName,
                                        new StringType()));
        bookmarks = getHibernateTemplate().findByCriteria(dc);

        cacheService.set(userBookmarksKey, bookmarks);
    }
    numberOfBookmarks = Utilities.safeNumberOfBookmarks(
                    offset, numberOfBookmarks, bookmarks);
    return bookmarks.subList(offset, numberOfBookmarks);
}
```

This method gets the username from the web session. Getting the bookmarks for that user is done with a Hibernate Criteria API call. This criteria helps Hibernate to generate a query that gets bookmarks by User ID. Because we don't have a User ID, only a username, we perform sub-select in the Criteria definition.

While it gets all of the bookmarks for a user, the method isn't very developer-friendly. At least it tries to put the user bookmarks in a side cache, if one exists. The usage pattern of this app is mostly "display a list of user bookmarks". This method gets called a lot. Let's start our refactoring here.

Because of the access pattern, "display a list of a user's bookmarks", does it make more sense to have User as the schema root? This means we partition on users with a partitioned data grid. An instance of User, and all Bookmarks belonging to that user, live in the same partition.

One consideration is that different users may have wildly differing numbers of bookmarks. Some users will prune while others hoard. Some users bookmark everything, and others bookmark only the most important pages. Partitioning on users puts all of their bookmarks in the same partition. If we monitor the grid with xsadmin or other JMX tools, we may see that some partitions use more memory and CPU than others. If our partitioning scheme is normal, the outliers shouldn't be *that far* out.

Let's define User and Bookmark as ObjectGrid Entities and JPA entities, since we're modernizing the code base. That means we need a WEB-INF/orm.xml file. Because this is our first attempt at inserting WebSphere eXtreme Scale in the software stack and we want to simplify the process, we drop URL from its own object and relationship with Bookmark in favor of making it a String field on Bookmark. There's no need to complicate the migration:

```xml
<entity-mappings
        xmlns="http://java.sun.com/xml/ns/persistence/orm"
        xmlns:xsi="http://www.w3.org/2001/XMLSchema-instance"
        xsi:schemaLocation=
            "http://java.sun.com/xml/ns/persistence/orm orm_1_0.xsd"
                version="1.0">
    <entity
      class="net.anthonychaves.bookmarks.dataobject.User"
      access="FIELD">
        <attributes>
            <id name="id"/>
            <one-to-many name="bookmarks">
                <cascade>
                    <cascade-all/>
                </cascade>
            </one-to-many>
        </attributes>
    </entity>
    <entity
      class="net.anthonychaves.bookmarks.dataobject.Bookmark"
      access="FIELD">
```

```
            <attributes>
                <id name="id"/>
            </attributes>
        </entity>
    </entity-mappings>
```

With two ObjectGrid entities defined, we should configure our ObjectGrid instance. We need a new `objectgrid.xml` file with a BackingMap for User and Bookmark:

```
<?xml version="1.0" encoding="UTF-8" ?>
<objectGridConfig xmlns:xsi="http://www.w3.org/2001/
  XMLSchema-instance" xsi:schemaLocation="http://ibm.com/ws/
  objectgrid/config ../objectGrid.xsd" xmlns="http://ibm.com/ws/
  objectgrid/config">
<objectGrids>
<objectGrid name="Bookmarks"
            entityMetadataXMLFile="bookmarkEntities.xml">
<bean id="TransactionCallback"
      className="{spring}jpaTransactionCallback" />
<backingMap name="User" pluginCollectionRef="User" />
<backingMap name="Bookmark" pluginCollectionRef="Bookmark" />
<backingMap name="NameToId" />
<backingMap name="HtmlFragments" />
</objectGrid>
</objectGrids>
<backingMapPluginCollections>
<backingMapPluginCollection id="User">
<bean id="Loader" className="{spring}userEntityLoader" />
</backingMapPluginCollection>
<backingMapPluginCollection id="Bookmark">
<bean id="Loader" className="{spring}bookmarkEntityLoader" />
</backingMapPluginCollection>
</backingMapPluginCollections>
</objectGridConfig>
```

Step one of the migration is complete. Our data model is fit to use with a data grid now!

The service layer

The `BookmarkService#getUserBookmarks` (sessionId, offset, numberOfBookmarks, force) method looks like it's doing some data access, as well as service-level pagination. This is an example of a poorly-defined data access layer. In fact, there isn't one! Data access is handled at the service level. We need to fix this. Because we decided that User is the schema root, it makes sense to start with the `UserDAO`:

```java
public class ObjectGridUserDAO implements UserDAO {

    private SpringLocalTxManager txnManager;
    private ObjectGrid grid;

    public void initialize(ObjectGrid grid) {
        txnManager.setObjectGridForThread(grid);
    }

    @Override
    public User find(int id) {
        txnManager.setObjectGridForThread(grid);
        EntityManager em = txnManager.getSession().getEntityManager();
        em.getTransaction().begin();
        User user = (User)em.find(User.class, id);
        em.getTransaction().commit();
        return user;
    }
    // getters and setters omitted
}
```

This looks almost like our `AccountDAO` class from Chapter 9. Two things should stand out. We inject an ObjectGrid instance at bean creation time, and we're not using declarative transaction management. This is a web application deployed to a web container. There is no driver application that calls the `UserDAO#initialize()` method. Instead, we rely on our Spring configuration to call initialize:

```xml
<bean id="userDAO"
    class="net.anthonychaves.bookmarks.dao.ObjectGridUserDAO"
    init-method="initialize">
    <property name="txnManager" ref="transactionManager"/>
    <property name="grid" ref="bookmarksGrid"/>
</bean>
```

The Spring bean life cycle init-method attribute makes Spring call the `ObjectGridUserDAO#initialize()` method so that the transaction manager uses the correct ObjectGrid instance.

Let's also define the `UserDAO` bean injected into the `bookmarkService` bean:

```
<bean id="bookmarkService"
      class="net.anthonychaves.bookmarks.service.BookmarkService">
    <property name="sessionFactory">
        <ref local="hibernateSessionFactory"/>
    </property>
    <property name="tagService">
        <ref local="tagService"/>
    </property>
    <property name="cacheService">
        <ref local="memcachedService"/>
    </property>
    <property name="userDAO">
        <ref local="userDAO"/>
    </property>
</bean>
```

Once we've got a `UserDAO` in the `bookmarkService`, we can create a method that uses it:

```
public List<Bookmark> getUserBookmarks(int userId) {
    User user = userDAO.find(userId);
    return user.getBookmarks();
}
```

This method signature is different from the other `getUserBookmarks` method. This one is not concerned with pagination. We only want a list of bookmarks to see if our integration steps work. Find a reasonably disruptive location to replace the old method call with the new method call (for now). Rebuild and redeploy your application, and see if it works:

```
protected ModelAndView handleRequestInternal(
                                  HttpServletRequest request,
                                  HttpServletResponse response)
                   throws Exception {
    String sessionId = request.getSession().getId();
    loginService.associateUserAndSession(
                request.getUserPrincipal().getName(),sessionId);
    bookmarkService.getUserBookmarks(
                request.getUserPrincipal().getName());
    return super.handleRequestInternal(request, response);
}
```

The most disruptive location I could find for this method call is in the login controller. Here we preload the user and all of their bookmarks from the database into the grid before performing any actions. There's also a small problem here that we'll address in just a moment.

We continue by looking for more locations as these new methods are useful. The UserService class has a getUserByName(String userName) method. The UserDAO has a find(userId) method. We don't have a User ID though, only a username. Ideally, we want our code to go from this:

```
public User getUserByName(String userName) {
    List userList = getHibernateTemplate().findByNamedParam(
                        "from User where userName = :userName",
                        "userName", userName);
    return (User)Utilities.getObjectFromListOfOne(userList);
}
```

To this:

```
public User getUserByName(String userName) {
    return userDAO.find(userName);
}
```

Not much of a change from an LOC perspective, but we're using the grid now. There's only one problem. The EntityManager#find method used by UserDAO#find(username) looks at a user by its primary key, which is the User ID and is not the username.

Storing data how it is used

The Primary key on the User class is its ID field. We look up for users based on their username. EntityManager.find(User.class, username) throws an IllegalArgumentException when called, because a username is not the primary key for a User object. Instead of changing the primary key field on User, we'll keep a username-to-User ID map.

The username is provided by the request principal after authentication. The request principal comes from the HttpServletRequest. The request principal obtained from the HttpServletRequest contains the username used in the login request after verifying the user's password according to our authentication configuration (we let JBoss authenticate the user for us). At this point, we only have a username, not the User ID.

The `UserDAO` interface and `ObjectGridUserDAO` need another find method. In this find method, we first look up the User ID in the name-to-id map, and then get the user object using the ID:

```
@Override
public User find(String username) {
    txnManager.setObjectGridForThread(grid);
    Session session = txnManager.getSession();
    EntityManager em = session.getEntityManager();

    try {
        ObjectMap nameMap = session.getMap("NameToId");

        session.begin();
        int id = (Integer)nameMap.get(username);
        User user = (User)em.find(User.class, id);
        session.rollback();

        return user;
    } catch(ObjectGridException e) {
        throw new ObjectGridRuntimeException(e);
    }
}
```

The `NameToId` map is configured in our `objectgrid.xml` file:

```
<backingMap name="NameToId" />
```

This map should contain an entry for each user that has signed up for the application. When the users sign up, they should be added to the map. This happens in the `SignupController`. Instead of directly calling a Hibernate save method, we should save the user with the new `UserDAO` interface:

```
@Override
public void addUser(User user) {
    txnManager.setObjectGridForThread(grid);
    Session session = txnManager.getSession();
    EntityManager em = session.getEntityManager();
    try {
        ObjectMap nameMap = session.getMap("NameToId");
        session.begin();
        nameMap.put(user.getUserName(), user.getId());
        em.persist(user);
        session.commit();
    } catch(ObjectGridException e) {
        throw new ObjectGridRuntimeException(e);
    }
}
```

The addUser(user) method does two things. It maps the username to the User ID in the NameToId map, and it saves the user object in the user map. Running this code shows that it has some bugs. The line em.persist(user) throws an OptimisiticCollisionException when we try to persist a second user.

The EntityManager takes care of converting entities to their key and value tuples and storing them in BackingMaps. Unfortunately, we don't have an ID for the user object yet. Before putting the grid in front of the database, our ORM framework relied on the database to generate a unique primary key for an object when it was saved.

The problem is that we're not using an ORM framework that gets unique IDs from the database anymore. Before inserting a new object into the BackingMap, it needs a unique ID. Prior to the em.persist(user) call, the user object must have an ID, or we'll encounter the OptimisiticCallbackException the second time we run this method. This is because an int without an assigned value defaults to 0. The EntityManager uses 0 as the key object. On the first method invocation, it appears to work as intended. The second method invocation throws the exception because the user object with ID 0 appears to have changed. Our intent was not to change the user object with ID 0, our intent was to create a new object with a new ID.

Grid/ORM hybrid

Alternatively, we need to consider the ID generation strategy which our application will use. If we want to keep our ORM-obtained IDs, then we need to take a hybrid grid/ORM approach. All persist operations on new user instances must first go through the ORM framework. This ensures that the user objects have a unique key obtained from the ORM-specified configuration:

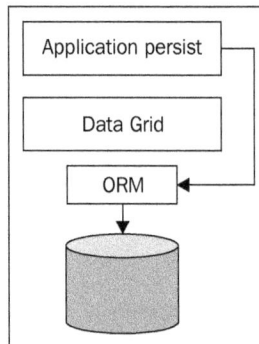

This saves a User object to the database, but does not put it in the grid. At first, you might think calling em.persist(user) is the right way to put the user object in the grid:

```
@Override
public void addUser(User user) {
    txnManager.setObjectGridForThread(grid);
    Session session = txnManager.getSession();
    EntityManager em = session.getEntityManager();

    getHibernateTemplate().persist(user);

    try {
        ObjectMap nameMap = session.getMap("NameToId");
        session.begin();
        em.persist(user);
        nameMap.put(user.getUserName(), user.getId());
        session.commit();
    } catch(ObjectGridException e) {
        throw new ObjectGridRuntimeException(e);
    }
}
```

Alternatively, the line em.persist(user) throws a DuplicateKeyException.
Because we have a loader configured on the User BackingMap, a write-through
(or -behind) is performed. We have already put the user object in the database with
a call to getHibernateTemplate.persist(user). When the remote ObjectGrid
partition performs the write-through, it executes the same SQL INSERT statement
used by the ORM persist method. The ORM framework provides the user object with
an ID. The EntityManager uses that ID inserting the user into the BackingMap. This
SQL INSERT statement contains the same primary key value as the SQL statement
executed by the ORM framework. Here, a DuplicateKeyException is thrown.

Alternatively, we take advantage of our newly-ORM managed user object, as it has
an ID that we call EntityManager#find(class, id):

```
@Override
public void addUser(User user) {
    txnManager.setObjectGridForThread(grid);
    Session session = txnManager.getSession();
    EntityManager em = session.getEntityManager();

    getHibernateTemplate().persist(user);

    try {
        ObjectMap nameMap = session.getMap("NameToId");
        session.begin();
        em.find(User.class, user.getId());
        nameMap.put(user.getUserName(), user.getId());
        session.commit();
    } catch(ObjectGridException e) {
        throw new ObjectGridRuntimeException(e);
    }
}
```

Having an ID for the object we want to find makes it possible to use the configured loader to our advantage. The call to `em.find(User.class, user.getId())` first looks to the near cache for a user object with this ID. Failing to find it in the near cache, ObjectGrid then makes a call to the remote partition to look for the ID in the remote BackingMap. Again, failing to find the object with that ID, ObjectGrid performs a read-through, thanks to the configured JPAEntityLoader on the BackingMap. The read-through performs an SQL query that finds the row with a primary key of the ID we're looking for. This row is transformed into the user object and loaded in the remote BackingMap:

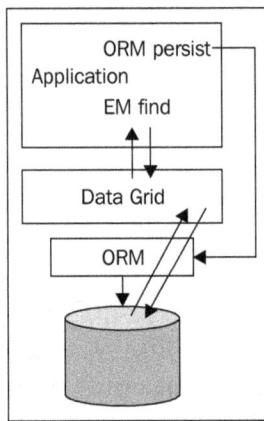

The hybrid approach is acceptable when other legacy applications depend on the same ORM and primary key generation schemes for interoperability. We're still bound to an ORM framework call in our data access layer, if this happens. We rely on the ORM call only for new objects that do not have an ID/primary key assigned to them yet.

The advantage of inserting ObjectGrid into the stack in a hybrid case is for objects that are **not new**, we then gain all of the advantages of a data grid. Though we still have a scalability bottleneck, it is isolated to the new object case. For read-mostly workflows, this should be acceptable.

If we are not bound to a legacy application, then we can generate object IDs in the application itself, as we've seen in previous examples. Since we already know how to use application-generated IDs, let's just say we'll do it for the rest of this example. Whatever strategy we use, we have one more issue to tackle before moving on to other parts of the application.

The `NameToId` map is the entry point to user objects. The workflow always goes through this map. When we start the application for the first time, and don't have any users, the application works as expected. Users sign up and get put in the NameToId map when their user object is saved. But what happens if we already have existing users? We are migrating an existing app, right?

Preloading data

We need to preload the NameToId map when the grid first starts. This needs to happen before the app servers come up and start making calls on the map. The preload is needed only once every time the grid comes up. The app servers can go up and down without requiring a map preload.

Rather than making the preload part of the app server startup process, we make it a separate process. This process should take a range of keys and load them from the database into the map. The range can include all keys in the table, or just a subset. We provide a range of keys so the preload process can run on multiple boxes. One box will not saturate the grid with put operations. The preload bottleneck is the preload process itself, if only one is running. When we break it up into multiple boxes working on a subset of keys, the preload goes much faster.

Let's create a MapPreloader class which takes rows from the database and loads them into the NameToId map. It needs to get usernames and IDs from the database table and load them into the NameToId BackingMap:

```
private void run(int start, int end) {
    loadMap(getRows(start, end));
}
```

First, we need to get the rows from the database.

```
private List getRows(int start, int end) {
    Session session = getSession();
    return session.createSQLQuery("select username,
            id from bookmark_users " + "where id >= :start " +
        "and id < :end").setParameter("start", start)
        .setParameter("end", end).list();
}
```

This method uses a Hibernate session, not an ObjectGrid session. This method only pulls the usernames and IDs from the database and returns them. The `loadMap(list)` method does the ObjectGrid work:

```
private void loadMap(List rows) {
   txnManager.setObjectGridForThread(grid);
   com.ibm.websphere.objectgrid.Session session =
                                     txnManager.getSession();
   try {
      ObjectMap map = session.getMap("NameToId");
      for (Object o : rows) {
         Object[] row = (Object[])o;
         session.begin();
         map.put(row[0], row[1]);
         session.commit();
      }
   } catch (ObjectGridException e) {
      e.printStackTrace();
   }
}
```

The Spring configuration for this bean is very simple:

```
<beans>
   <import resource="objectgridbeans.xml"/>
    <bean id="localHibernateSessionFactory"
                        class="org.springframework.orm.hibernate3
                        .LocalSessionFactoryBean">
      <property name="configLocation"
               value="/META-INF/hibernate.cfg.xml"/>
   </bean>
   <bean id="mapPreloader" class="net.anthonychaves.bookmarks
                              .batch.MapPreloader">
      <property name="sessionFactory"
               ref="localHibernateSessionFactory"/>
      <property name="grid" ref="bookmarksGrid"/>
      <property name="txnManager" ref="transactionManager"/>
   </bean>
</beans>
```

Improving responsiveness

This preloader does the bare minimum required for our web app to function. It only loads the NameToId map. Is there a way to make it more useful? Think about how the app works:

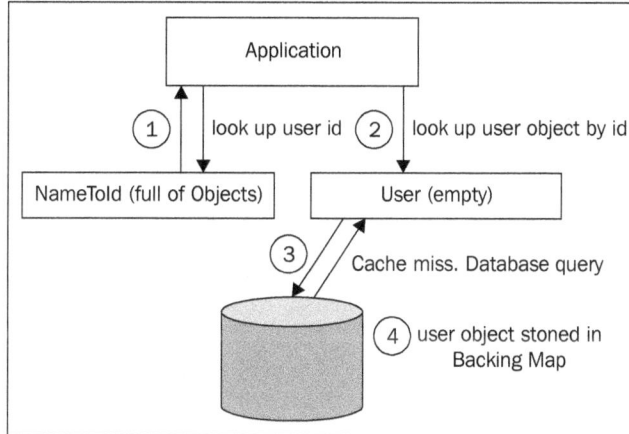

Because the User BackingMap is empty, we incur a database hit every time we lookup at the previously unused user. This is a prime candidate for inclusion in the preload process. If we can fit most, or all of the User objects in the grid, then we avoid the database lookup.

The preload process changes a little bit. Instead of looking up only usernames and IDs from the database table, we get the User objects from the ORM. The LoadMap method changes a little bit:

```
private void loadNameToIdMap(List<User> users) {
    txnManager.setObjectGridForThread(grid);
    com.ibm.websphere.objectgrid.Session session =
                                        txnManager.getSession();
    try {
        ObjectMap map = session.getMap("NameToId");
        for (User user : users) {
        session.begin();
            map.put(user.getUserName(), user.getId());
            session.commit();
        }
    } catch (ObjectGridException e) {
        e.printStackTrace();
    }
}
```

We need a new method to preload users. The preload process already has a collection of user objects, thanks to the getRows(start, end) method. It would be wasteful to get the users from the database, and then perform a find operation on each during the preload process. Instead, we use the objects we already have. We put them into the grid with a ReduceGridAgent.

First, let's look at the workflow:

```
private void run(int start, int end) {
    List<User> users = getRows(start, end);
    loadNameToIdMap(users);
    loadUsers(null);
}


private void loadUsers(List<User> users) {
    txnManager.setObjectGridForThread(grid);

    Map<Integer, List<User>> partitionedUsers =
                                    partitionUsers(users);
    runAgents(partitionedUsers);
}
```

The ReduceGridAgent is run from the runAgents(users) method. Recall from Chapter 7 that grid agents are serialized and sent to the grid. This means their instance objects are also sent to the grid. Our goal is to take the users we already have, and send them to the grid along with the grid agent. Once in the grid, we insert them into the appropriate BackingMap.

Let's take a look at the grid agent:

```
public class UserPreloadReduceAgent
                    implements ReduceGridAgent, EntityAgentMixin {

    private Collection users;

    @Override
    public Object reduce(Session session, ObjectMap map) {
        System.out.println("Preloading Users");
        try {
            Session s = session.getObjectGrid().getSession();
            EntityManager em = s.getEntityManager();

            s.beginNoWriteThrough();

            for(User user : users) {
                em.persist(user);
            }
            s.commit();
```

```
        } catch (Exception e) {
           throw new ObjectGridRuntimeException(e);
        }
        return Boolean.TRUE;
    }

    @Override
    public Object reduce(Session session,
                                    ObjectMap map, Collection keys) {
        // This method should not be called
        return Boolean.FALSE;
    }

    @Override
    public Object reduceResults(Collection arg0) {
        System.out.println("Finished user preload!");
        return null;
    }

    @Override
    public Class getClassForEntity() {
        return User.class;
    }

    public Collection getUsers() {
        return users;
    }

    public void setUsers(Collection users) {
        this.users = users;
    }
}
```

The agent has a collection of users along with appropriate getter/setter methods. The `reduce(session, map)` performs the user inserts. We use this method because we do not provide the key list for the `reduce(session, map, keys)` method. This seems strange! We have the user objects and their keys from the ORM framework. Why don't we provide the key list when we run the agent?

This agent implements the `EntityAgentMixin` interface. This interface gives us the `getClassForEntity()` method. In Chapter 7, we saw that this method is called by ObjectGrid before we work with the key list. This transparently transforms the Entity metadata into the Entity object we work with. The caveat is, this only works for Entities that already exist in the partition. If we had user objects that were already loaded in their partitions, our reduce method would look different.

Instead of iterating through the key list, we work with User objects. Before running the agent, we set the list of users the agent works with. Once in the grid, we use that list to insert the user objects into their BackingMap.

```
s.beginNoWriteThrough();
for (User user : users) {

    em.persist(user);
}
s.commit();
```

The excerpt above from the `reduce(session, map)` method includes a call to `Session#beginNoWriteThrough()`. This method is meaningful only within grid agents. It disables the loader write-through (and -behind). Remember the last time we tried to insert a user object into the grid and got a `DuplicateKeyException` from the database? With `beginNoWriteThrough()`, we avoid that problem. The BackingMap Loader is not called, and the user object is put in the BackingMap without a thrown exception. The user already has a row in the database. Therefore, there is no need to insert it again.

We avoid sending all users to all partitions by pre-partitioning users based on their key in the MapPreloader class:

```
private Map<Integer,List<User>> partitionUsers(List<User> users) {
    HashMap<Integer, List<User>> partitions =
                                new HashMap<Integer, List<User>>();
    for (User user : users) {
        BackingMap bm = grid.getMap("User");
        int p = bm.getPartitionManager().getPartition(user);
        List<User> list = partitions.get(p);
        if (list == null) {
            list = new ArrayList<User>();
            partitions.put(p, list);
        }
        list.add(user);
    }
    return partitions;
}
```

This should look familiar to the code which we used in Chapter 7. Iterating over the list of User objects, we use the PartitionManager associated with the User BackingMap to map a user to a partition. We keep all of the users associated with a partition in a list keyed by the partition ID, and return the map of partition id-to-user list:

```
private void runAgents(Map<Integer, List<User>> partitionedUsers) {
    Iterator<Integer> iter = partitionedUsers.keySet().iterator();
    while (iter.hasNext()) {
        UserPreloadReduceAgent agent = new UserPreloadReduceAgent();
        List<User> users = partitionedUsers.get(iter.next());
        agent.setUsers(users);

        try {
            ObjectMap map = txnManager.getSession().getMap("User");
            map.getAgentManager().callReduceAgent(agent);
        } catch (UndefinedMapException e) {
            e.printStackTrace();
        }
    }
}
```

The runAgents(users) method is not the optimal implementation. The agents are created and run sequentially. Though it's not as noticeable when the preload process runs on multiple boxes, we can do the job much faster by creating the agents and running them in parallel:

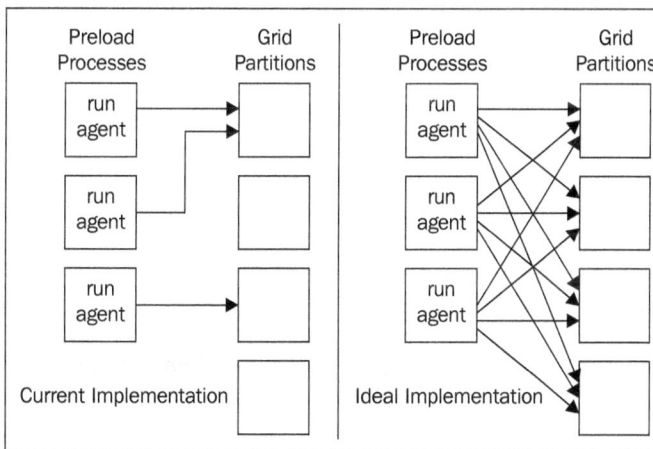

Each preload process should run its grid agents in parallel.

At this point, we have a good start integrating a data grid with an existing project. Obviously, unit tests and integration tests point out areas where the changes we just made cause problems. If you're going to integrate WebSphere eXtreme Scale with an existing project, it is a good idea to create a new branch in your SCM. The build will break and tests will fail. With good test coverage and small methods, fixing it should be straightforward. For the Bookmarks project, I now need to fix the build before migrating further towards ObjectGrid. Once the build is fixed, and all of the tests passed, I'm free to migrate my service layer further toward the ObjectGrid APIs. We won't cover any more service-level migrations because you should have the hang of it by now. Instead, we'll look at the more interesting things we can do with a data grid and a web app.

Caching more than ORM

Though we cache a lot of objects that map to database tables through an ORM framework, we are not limited to ORM'd objects. The NameToId map is an example of this. It does not have a corresponding table in a database. Instead, it is an intermediate map between users and their data. The user data doesn't necessarily need to be the user object and the bookmarks that go along with it. We can cache HTML fragments instead.

Which HTML fragments? A user looks at their bookmarks in a browser. If a user hasn't changed their bookmarks since the last cache hit, then we store the HTML view of those bookmarks in addition to the data objects. This moves the cache one logical layer closer to the user. Instead of assembling HTML in the controller, we perform a lookup in a BackingMap:

```
<backingMap name="HtmlFragments" />
```

That's it! Now our controllers can build the HTML that represents a list of bookmarks and store them in this map.

In fact, at any time, caching closer to the presentation is worthwhile. Caching HTML fragments in this application is probably the best reward for the effort we'll see. Other places that help are caching remote service calls. Caching a web API result from Twitter, Digg, or Facebook is much better than repeatedly calling the API.

Forgetting the web for a minute, caching ESB calls, perhaps from another JavaEE-based app, .NET or another platform, is worthwhile.

The size of all of these calls varies. Even the same API method can return results of wildly varying sizes. Working with these result sets is made easier with map-based pagination. Let's take the results of a database query as an example. A query can return 1 row, 10 rows, or 10,000 rows. We store the results in a BackingMap with some known key and the raw string form of the database rows.

Getting a result set by key may copy a small object to the client if the result set is small. For a large result set, the entire large result set is copied to the client. When the client doesn't use the entire result set, this is wasteful. It's also wasteful if multiple clients use a portion of the result set.

A common pattern we see when working with a data grid is the push for consistency. Consistent partition sizes, consistent container load, and consistent node access. This concept helps us when dealing with large result sets, whether from database queries, stored procedures, or remote API calls. Instead of storing the entire result set as one key/value pair in the BackingMap, we break it up into consistently-sized chunks.

We use one BackingMap and store key/list of keys, instead of a key/result set. The key remains the same. It must uniquely identify this API call. A good key convention is `api name:method name:method parameters`. The value is a list of additional keys that each point to a subset of the result set.

This breaks up a 10,000 row result set into 1,000 map entries that have 10 results each. If 10 results are too small, it could be 100 map entries of 100 results each. Size the result entries based on application usage.

The advantage to this approach is that the entire result set does not need to be reproduced via a remote call until we're sure the results are invalid. Instead, the results are always exactly two hops away. This is very fast and predictably scalable. Our eXtreme Scale client first makes a "find result keys" call for the method call and obtains a 1,000 entry list. This list contains another key to the same map. Performing a lookup on this key gives the result page we're looking for:

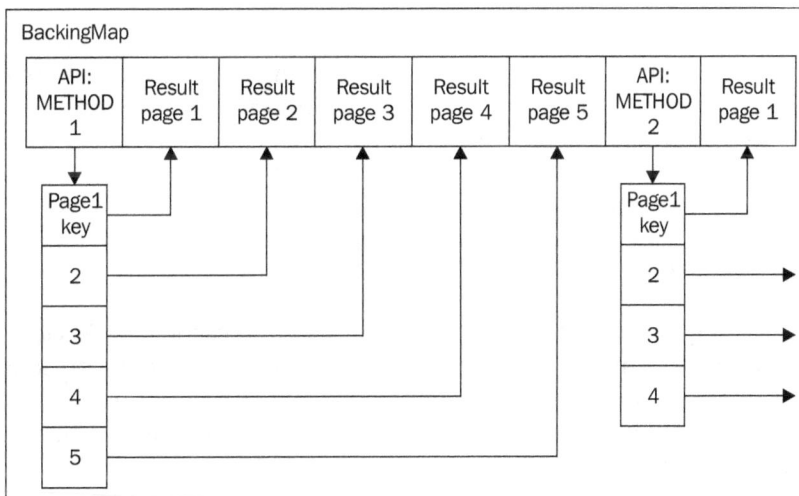

Summary

This chapter covered some familiar material, as well as some new material. By now, you should be comfortable using the WebSphere eXtreme Scale APIs, and working with local and remote ObjectGrid instances.

We started this chapter with an existing project that was in poor condition. As we worked through the examples, we made some design decisions which allowed us to use WebSphere eXtreme Scale. We didn't just migrate all at once though. Instead, we saw how we migrate an application where we gain the most value from a distributed cache.

We made the decision to use the data grid in a fairly disruptive place in the project. It required rethinking of the original data access patterns and application workflow. Integrating with a data grid isn't just changing existing patterns. It requires knowledge of additional patterns using data grids. The preload process makes the application much more responsive without a long warm-up period.

Preloading the NameToId map is required due to the design decision to access users by username, instead of performing a query across all grid partitions. This slows the entire grid, instead of making at most two hops for every user access. 100 clients saturating the grid running the same query, and most partitions return no results, is an inefficient use of the grid. Instead, we know how to store data in the way it's accessed. This gives us predictability and consistency.

We also looked at caching non-ORM'd objects. Caching data close to where it is used makes applications more responsive by reducing latency. Keeping code and data as close together as possible is the prevailing concept behind the DataGrid API. We co-locate code and data in the same process. We take this concept a little further by applying it to remote calls. Any remote call is a candidate for caching. Is the result expensive to build? Does it travel a long way to get to our code? Caching the result makes sense.

Rather than storing only ORM-related objects, we should cache data as close to it's final form as possible. This means storing it as close as possible to its presentation, HTML, CSV, XML, or whatever the format. It also means co-locating the data where it is used. A near cache in a web container can get HTML fragments much faster than a call to a remote partition.

Index

Q

query.getPlan() method 79
Query API 59, 73-75

R

RDBMS 93
ready(...) method 80
reduce concept 170, 171
ReduceGridAgent
  writing 178
ReduceGridAgent#reduce(session, map)
    method 181, 183, 187, 204
ReduceGridAgent#reduce (session, map,
    collection) method 204
ReduceGridAgent#reduce(session, map,
    keys) method 179, 181, 187
ReduceGridAgent#reduceResults(
    Collection results) method 188
ReduceGridAgent#reduceResults(results)
    method 180, 188
reduce method 171
reference data 200-202
remove(Object key) method 48
removeAll(Collection keys) method 48
remove method 68
replica shard 153
replication
  about 146
  replicaReadEnabled attribute 146
reportStates() method 81-83
root entity 197
runAgents(users) method 265
runReport(EntityManager em, MapIndex
    idx) method 83

S

scale-out deployments 195
scale-up deployments 195
schema root
  about 196-199
  guidelines, for selecting 200
schemaRoot attribute 73

schemaRoot property 197
Session#getEntityManager() method 62
session.begin() 21, 32
session.commit() 21, 32
session.commit() method 32
Session argument 172
setLockTimeout(int seconds) method 39
setTimeToLive(int ttl) method 49
setWriteBehind("time; conditions") method
    105
setWriteBehind method 105
shard placement
  -containers 147
  -hosts 147
  -mapsizes 147
  -mbeanservers 147
  -primaries 147
  -unassigned 147
  about 146-151
  failover 154-158
  lost shards 154-158
  shard start-up 153
  xsadmin tool used 146
shards 118, 119, 141, 143
shard start-up, shard placement
  about 153
  copy-on-write/merge process 154
  copy-on-write mode 153
  peer mode 153
  primary shard 153, 154
shared lock 36
single-threaded application 11
Singleton design pattern 13
S lock. *See* shared lock
soft-reference 209
Spring
  ObjectGrid instances, injecting 220
  transaction management 227
Spring-managed eXtreme Scale
    configuration 226
StateReportIndex.ready() method 83
StateReportIndex class 81, 82
StateReportRunner.runReports() 84
strategy pattern 227
sum function 77
sync 105

[PACKT] PUBLISHING

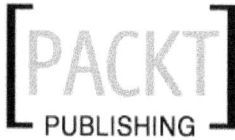

Thank you for buying
IBM WebSphere eXtreme Scale 6

About Packt Publishing

Packt, pronounced 'packed', published its first book "*Mastering phpMyAdmin for Effective MySQL Management*" in April 2004 and subsequently continued to specialize in publishing highly focused books on specific technologies and solutions.

Our books and publications share the experiences of your fellow IT professionals in adapting and customizing today's systems, applications, and frameworks. Our solution based books give you the knowledge and power to customize the software and technologies you're using to get the job done. Packt books are more specific and less general than the IT books you have seen in the past. Our unique business model allows us to bring you more focused information, giving you more of what you need to know, and less of what you don't.

Packt is a modern, yet unique publishing company, which focuses on producing quality, cutting-edge books for communities of developers, administrators, and newbies alike. For more information, please visit our website: www.packtpub.com.

Writing for Packt

We welcome all inquiries from people who are interested in authoring. Book proposals should be sent to author@packtpub.com. If your book idea is still at an early stage and you would like to discuss it first before writing a formal book proposal, contact us; one of our commissioning editors will get in touch with you.

We're not just looking for published authors; if you have strong technical skills but no writing experience, our experienced editors can help you develop a writing career, or simply get some additional reward for your expertise.

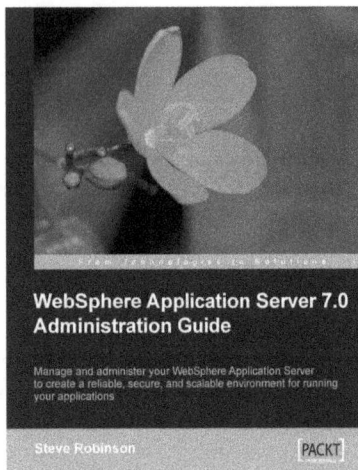

WebSphere Application Server 7.0 Administration Guide

ISBN: 978-1-847197-20-7   Paperback: 344 pages

Manage and administer your WebSphere application server to create a reliable, secure, and scalable environment for running your applications

1. Create a reliable, secure, and flexible environment to build and run WebSphere applications efficiently

2. Learn WebSphere security, performance tuning, and debugging concepts with a variety of real-life examples

3. Thoroughly covers Java messaging, administrative agent, and product maintenance features

4. # No previous knowledge of WebSphere is expected

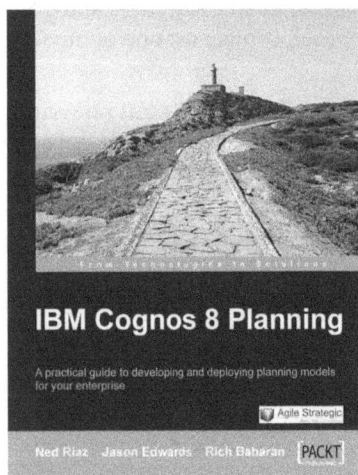

IBM Cognos 8 Planning

ISBN: 978-1-847196-84-2   Paperback: 424 pages

Engineer a clear-cut strategy for achieving best-in-class results

1. Build and deploy effective planning models using Cognos 8 Planning

2. Filled with ideas and techniques for designing planning models

3. Ample screenshots and clear explanations to facilitate learning

4. Written for first-time developers focusing on what is important to the beginner

Please check **www.PacktPub.com** for information on our titles

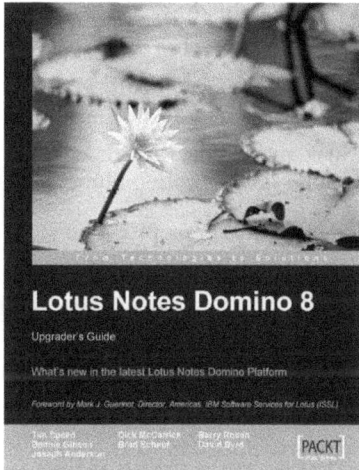

Lotus Notes Domino 8: Upgrader's Guide

ISBN: 978-1-847192-74-5   Paperback: 276 pages

What's new in the latest Lotus Notes Domino Platform

1. Upgrade to the latest version of Lotus Notes and Domino

2. Understand the new features and put them to work in your business

3. Appreciate the implications of changes and new features

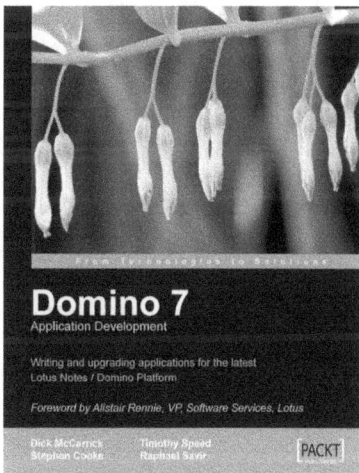

Domino 7 Application Development

ISBN: 978-1-904811-06-0   Paperback: 228 pages

Writing and upgrading applications for the latest Lotus Notes Domino Platform

1. Get to grips with all of the major new developer features in Lotus/Domino 7

2. Use DB2 as your Domino data store, optimize your code for performance, adopt best practice

3. Domino Designer 7, agent profiling, remote Java debugging, web services, and more

Please check **www.PacktPub.com** for information on our titles

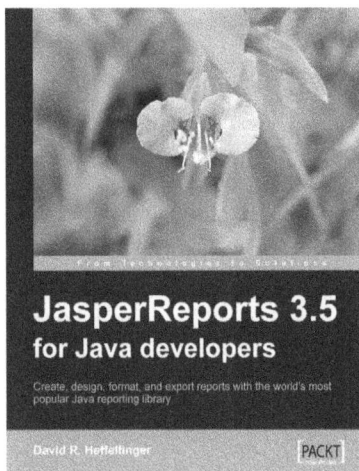

JasperReports 3.5 for Java Developers

ISBN: 978-1-847198-08-2   Paperback: 368 pages

Create, Design, Format, and Export Reports with the world's most popular Java reporting library

1. Create better, smarter, and more professional reports using comprehensive and proven methods

2. Group scattered data into meaningful reports, and make the reports appealing by adding charts and graphics

3. Discover techniques to integrate with Hibernate, Spring, JSF, and Struts, and to export to different file formats

4. Written in a lucid and practical manner, this book introduces you to JasperReports and gets you creating complex and elegant reports

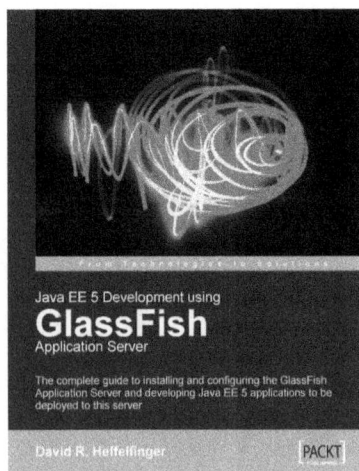

Java EE 5 Development using GlassFish Application Server

ISBN: 978-1-847192-60-8   Paperback: 424 pages

The complete guide to installing and configuring the GlassFish Application Server and developing Java EE 5 applications to be deployed to this server

1. BConcise guide covering all major aspects of Java EE 5 development

2. Uses the enterprise open-source GlassFish application server

3. Explains GlassFish installation and configuration

4. Covers all major Java EE 5 APIs

Please check **www.PacktPub.com** for information on our titles

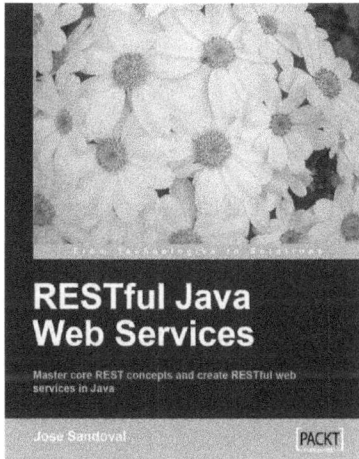

RESTful Java Web Services

ISBN: 978-1-847196-46-0   Paperback: 260 pages

Master core REST concepts and create RESTful web services in Java

1. Build powerful and flexible RESTful web services in Java using the most popular Java RESTful frameworks to date (Restlet, JAX-RS based frameworks Jersey and RESTEasy, and Struts 2)

2. Master the concepts to help you design and implement RESTful web services

3. Plenty of screenshots and clear explanations to facilitate learning

4. A developer's guide with practical examples to ensure proper understanding of all concepts and the differences between the frameworks studied

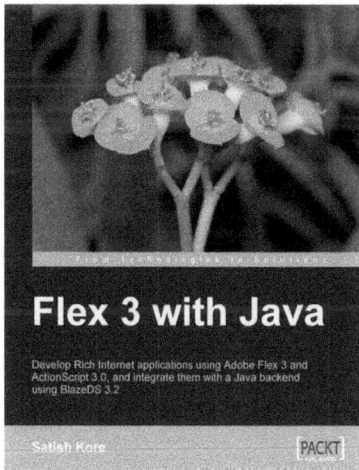

Flex 3 with Java

ISBN: 978-1-847195-34-0   Paperback: 304 pages

Develop rich internet applications quickly and easily using Adobe Flex 3, ActionScript 3.0 and integrate with a Java backend using BlazeDS 3.2

1. A step-by-step tutorial for developing web applications using Flex 3, ActionScript 3.0, BlazeDS 3.2, and Java

2. Build efficient and seamless data-rich interactive applications in Flex using a combination of MXML and ActionScript 3.0

3. Create custom UIs, Components, Events, and Item Renders to develop user friendly applications

Please check **www.PacktPub.com** for information on our titles

www.ingramcontent.com/pod-product-compliance
Lightning Source LLC
Chambersburg PA
CBHW061345210326
41598CB00035B/5887